E. Œ. Somerville and Martin Ross
female authorship and literary collaboration

E.Œ. Somerville and Martin Ross

female authorship and literary collaboration

ANNE JAMISON

CORK UNIVERSITY PRESS

First published in 2016 by
Cork University Press
Youngline Industrial Estate
Pouladuff Road, Togher
Cork
T12 HT6V
Ireland

British Library Cataloguing in Publication Data
A CIP record for this book is available from the British Library.

ISBN 978–1–78205–192–3

Printed in Malta by Gutenberg Press
Print origination & design by Carrigboy Typesetting Services, www.carrigboy.com

www.corkuniversitypress.com

To Adel and Margaret Shafiq

Contents

Acknowledgements

The research and writing of this book has taken many years and spanned several institutions, it has also relied on the expert knowledge, guidance and encouragement of many friends and fellow scholars. Its final revisions were generously facilitated by a Researcher Development Grant awarded by Western Sydney University and much of its foundational archival research was funded through a DEL Postgraduate Studentship in Northern Ireland. Without the above financial assistance none of the following would have been possible.

The research for this book happily took me to several archives and libraries and I am very grateful for the assistance and knowledge of library staff and archivists in many places, notably the Special Collections department at Queen's University Belfast, the Manuscript Department at Trinity College Dublin, and the Berg Collection Department at New York Public Library. I would particularly like to thank Mary Kelly and Deirdre Wildy for their generosity and trust in facilitating privileged and unhampered access to the Special Collections archives in Belfast. Deirdre's energy and vision for the Somerville and Ross manuscript papers at Queen's remains inspiring and I continue to be grateful for her support and collaboration. I am further obliged to Christopher and Celia Somerville for their kind welcome to Drishane House. Christopher's tales of his 'Great Aunt Dee' and his tour of her restored art studio are treasured memories.

I also owe a great debt to all those people whose teaching, enthusiasm, support, collegiality and scholarly influence I have been fortunate to benefit from over the last decade and more. Neal Corcoran's inspirational teaching at the University of St. Andrews catalysed my initial interest in Irish literature, and staff in the School of English at Queen's University Belfast gave me my first insight into the fascinating writers and texts of nineteenth-century Ireland. They are too numerous to list, but I wish especially to thank Eamonn Hughes, Colin Graham and Dominic Bryan who all supported this project and its offshoots in a variety of instrumental ways, especially in its earliest stages. It remains a privilege and a delight to benefit from Eamonn's continued friendship and limitless knowledge. Margaret Kelleher's sustained enthusiasm for this project has also been greatly appreciated and I can't thank her enough for her ongoing personal and intellectual generosity and support.

My former colleagues at the University of Ulster, where most of this book was written, are much missed for their camaraderie, intellectual sharpness and brilliant sense of fun. Jan Jedrzejewski's support and mentorship has taken me much further than I ever expected to go. In the same vein, I also extend thanks to colleagues at Western Sydney University, so many of whom kindly offered assistance and a great welcome, all of which helped the final writing of this book take place. My affectionate gratitude goes to Matt McGuire, James Gourley and Helen Koukoutsis who have proved the best of colleagues and friends; they have made the move from Belfast to Sydney so much easier than it might otherwise have been.

Special thanks to the editorial and publishing team at Cork University Press who have been unfailingly patient and professional. Mike Collins and Maria O'Donovan, in particular, have given so much of their time and expertise in bringing this book to fruition and have made the process between submission and publication an enjoyably smooth one. My thanks are further due to Tom Dunne for accepting my original book proposal at the press, as well as to the anonymous readers of my book manuscript, both of whom provided such valuable suggestions.

My dearest thanks and esteem go to my wonderful Belfast pals; Sinéad Sturgeon, Conor Wyer and Neal Alexander. Our enduring conversations and your astute ideas are all somewhere in this book. My heartfelt thanks go to Sinéad for her untiring and generous work in libraries and archives on my behalf, as well as for her friendship which I could not be without.

My brothers and sister, Amere, Tariq, and Tara, sustain me in more ways than they know and, without their support, this book would not have been possible. Rubin, Maggie-Rose, and Reem – my beautiful children – were all born between these pages and their love, laughter and playfulness has brought me much joy and sustenance throughout the research and writing of this book. My most incalculable debt goes to Richard whose love and support always makes him the best and truest partner in everything I do.

This book is finally dedicated, with deepest affection, to my wonderful parents; Adel and Margaret Shafiq. Their lives are a constant source of strength and inspiration and their love, thoughtfulness and support are always unfailing. It is to them that I owe everything.

Sydney, May 2016

Introduction

In his 1920 essay on the Renaissance dramatist Phillip Massinger, T. S. Eliot described the collaborative ethic which he believed governed the compositional methodologies of Elizabethan drama. Eliot defined this form of collaboration as 'the threads of authorship and influence', which float below the surface of the dramatic text, and concluded that in order to understand such drama, the critic must 'ponder collaboration to the utmost line'.[1] This book strongly aligns itself with a very similar kind of critical pondering. Throughout history, literary critics have certainly deliberated on the nature and authenticity of the collaborative text and its authors: validating in the neo-Classical and Renaissance periods the passive scribe in thrall to a collaborating muse or God; turning with horror during the reign of the Romantics and the Victorians from the labouring collaborator's desecration of the originating hero-artist; and, more recently, effecting a minor reconciliation with multiple authorship in a world which admits to the Barthesian maxim that 'a text is not a line of words releasing a single "theological" meaning (the "message" of the Author-God), but a multi-dimensional space in which a variety of writings, none of them original, blend and clash'.[2]

This book considers a very specific and public collaboration, one which challenges from the outset the very idea of an 'Author-God' and is now recognised as one of the most well-known and successful female literary collaborations at work in the late nineteenth century.[3] The collaboration of Irish authors Edith Œnone Somerville (1858–1949) and (Violet) Martin Ross (1862–1915) spanned just under three decades between 1888 and Ross' premature death in 1915. During this period, Somerville and Ross jointly published five novels, five collections of short stories and essays, four travel memoirs and numerous other periodical literature, all under the male soubriquet of 'E.Œ. Somerville and Martin Ross'. The ambition of this book is, in part, to reorient traditional thinking about Somerville and Ross' partnership and rethink the collaboration beyond a purely domestic and personal affair. It will consider the ways in which Somerville and Ross' literary collaboration was a significant part of the two women's lifelong but always complex feminist ethic, as well as a professional literary partnership. This analysis of the collaboration recognises Somerville and Ross' dual authorship as a challenge to dominant nineteenth-century conceptions of the post-Romantic author as male, originary and singular. As such, this book attempts to open up ways of thinking about women's literary collaborations as a defiant cultural position within Irish and Victorian literary society more generally and, in particular, examine how Somerville and Ross' partnership significantly influenced both the gender and national politics of their writing.

Somerville and Ross were second cousins and descendants of well-established Protestant Ascendancy families in Cork and Galway. They met in 1887 and, from humble beginnings which saw the duo collaborating on a family dictionary, went on to publish their first professional novel, *An Irish Cousin*, in 1889 to popular and critical acclaim. The novel is written in the style of a Victorian 'shilling shocker' set on an Irish country estate. Despite its sensationalist gothic tone, however, it firmly exposes Somerville and Ross' serious and lifelong literary interest in the gender conventions of their time, as well as in Anglo-Irish society and the depiction of Irish character across a broad spectrum of class and race. Building on the initial success of their debut publication, the two authors eventually published what is now one of the most critically acclaimed Irish novels of the late nineteenth century, *The Real Charlotte* (1894), as well as a long-running and enduringly popular series of sporting comic short stories based around the experiences of an English resident magistrate in Ireland: *Some Experiences of an Irish R.M.*, *Further Experiences of an Irish R.M.*, and *In Mr. Knox's Country* (1899–1915). Despite the divergent tone and genre of *The Real Charlotte* and Somerville and Ross's Irish R.M. tales, these texts all document and interrogate the intriguing complexities of the social, cultural and gender politics in turn-of-the-century Ascendancy Ireland and, in this sense, represent the heart and drive of Somerville and Ross' entire literary oeuvre.

Somerville continued to use the dual signature after Ross' death, validating her practice by utilising the literary notebooks compiled with Ross during the latter's lifetime, as well as deriving new literary material through spiritualist communications with her dead collaborator. Somerville eventually published another fourteen books under the dual signature, including the noted *The Big House of Inver* (1925), but the literary partners are now largely remembered for the publications jointly produced during Ross' lifetime. Outside their literary activities, the two authors were also ardent huntswomen, farm managers, active suffragettes and, in the case of Somerville, a professional painter and illustrator.

All these activities had a bearing on their writing and, moreover, revolved around a significant feminist ethos. As a young woman attempting to pursue a career as an artist, Somerville fended off the gender-based disapproval of her family to study in the studios of Paris and Düsseldorf. She eventually succeeded in showing her work at several major exhibitions in London, Dublin and the United States in the 1930s and 1940s. Similarly, Somerville and Ross' initial attempts at professional authorship also suffered familial censure and the two women had to pursue their writing in the face of practical disruptions and the knowledge that 'every man's hand was against' them.[4] Continually undeterred by social dictates, Somerville became Ireland's first female master of foxhounds in 1903 and, with Ross as her vice-president, founded the Munster Women's Franchise League (MWFL) in 1910. The duo organised sixteen meetings of the MWFL in their first year, and also established two further branches of the league across the southwest of Ireland. However, these activities all took place within the patriarchal and conservative framework of the Protestant Ascendancy and were thus often complicated by the overt support the two women maintained for the sustenance of their social position in Ireland.

Throughout their writing careers, Somerville and Ross' collaborative practice was also complicated by a disjunction between what their joint methodology literally represented in the public domain, and the ways in which they were aware of its social and literary inadequacy as a high aesthetic and Romanticised practice. Such a disjunction is nowhere better expressed than in Ross' ecstatic response to Richard Bentley's commercial agreement to publish her and Somerville's first novel in 1889. Ross jubilantly commands her co-author to 'take' together their home region of Carbery and 'grind its bones to make our own bread': 'cut, my dear! – It would be new life to me to cut it – and we will – and we will serve it up to the spectator so that its mother wouldn't know it.'[5] With this desire to make the most of their new-found and publicly acknowledged talents, Ross explicitly echoes John Locke's seventeenth-century rhetoric of possessive individualism: the derivation of private property through an individual's labour upon the common store of nature.[6] By the late nineteenth century, Locke's political philosophy was a recognised cornerstone discourse in the development of an author's rights over their literary property, and Somerville and Ross' claim to ownership, as well as the increasingly professional status of that ownership, was assumed to be protected by these legal and aesthetic developments.

Ross' euphoric declaration of authorship thus confidently appeals to the Victorian conception of the professional author as a respectable person of letters with just rights to generate and protect the economic and cultural value of their works. This places authors in a vocational rank whereby they can 'command an income and a position quite equal to those' of society's other recognised professions and reap the benefits of the late-nineteenth-century's blooming literary professionalism.[7] The fruits of their collaborative labours, Somerville and Ross believed, would be the bread that legally guaranteed to provide the necessary financial and intellectual remuneration to be both independent and resident in Ireland. As this book will go on to argue, however, such a claim remained severely compromised by the two authors' collaborative and gender status.

The cousins' proprietary standing as both authors and Ascendancy house mistresses was severely undercut by the very legal and aesthetic institutions that Locke prefigured in his seventeenth-century political tract, and to which the two author-chatelaines were culturally and legally bound, even in late-nineteenth-century Ireland. While financial endurance did indeed secure the aristocratic tradition of familial inheritance, at least in Somerville's case, the authorial figures the collaborative duo cut failed to assure a corresponding level of intellectual and literary authority. Despite their belief in the resultant superiority of their dual- over single-authored works, Somerville and Ross' literary practice was confined by a social and legal system that dictated an author's primary and almost exclusive role in the creation of a text. In aesthetic and legal discourse, collaborative authorship was posited as an inferior and aberrant method of textual production that was publicly configured in opposition to the sanctioned and singular author figure. Sir Walter Besant, founding member of the Society of Authors and leading public champion for the professionalisation and legal protection of authorship in late-nineteenth-century Britain, maintained in 1892 that:

> two men talking together, using the same words, on solemn subjects, like a church congregation, might look ridiculous. One must alone, speak to the alone ... Satire, fun, humour, pathos of a kind, all may be exhibited at their best in partnership. But some things cannot be treated at all in this way ... [joint authors] are first and foremost, and always, storytellers ... Neither in the study of the wanderings and development of the individual soul, nor in the development of character, nor in the work of pure and lofty imagination, is collaboration possible.[8]

Besant's attitude reflects the socially and culturally prominent idea of the singular hero-artist of the late nineteenth century, a conception which engendered vigorous public legal and aesthetic debate over what constituted an author.

The origins of this particular doctrine appear to stem from an over-simplification of Romantic tenets of originality and authorship which mythologise the originating individual as literary genius. Aesthetes such as Edward Young and William Duff, as well as major legal figures such as William Blackstone and Francis Hargrave, are often cited as the precursors of this rhetoric. This is largely due to their public challenge in the previous century of the more multifaceted Renaissance and neo-Classical conceptions of the author as either a craftsman or inspired and both equally subject to independent sources. The author is, here, a mere 'vehicle or instrument' to a higher religious muse.[9] The eighteenth and nineteenth centuries' departure from this more versatile form of writing diminished the element of craftsmanship in favour of the inspired individual, but more significantly it also modified the source of this inspiration. As legal-literary theorists have repeatedly noted, this had broader implications not only for aesthetic definitions of authorship, but also for the development of English copyright law and the legal classification of an author's relationship with their work: 'inspiration came to be regarded as emanating not from outside or above, but from within the writer himself. "Inspiration" came to be explicated in terms of "original genius", with the consequence that the inspired work was made peculiarly and distinctively the product – and the property – of the writer.'[10]

The rapid technological printing advances and educational reforms of the nineteenth century, which enabled a proliferation of authors of all abilities and type, spawned a consolidation of this legal-aesthetic rhetoric in an attempt to safeguard the prestige of the inspired artist against the material conditions of the burgeoning Victorian publishing trade. The Romantic ideal of original authorship, which this rhetoric championed (and indeed helped to belatedly construct), was further institutionalised in domestic and international copyright law, most prominently in the form of the revised Copyright Act of 1842 and the ratification by nine countries of the Berne Convention in 1886 respectively.[11] Terry Eagleton understands these cultural and legal developments as a kind of 'spiritual compensation' for the debasement of the artist to a 'petty commodity producer', a point additionally borne out by the founding of the Society of Authors in 1884 which was, in part, an institutional manifestation of this divine recompense.[12] The society's central function was to protect authors from economic exploitation and implicitly recognise their professional status and legal rights. More pertinently to this study, it also worked to make a subtle distinction between an author's high art practice and the necessary mercantile trading which made an author's work available to the public and profitable to the author.[13] These distinctions contributed to, and in many ways prefigured, the growing separation of popular (mass) from high (elite) art and culture that distinguished the later modernist period and which flooded the cultural imagination of the 1890s, particularly in its preoccupation with preserving the honour of *succès d'estime* from the taint of fashionable recognition and economic reward.[14] Moreover, the patterning of this split along lines of gender and genre included the disenfranchisement of communal and collaborative norms of creativity which have arguably sustained artistic production throughout much of literary history.

Romantic doctrines of authorship that validate the hero-artist leave the collaborative author confined to 'satire, humour, fun, pathos', with the work of the 'pure and lofty imagination' far beyond these authors' inventive reach. This aesthetic division effectively pits the supposedly popular collaborative author against the elite singular artist. Such an argument is further sustained by the procedural and figurative execution of the collaborative process: the imagined visibility of two hands working together versus the assumed cerebral outpourings of the singular author. This illusory image of artistic hierarchies once again realigns collaborative literary endeavour with craftsmanship, rather than with inspiration. Dual authorship's requisite labours are, therefore, far from commensurate with the usual cultural status and financial rewards conferred on singular authors. This discordance further pushes collaborative practice and its merchandise out into the margins of the literary elite's body of serious literature. Myriam Boucharenc maintains that the position of the collaborative author has largely remained unchanged in contemporary culture: 'whatever creative or editorial operations it results from, and whether the community it embodies is avowed or inadmissible, private or political, real or symbolic, the plural author appears as a dissident in relation to the official figure of the Author.'[15] Many legal theorists also insist that idealised Romantic authorship and its implications remain 'deeply embedded in legal consciousness' and hence contemporary copyright laws still struggle to acknowledge the existence of joint authorship. These scholars forcibly maintain that 'no [modern] copyright can exist in a work produced as a true collective enterprise.'[16]

Despite (or indeed because of) its alleged illegality, however, reading collaborative authorship as a type of authorial dissidence becomes suggestive of the subversive cultural and literary power of the collaborative stance. This book explores authorial dissidence as a literary concept in the dual artistic practice of Somerville and Ross, a writing partnership that occupied and exploited the collaborative position in turn-of-the-century Ireland. It does so in order to examine and reassess the impact of Somerville and Ross' self-conscious authorial position on the cultural politics of their writing, as well as on historical and contemporary critical responses to their work. It further attempts to understand the 'double marginalisation' which Bette London recognises at work in women's collaborations of this period but, in addition, further seeks to investigate the ways in which the minor position of the female collaborator becomes a site of cultural authority and feminist ideals.[17] Chapter 1 investigates how specific discourses of the Romantic period concerning authorship and literary originality have contributed to a long-standing singular and proprietary ideal of the author figure. It examines the moral, philosophical and aesthetic foundations for the conceptualisation of this figure, as well as the associated beginnings of copyright law, and considers how these ideas contributed to delegitimising collaborative authorship in the nineteenth century. It also utilises the historical literary partnership of William Wordsworth and S. T. Coleridge as a case study for understanding the contradictions and complications between the law's understanding of authorship and the practicalities of collaborative authorial practice. This partnership also exposes the burgeoning split between 'high' and 'low' art forms, a division (this book argues) that compounds the aesthetic downgrading of Somerville and Ross' literary collaboration. Set alongside these eighteenth-century legal and literary developments, Somerville and Ross' collaborative methodologies and self-aware literary philosophies clearly represent a departure from sanctioned notions of authorship. Launching their writing careers into a cultural climate that was feverishly debating what it meant to be an author, and ostensibly privileging the individual hero-artist at the same time, caused multiple ideological and physical hardships for Somerville and Ross and their repeated attempts to publicly articulate and maintain their professional and intellectual dual identity.

Previous studies of the duo's literary practice have largely glossed over the collaboration as a domestic and/or sexual affair and this has unfavourably denied the textual and theoretical aspects of Somerville and Ross' authorship any serious consideration.[18] Chapter 2 attempts to reassert the intertwined intellectual and emotional contexts of Somerville and Ross' literary collaboration, as well as their own public and private definitions of coauthorship, in order to both complicate such critical discourses and provide a necessary reassessment of the sexual-textual dynamics of the duo's partnership. In so doing, it also pays specific attention to the personal and socioeconomic empowerment primarily achieved through Somerville and Ross' partnership, a partnership which became the bedrock and mainstay of both their collaboration and friendship, but which is frequently and prematurely collapsed into a discourse on female sexuality and homoerotic desire.

Janice Raymond's ground-breaking study of the 'philosophy of female affection', *A Passion for Friends* (1986), argues that female friendship needs to be studied and understood 'beyond the intimacy of a personal relationship' and regarded in the light of 'a politically affective state of being'.[19] Unsurprisingly, ethical and political discourses in Western philosophy and literature have long privileged male friendship within the latter context, from Aristotle and Plato through to Bacon, Montaigne, Kant, Nietzsche, Freud, and beyond. Female friendship, however, has largely been discounted from the fraternal bonds which such writers and thinkers have aligned with the founding of nation states and political communities, as well as the quest for self-identity and the source of moral awareness. This chapter moves towards a reintegration of the erotics and politics of female friendship in an attempt to fully comprehend the emotional intimacy that existed between Somerville and Ross, as well as the 'politically affective state of being' into which the friendship and subsequent literary collaboration moved the writing couple. The chapter further explores the duo's second novel, *The Silver Fox* (1897), as a literary representation of these friendship dynamics within the colonial context of nineteenth-century Irish politics and social relations. It finally attempts to reanimate both the oral and textual communications of their living partnership and, in so doing, explicitly reveal the significance of female letter-writing in the processes of joint creativity and the assertion of a public authorial identity. Somerville and Ross' coauthorship here becomes a site of what Marilyn Friedman has termed 'socially disruptive possibilities', whereby the collaboration enables Somerville and Ross to challenge the gendered expectations and ascribed roles of their given Anglo-Irish communities, as well as Victorian society more generally.[20]

While not necessarily refuting outright, therefore, the sexual readings of Somerville and Ross, this book argues for a widening of the boundaries within which such interpretations operate, in order to accommodate and appreciate the multiple determinants and contexts that necessarily problematise this straightforward historical and sexual conditioning of Somerville and Ross and their works. It also seeks to relocate Somerville and Ross' dual practice within the commercial, domestic, aesthetic and legal contexts in which that practice surfaced and which broadly attempted to define and marginalise literary collaboration as amateurish. Chapter 3 exposes the complexities and professional *savoir-faire* of the merchant negotiations between Somerville and Ross and their publishers, editors and agent, and puts back into radical circulation the public and private narratives which credit Somerville and Ross with a critical self-fashioning of their dual practice. The chapter further utilises Somerville and Ross' legal allegations of plagiarism in 1913 against the authors of a collection of Irish comic short stories, *By the Brown Bog*, in order to render explicit the intertwined legal and literary discourses which served to undermine the duo's collaboration. This legal case is also seen to highlight the ways in which the gendering of literary genres in this period fed into these discourses and did further damage to the collaborators' professional status.

Somerville and Ross' determination to assume their literary position in relation to the aesthetic and cultural debates that surrounded their authorial debut, as well as navigate the material conditions that this position entailed, places them alongside many of their more critically acknowledged female predecessors and peers. Literary historians and critics of the Victorian period, such as Catherine Gallagher, Linda Peterson, Betty Schellenburg and Gaye Tuchman, have persuasively argued and illustrated the influence of the commercial literary marketplace in eighteenth- and nineteenth-century women's attempts to forge an artistic and professional career. Jane Austen, Fanny Burney, Charlotte Brontë, Maria Edgeworth, Charlotte Riddell, Harriet Martineau, Margaret Oliphant, to name but a few, have all been shown to take different approaches to authorship and yet within these myriad approaches scholars have also exposed how they each 'articulated their role as authors, negotiated the material conditions of authorship, and constructed myths of the woman author, often against the material realities'.[21] Somerville and Ross' anarchical and successful exploitation of their enforced cultural and literary marginality enriches and sometimes complicates these debates by inserting into the mix an alternative mode of authorial practice which has hitherto been largely unstudied in any detail in this context.

This wholesale reconsideration of Somerville and Ross' dual authorship further suggests that the collaboration is not just a physical practice born of domestic convenience and affectionate like-mindedness, but a literary practice central to any critical understanding of their writing. Studies of female literary collaboration have variously recruited Somerville and Ross as a significant nineteenth-century case study in the development of a much more theoretically engaged approach to women's collaborative life and work. While this has its benefits in terms of understanding the significance of Somerville and Ross' collaborative practice within a broader social and literary context, as well as aiding the enhancement of critical theories crucial to highlighting the particularities and complex dynamics of female authorship, the overall effect has been to disembody the duo's collaborative practice from both its historical roots and the cultural politics of the texts that it engendered.[22] This study will suggest that the two are inextricably intertwined and that the collaborative

mindset was one which seems to have had an impact on Somerville and Ross'
attitude to both domestic and national issues.

Chapter 4 thus undertakes a detailed study of the duo's early travel literature
and argues for such works as a crucial embryonic stage in their dual writing
style. In these texts the double voice and dual persona of the collaborative
stance is often explicitly rendered through the texts' fictionalised travelling
companions who purport to represent both the actual and fictional 'We/I'
of the narrative voice. As a result, Somerville and Ross' employment of the
traveller text, particularly their recorded tour of the west of Ireland in *Through
Connemara in a Governess Cart* (1892), serves as a means of experimenting
with the multiple literary possibilities of the dual narrative voice in relation
to their home country. Somerville and Ross' depiction of Ireland in the text
as a shifting locus of national loyalties and hybridised local identities becomes
knitted to, and in fact reliant upon, an appreciation of the dual narrative voice
and its ability to hold in constant tension the multiplicity of an otherwise
static and singular authorial subjectivity. The fractured (yet always united)
authorial voice is not just a simple metaphor for the state of Anglo-Ireland's
national identity, but a physical practice governed by a working ideology which
permanently colours Somerville and Ross' cultural and political outlook on the
Irish nation. This further embeds the collaboration within the cousins' texts, as
well as those texts' material history, and the merchant and domestic processes
which initially brought those texts to the public arena.

With regard to the alternative critical narrative which the previous chapters
attempt to assert over Somerville and Ross' partnership, Chapter 5 finally
endeavours to resuscitate and interrogate Somerville's post-Ross and largely
self-styled spiritualist narrative of collaborative life and work. The preceding
chapters contextualise Somerville and Ross' literary and personal bond
within prevailing late-nineteenth-century legal, aesthetic and gender norms,
which significantly influence contemporaneous definitions of authorship.
The explicitly textual performances of this collaboration are also seen to
serve as a space for working out and defining Somerville and Ross' own
parameters of authorial identity and, this last chapter will argue, the spiritualist
manifestations of collaboration after Ross' death are a significant extension and
imitation of these various modes of coauthorship. Somerville's adoption of
the role of medium establishes an out-of-this-world continuation of a textual
discourse which sustains and fortifies the living collaboration. This latter half
of the collaboration, however, has lacked a certain seriousness of consideration
within critical circles and, rather than a continuation, it is somewhat severed
from the more corporeal joint authorship.[23] This final chapter, therefore,

interrogates the particular social and historical nexus of spiritualist practice and psychical enquiry that influenced Somerville long before Ross' death and came significantly to the fore after it. It finally suggests that Somerville's psychic literary collaboration was not just an indistinct simulacrum of the former animate coauthorship but a corresponding, if less successful, otherworldly collaborative practice that shifted the parameters once again of the monolithic author, and stretched the boundaries of normative literary collaboration itself.

From Ross' joyous declaration of authorship on the publication of her and Somerville's first novel, then, to Somerville's determination to utilise the dual signature beyond the grave, both women explicitly recognise that 'collaboration does not foreclose the demand for an author'.[24] Somerville and Ross repeatedly meet this demand throughout their working lives, but they also significantly revise the author figure who sits at the receiving end of such mandates and are, therefore, forced to mediate between acquiescing to, and challenging, their ascribed public and professional status as authors. This book's interrogation of that cultural dynamic recognises that the collaboration is a result both of specific ideological conditions, and the economic and social position of women writing in the late nineteenth century. In this light, Somerville and Ross' dual authorship, and collaborative authorship more broadly, has the potential to deepen and perhaps challenge current literary history's wider understanding and treatment of nineteenth-century female authorship and literary production in particularly resonant ways.

CHAPTER ONE

The legality and aesthetics of Victorian authorship

Questioned about his extensive authorial collaboration with Félix Guattari, the late twentieth-century philosopher, Gilles Deleuze, stated that, 'theft of thoughts [was] what I had with Félix. I stole Félix, and I hope he did the same for me.'[1] Deleuze here admits to the legal rhetoric which would effectively disenfranchise the dual signature of 'Deleuze and Guattari', and takes to the extreme the legal position of dual authorship when set against the sanctioned singular author figure. Textual collaboration is in effect reduced to a kind of intellectual plagiarism, a mutual stealing of thoughts. Deleuze, however, simultaneously defies this legal rhetoric by recontextualising it within an atmosphere of creativity that inscribes the legitimacy of collaborative authorship, and lays bare the revolutionary potential of such a practice: 'We were only two, but what was important for us was less our working together than this strange fact of working between the two of us. We stopped being "author".'[2] This celebrated ending of authorship recognises the collaborative position as one which bypasses the traditional legal and aesthetic construction of authorship and hence refuses to indulge in what Michel Foucault has termed the author's 'privileged moment of individualization'.[3] Deleuze and Guattari's 'working between the two of us' creates an artistic space whereby the authority of the individual writer in partnership is not simply doubled ('less our working together'), but fully dispersed ('working between the two of us').[4]

Yet, not unlike their Irish nineteenth-century predecessors, Deleuze and Guattari have had to face the ongoing legacy of the individual hero-artist in the academic establishment's attempts to subordinate or simply disengage altogether the name of Guattari to and from Deleuze. By using the Deleuzian corpus as the standard-bearer of Deleuze's mutual collaborations with Guattari, Gary Genosko argues that cultural and intellectual authority has been forced to 'pool around the figure of Deleuze'. As a result, the 'creative mutual enhancement of intellectual powers' which the collaborative alliance otherwise represents is misinterpreted through a publicly constructed power relation that explicitly 'subordinates Guattari'.[5] The implication is that Deleuze is the inspired genius and Guattari his labouring sidekick or, even more maliciously, that Deleuze's academically approved theoretical thinking is deformed by the militant analytical and political leanings of Guattari. The philosophical tomes of *L'Anti-Oedipe* and *Mille plateaux*, which bear the joint authorial name of 'Deleuze and Guattari', are thus rendered more politically and institutionally valuable, as Guattari himself admits, by quite simply omitting the latter's name.[6]

During their lifetimes and after, Somerville and Ross were similarly not immune to such a disentangling of their writing partnership, the latter of which was coupled with a determination to seek out the more talented author behind the collaboration. At the height of the elite but nonetheless fêted success of *The Real Charlotte* in 1895, the revered critic, folklorist and literary editor, Andrew Lang, encouraged Ross to privately admit to him that she was the one 'who did the writing'.[7] Lang was not alone in his suppositions. An early admirer of the duo's *An Irish Cousin* suggested that 'the next novel ought to be by *one* of them' because one of the hands was surely 'the better of the two'.[8] Katharine Tynan's obituary notice in December 1915, on the death of Ross, even went as far as erasing Somerville's literary input altogether by implying that 'beyond the illustrations', Somerville played no part in the actual writing of the stories. '[T]he collaboration is at an end' not because one of the partners in its success has passed away but, Tynan implies, more because the better of the two partners (the genius of Ross) has been lost.[9]

Such comments were also accompanied by a disbelief in the shared mechanics and dispersed thought processes of joint authorship. The repeated question of 'which of you holds the pen?' attempted to divide Somerville and Ross' texts into individually executed lots and always carried with it the assumption that, at some level, individual literary control had to be the driving force of the partnership.[10] In 1904 Somerville found herself being asked by a devoted reader: 'is it you that do the story and Miss Martin the words?'[11] Even Somerville and Ross's publishers found it difficult to understand the collaboration beyond a simple process of division of labour. In his massive enthusiasm for the cousins' sporting comic short stories, the editor of the *Badminton Magazine* 'attacked' Somerville to know which partner 'wrote which parts' during an editorial meeting in London in 1897.[12] In their inability to appreciate Somerville and Ross' coauthorship on both an ideological and practical level, these lines of questioning were both a source of bemusement and frustration to the two women and they eventually coined it 'the usual old thing', relegating it to the ranks of 'senseless curiosity'.[13] But such public curiosity was recognisably profitable, too, and the two authors became adept at channelling it to their advantage in the promotion of their works by way of the nascent celebrity culture of the Victorian literary marketplace.

Despite the complexity, then, of Somerville and Ross' attitude towards the parsing of their collaborative efforts, more recent critics (like their earlier counterparts) have still not been averse to an empirically-based reduction of the collaborative process to a simplistic division of labour, as well as the site of a dominant and single authorial consciousness. In the 1970s and 1980s, academic studies of Somerville and Ross were largely dominated by critical biographies which often attempted to both divide the collaboration into its assumed individual shares, and articulate a watertight division of labour. Gifford Lewis declared that Somerville was 'the major partner' in the duo's writing and both Violet Powell and Maurice Collis spent disproportionate amounts of time attempting to disentangle the textual threads of the partnership.[14] These foundational works still seem to have an effect on more contemporary thinking on Somerville and Ross' collaboration and, at least within Irish studies, attitudes towards the cousins' dual authorship, from the 1990s onwards, betray a subtle anxiety to construct a superior literary figure within the collaboration. In his *Life of W. B. Yeats*, Terence Brown's passing remark on the two authors cites Somerville as Ross' 'friend and literary co-adjutor', and Julie Anne Stevens posits Ross as 'a Bishopess of a High Comic Art, assisted by Somerville in the various rites of a cultural mission in Ireland'.[15] Declan Kiberd adds a further perspective through his comparison of Somerville and Ross' social critiques and the biting satires of Jane Austen. Up against the 'steely' individualism of Austen, Somerville and Ross' collaboration is cited as a form of literary and social weakness: '[a]s a duo they could form a sort of alternative society, offering one another mutual protection and support: only an *individual* as steely as Austen could hold out against the mindless sociable consensus [emphasis in original].'[16]

Concomitant with this later criticism, however, is a rising body of work which can be found within the fields of collaboration theory, legal-literary history, and women's studies, all of which have begun to dismantle such attitudes. Amid this work and significantly drawing on poststructuralist theories of authorship, critics such as Lorraine York, Holly Laird, Bette London and Jill Ehnenn have initiated a reorientation of critical approaches to Somerville and Ross (and women's creative collaborations more generally) in order to read and understand co-authored texts as the realisation of a consciously shared authorship instead of a means to dissect the 'relationship behind the writing'.[17] These latter studies are beginning to recognise the ways in which both historical and contemporary critical attitudes towards coauthorship derive from and arguably maintain the myth of the singular author-genius by either sundering literary partnership into its assumed constituent parts (hero-artist and hack assistant), or setting up the collaboration as a whole against the simulated literary greatness of a singular author figure. They also significantly acknowledge that social anxieties about lesbian desire have played their part in some of this critical fashioning of female co-authors, particularly in attempts by contemporary critics to unravel the textual authority of shared writing in order to 'disentangle the legs and arms' responsible for that writing: 'the spectacle of two women "holding the pen" may have suggested all too easily the notion that they might hold each other too.'[18]

Many of these studies, however, only utilise Somerville and Ross as an appropriate case study, often clustered among an ahistorical grouping of other female collaborators. The impact of such studies, therefore, has been somewhat minimal in terms of forcing a wider rethink of Somerville and Ross' overall collaborative life and professional practice and the latter's significance in interpreting and understanding their writing. Regardless of its sexual/textual origins, then, and aside from these important but all too brief inroads into reinterpreting Somerville and Ross' collaborative practice, the dominant critical ideology of collaboration still seems to prevail. The duo's coauthorship is more often than not either domesticated and deemed irrelevant, or forced to locate what Richard Badenhausen has termed 'a dominant voice', one that is 'finally privileged and identified by its signifying name right below the title'.[19] Badenhausen further maintains that by designating literary collaborations in this way, they are forbidden the 'construction of a more complicated (yet more tenuous) collaborative relationship where partners share artistic authority', an authority which evolves and resists 'being fixed, defined, and separated'.[20] Historical and contemporary denials of this 'more tenuous' relationship by the majority of Somerville and Ross' critics thus limit their literary collaboration to a sort of artistic developing ground, an amateur playing field which continuously hints at the possibility of one or other partner rising out of the collaborative rubble to assume a 'dominant voice' within a professional, singular and (metaphorically at least) heterosexual position.

Deleuze's legal-literary analogy neatly summarises the consequences of refusing this kind of singular authorship and its Romantic poetics. This analogy also crucially echoes Hélène Cixous' determination of female writing as a kind of 'working (in) the in-between', an 'ensemble of one and the other, not fixed in sequence of struggle and expulsion ... but infinitely dynamized by an incessant process of exchange from one subject to another'.[21] As a result, Deleuze seems to consciously align his collaborative ethic with the erotic and imaginative bonds which Cixous cites as the foundational bedrock of the female intellectual and creative impulse. Writing is here not a narrative, but a process of continual exchange which respects the desire for alterity within an empathetic identification with another subject. Deleuze's definition of collaboration thus allows for a much more fluid and open interpretation of the sexual/textual dynamics of coauthorship, and defies the critical tendency to untie the arms, legs and textual threads of creative partnerships.

For the purposes of this chapter, it also importantly highlights the significance of the historical interplay between legal and literary definitions of authorship and subtly recognises the cultural reinforcement derived from this twin discourse in the sustenance of a particular authorial type. As both Catherine Seville and Paul K. Saint Amour note, the birth of the profession of authorship witnessed in the nineteenth century, and to which Somerville and Ross forcefully subscribe, significantly coalesced around the legal issue of copyright: 'copyright was indispensable to the development of the author as a propertied, professional, and financially self-sufficient figure.'[22] A history of copyright law and its relationship to developing aesthetic definitions of authorship thus becomes a necessary preface to understanding Somerville and Ross' dual entry into the authorial marketplace in 1889, as well as their attempts to be recognised as professional authors. The following section of this chapter will examine the history of the development of copyright law in Britain across the eighteenth and nineteenth centuries, and analyse how the moral, philosophical and aesthetic foundations of this law delegitimised collaborative literary practice as a legally and publicly valued form of authorship.

Copyright and its discontents

Broadly viewed, the historical and ongoing rationale for copyright is to encourage aesthetic and intellectual works of public value through the appropriate encouragement and reward of private intellectual labour. To facilitate such a creative environment, copyright law is intended to create a fair legal balance between private reward, which is usually considered in both financial and moral terms, and public benefit. As a result, however, copyright law has had to both produce and legitimise a particular kind of author, usually singular and involved in an endeavour to create works of an original nature ('original' as defined by the courts) and in so doing it affects and conditions literary and other artistic production.[23] The first copyright law was introduced in Britain through the Statute of Anne (or the Act for the Encouragement of Learning) in 1709 and was, in effect, an attempt by the leading booksellers in London to regain their general monopoly over the publishing trade. This monopoly had been significantly reduced by a lapse in the Licensing Acts in 1694, as well as the piratical book trading of Britain's provincial booksellers.[24] Prior to this, a system of printing privileges granted by the Crown and based on the idea of artistic patronage was in operation under the auspices of the Stationers' Company. The company both regulated the book trade by controlling the printing and dissemination of an author's work, and acted as moral and royal censor.

As a consequence, a small but powerful coterie of London booksellers and printers acquired virtually perpetual rights over the printing and reprinting of authors' works and held some of the most lucrative rights in the business. The new statute placed a time limit on these rights (fourteen years in the first instance, followed by a fourteen-year renewal term) and eventually transferred them to the author, but many continued to cede their rights to the booksellers for a fixed fee on publication and this restored an albeit restricted level of control and profitability back to the London booksellers.[25] Edward Young's and Williams Duff's privileging of the inspired and proprietary individual author was to some extent heralded by this legal precedent, which gradually abolished the Royal Privilege and, more importantly, focused attention on the discussion of authors' common-law rights (i.e. natural rights, which supersede rights granted through statute law) and the desire to have those rights formally instituted.

Debates over the term of copyright continued throughout the century and the booksellers sustained their attempts to 'safeguard the perpetuity for their copyrights by treating the property rights of authors who ceded their manuscript to them as a common-law right'.[26] This argument drew strongly on Locke's discourse of rights-based property ownership and often echoed his rhetoric and philosophical bearing. Writing in the mid-1770s, for example, the lawyer, William Enfield, wrote that, '[l]abour gives a man a natural right of property in that which he produces: literary compositions are the effect of labour; authors have therefore a natural right of property in their works.'[27] But as an effect of intangible labour, rather than mechanical endeavour, artistic composition is extracted from the complex literary, social and commercial relations that sustain it and is thus viewed as a special type of property. Even so (and not without difficult contradictions), this literary property is still offered, in its more concrete form, the same kinds of legal protection as its more physical counterparts. If the incorporeal nature of literary ideas could not be owned or protected by the law, the argument went, the expression (style and sentiment) of those ideas definitely could.[28] Moreover, the right of that expression and its originality belonged to its author in perpetuity and this treats the literary work as both an economic commodity and an Hegelian extension of the self that demands legal protection by natural right.

Much of the legal struggle over an author's property rights in the 1760s and 1770s, largely witnessed through prominent court arguments and polemical pamphlets, predates but nonetheless gestures towards Hegel's formalisation in 1821 of property as an adjunct of individual will.[29] Lawyer and judge, William Blackstone, asserted in 1769 that '[s]tyle and sentiment are the essentials of a literary composition. These alone constitute its identity.'[30] By ascribing a recognisable 'identity' to 'literary composition', one that is the sole effect of an author's invention and labour, Blackstone effectively begins to minimise the ontological distinction between the author and the work. Francis Hargrave would later pursue this idea in his pamphlet *Argument in Defence of Literary Property* (1774), and realign much more firmly the author's unique personality with the physical effects of the author's labours:

> Every man has a mode of combining and expressing his ideas peculiar to himself. The same doctrines, the same opinions, never come from two persons ... A strong resemblance of stile, of sentiment, of plan and disposition, will be frequently found; but ... a literary work *really* original, like the human face, will always have some singularities, some lines, some features, to characterize it, and to fix and establish its identity [emphasis in original].[31]

The literary work and the personality behind that work become ever more intricately entwined in Hargrave's invocation of the individual human face as a metaphor for the literary work's now anthropomorphic 'modes of thinking and writing', 'connection of ideas', and 'use and arrangement of words' which, like the lines and features of a human face, are both original and constitutive of that face's physical identity. The cognitive leap is but a small one from these late eighteenth-century attempts to justify literary property as a natural right, to Hegel's much more explicit assertion in the early 1820s that property more generally is always an expression of individual will: 'an *embodiment* of personality [emphasis in original]'.[32]

Hegel's philosophy had a direct and swift impact on continental Europe's development of copyright law, particularly in France and Germany, and would later significantly influence English law by grounding itself within a moral rights argument. The work of Hargrave and Blackstone, as well as the growing consolidation of their argument in public and court circles, had arguably ripened the ground for this belated welcome of Hegel's philosophies within English legal thinking. Moreover, Hargrave and Blackstone also notably rely on Locke's dual theory of labour and occupancy with regard to their own justifications of an author's natural right in their work, as had Young before them, and thereby insist that the cultivation of the mind is no different to the cultivation of a piece of land. All three critics create an analogy between propertied land and literary composition whereby the 'mind of a man of Genius' becomes 'a fertile and pleasant field', and the former's original compositions that field's 'fairest flowers'.[33] Literary properties are here defined as material goods – flowers to be picked – but in also arguing for them as Hegelian signs of personality, such properties become seemingly physical and immaterial at the same time, both objective and subjective: '[t]he commodity that changed hands when a bookseller purchased a manuscript or when a reader purchased a book was thus personality no less than ink and paper.'[34] Via the legal debates of the eighteenth century, then, copyright law eventually conflates Locke's and Hegel's characteristically rights-based validations of private property, and this is despite Hegel's rejection of Locke's belief in man's ownership of self as a natural given in the state of nature. The right to property exists in both cases by being the proprietor of one's own body and mind, regardless of the divergence between how and when that possession takes place. As a result, literary properties are protected as both a reward for the effort of individual labour, and a necessary condition for (and manifestation of) the right to life and liberty.

The future difficulty for collaborative authorship already begins to become apparent here. Property as an expression of individual will disallows joint authors a legal claim to the fruits of their labours by refuting the possibility of the individual as an incarnation of shared (as opposed to exclusive) consciousness. Copyright law's incorporation of these metaphysics of rights-based ownership, which consequently define authorship, originality and literary work, thus struggles to protect the product of an individual's labour where the mechanical process (style and sentiment) and intentionality of that labour cannot be physically distinguished. In other words, where that mechanical process is part of an inherently collaborative and intersubjective system of creative activity, one that does not recognise mine and yours in a jointly authored work, the long arm of the law is suddenly shortened.

The very public ontological and ethical questions which these arguments consequently engendered about the nature of authorship – the origins of literary work, artistic composition and property – and the relationship between an author and the marketplace, had a lasting and powerful impact. The force of the booksellers' reasoning bypassed, albeit metaphorically, the now infamous landmark ruling of *Donaldson v. Becket* in 1774, which saw the courts finally rule against the booksellers' claims for authors to be entitled to a common-law right in their work. Despite the ruling, the London booksellers managed to successfully use their arguments to develop the 'representation of the author as proprietor' and force this representation into the public and legal consciousness: 'the [court's] decision did not touch the basic contention that the author had a property in the product of his labor. Neither the representation of the author as a proprietor nor the representation of the literary work as an object of property was discredited.'[35]

The influence of this representation continued to be felt in the following century, notably resurfacing in the build-up to the 1842 revision of copyright law, which significantly witnessed the active involvement of authors opposed to booksellers in the renewed agitation for perpetual, or at least extended, copyright. William Wordsworth, Thomas Carlyle, Robert Southey, Charles Dickens, Robert Browning and Thomas Arnold all offered their support to author, judge and MP, Sir Thomas Noon Talfourd, and his parliamentary bill to revise the term of copyright to the life of the author plus sixty years, marking a zenith in the conflation of aesthetic and legal discourse over authorship, originality and literary property. Wordsworth's often contradictory public stance in particular offers material insights into the actual and theoretical difficulties that would go on to plague and disinherit collaborative authors later in the century, such as Somerville and Ross.[36]

Coupled with his role as poet, Wordsworth's legalistic familial background also encouraged a lifelong dialogue between the discourses of law and literature. This dialogue is important for understanding how the commercial literary marketplace of the nineteenth century developed and why the careers of writers like Somerville and Ross suffered under its professionalisation of their trade. As Mark Shoenfield has pointed out, this specific dialogue locates Wordsworth as a key transitional figure between the overt professionalisation of authorship to which the late nineteenth century bore witness, and in which Somerville and Ross' early career played out, and modernist anxieties over high and low art forms. This dialogue also demonstrates the legal and material developments of eighteenth-century commerce, which augured that professionalisation.[37] Wordsworth's active control over his own copyrights, and his marshalling of his words into what Shoenfield terms 'a symbolic capital', suggest a relatively new concept in the management of a poetic career, one which is forced to make the difficult reconciliation between idealised Romantic aesthetics and the increased commodification of authorship.[38] This is a reconciliation that Somerville and Ross and other collaborative authors found doubly difficult to make given the cultural downgrading of their dual practice.

Wordsworth's literary partnership with S. T. Coleridge in the publication of the 'most famous co-authored book in English literature', the *Lyrical Ballads*, further makes Wordsworth's pronouncements on original authorship significant and necessary.[39] In two key essays published in the 1990s, Alison Hickey points out that 'collaborative relations are an indisputable fact of the Romantic period', and the 'still-prevalent assumption that creation is a solitary process owes much to insufficiently-considered notions of Romanticism as the flourishing of individual genius'.[40] Both historical and contemporary critics, including those involved in the history of the rise of the professional author and consolidation of English copyright law, have arguably been guilty of assenting to and further advocating the public centrality of such notions with little regard for the private dynamics of compositional practice that the Romantic era exposes. Wordsworth, Coleridge and their respective wider circle of collaborative relationships played a key part in this prevailing public discourse of originality and authorship. Any attempt to understand, however, the aesthetic and legal ideologies of literary partnership, as well as resuscitate the historical narrative of joint authorship's increasing alienation from dominant definitions of the author figure, crucially relies on a much more ambiguous narrative.

The next section of this chapter argues that such a narrative resurfaces in the incongruity between dominant public aesthetic discourses and the much more untidy and often acrimonious textual, commercial and collaborative practices that lay beneath the surface of those discourses. It makes this argument by analysing Wordsworth's attitude towards copyright, literary genius and the professionalisation of authorship in this period, as well as utilising Wordsworth's public literary collaboration with S. T. Coleridge as a brief case study. This analysis provides a means of understanding how the period's changing copyright laws later began to affect the legitimacy of collaborative authorship in the nineteenth century; it also looks towards the very specific difficulties that Somerville and Ross faced as they attempted to forge a literary career in the wake of these legal and aesthetic developments.

The anxieties of joint authorship: Wordsworth and Coleridge

Fuelled by the dismal sales of his *Poems, in Two Volumes* (1807), Wordsworth argued that every author, 'as far as he is great and at the same time *original*, has had the task of *creating* the taste by which he is to be enjoyed' [emphasis in original].[41] The 'proof' of genius lies in doing 'well what is worthy to be done' and, more importantly, doing 'what was never done before':

> there never has been a period ... in which vicious poetry, of some kind or other, has not excited more zealous admiration, and been far more generally read than good, but this advantage attends the good, that the *individual*, as well as the species, survives from age to age; whereas, of the depraved, though the species be immortal, the individual quickly *perishes* [emphasis in original].[42]

The general unpopularity of Wordsworth's work is here secured as a sign of his individual genius – a literary authority which surpasses the faddish tastes of the reading public and ensures the kind of individual artistic posterity that Wordsworth desires. Perpetual (or at least substantial) copyright becomes ever more necessary in attaining, in the words of Talfourd, 'that justice which society owes to authors [especially those] whose reputation is of slow growth and enduring character'.[43]

Wordsworth's immediate and impending financial needs, however, were not enough to discourage a certain reticence over being seen to favour in public Talfourd's new copyright bill in the early decades of the nineteenth century.[44] This reticence is telling. In order to guarantee his future posterity, Wordsworth's living authorship and published works had to be consistent with the claims that he made for them and thus had to avoid the taint of private financial aspiration. Lord Camden's courtroom slur on those seeking everlasting common-law rights for authors in 1774 was well known: '[i]t was not for gain that Bacon, Newton, Milton, and Locke instructed [and delighted] the world; it would be unworthy [*sic*] such men to traffic with a dirty bookseller for so much a sheet of letterpress.'[45] In order to sidestep such accusations, Wordsworth reasoned that his interest in the proposed copyright bill lay in its justice, rather than in its individual economic gains for authors, and conversely invoked a similar argument to Camden in support of Talfourd's bill.

Wordsworth's argument indirectly suggests that precisely because an author does not want to have to 'traffic with a dirty bookseller', he should be entitled to an unending or at least substantial right to oversee the publication and propagation of his work in order to ensure its posterity in the form in which it was originally created.[46] Furthermore, Wordsworth implies, in order to achieve the much-coveted posterity that Camden rigorously affirms as the only honourable remuneration available to an author, substantial legal protection and its by-product of economic gain become essential. Denial of this legal protection places in jeopardy the ability of 'a conscientious author' with familial obligations to produce 'good books': '[d]eny it to him, and you unfeelingly leave a weight upon his spirits, which must deaden his exertions; or you force him to turn his faculties ... to inferior employments.'[47] Returning, as many did, to the conflation of literary and all other property, Wordsworth finally argues that poems as property increase the reputation of 'Authors as a Class': 'the possession of Property tends to make any body of men more respectable'.[48]

Wordsworth thus ensures personal and (more importantly) social development through the respect derived from property ownership; a respect notably linked to the founding principles of property ownership espoused by Locke and which had previously paved the road for copyright's original initiation. As James Holston notes of Locke's rights-based property owners: '[they] are more likely to think responsibly about the consequences of their actions because they naturally want to leave their property to their descendants and do not want irresponsible behaviour to compromise its perpetuation. Thereby, property ownership generates responsible citizens with real stakes in the future of the nation.'[49] This implied national debt owed to authors was further amplified by Trevelyan imperial politics and British territorial conquest in the mid- to late nineteenth century. In his article on the 'Copyright Question' for *Blackwood's Magazine* in 1842, for example, Scottish author, Archibald Alison, harnessed British colonial policy to advance the argument for perpetual rights for authors:

> A nation which aspires to retain its eminence either in arts or in arms, must keep a-breast of its neighbours; if it does not advance, it will speedily fall behind, be thrown into the shade, and decline. It is not sufficient for England to refer to the works of Milton, Shakespeare, Johnson, or Scott; she must prolong the race of these great men, or her intellectual career will speedily come to a close.[50]

In addition, Matthew Arnold's later attack in 1880 on America's piratical book trade expands the underlying premise of Alison's argument by suggesting that 'the proprietary right of the author' is crucial to the overall civilising process. America's refusal to submit to an international regulation of copyright is here interpreted as a lack of 'a spirit of delicacy' which holds the nation back from being 'truly and thoroughly civilised'.[51] Copyright, therefore, was not simply viewed as a mercantile refinement, but a vital indicator of national maturity. As a consequence, the professional and social aspirations that Wordsworth ascribes to authors in the early nineteenth century's quarrel over copyright reform not only deflect attention from the personal gains of the individual under an extended term of copyright, but significantly reorient the public's attention to the communal cultural and potentially national benefits instead, benefits that would be latched on to by future proponents of perpetual copyright for authors, such as Arnold and Alison.

In these early decades of the nineteenth century, copyright is thus accordingly justified as a cultural and potentially national, rather than simply economic, essential and the benefits are primarily public rather than private. The legal protection here proffered to authors further endorses private ownership of literary products and, as a consequence, redefines literary originality as that which 'was never done before' and which significantly antedates the public taste and comprehension by which it will eventually be known. But this almost Kantian definition of originality as an 'exemplary' or 'fanatical' type of originality is a far cry from copyright's now seemingly modest initial aspiration, which was to simply prevent the unlawful and direct copying and sale of an already published work.[52] While it is undeniable that copyright is necessary to ensure fair remuneration to authors, and collaborative authors are no exception to this, this definition of originality damagingly conceals the collaborative state of affairs that often governs the site of literary production and propagation (whether singular or collective), and does so by effectively denying historically approved compositional techniques that rely on imitation, tradition, assimilation and communal models of thought. It was exactly this explanation of originality that W. B. Yeats would later rage against, recognising in its execution a denial of tradition's rightful place in poetic activity and a fallacious cultivation of the originating individual.[53] Yet Wordsworth's instrumental support for and ideological fostering of the 1842 Copyright Act and its foundational philosophies, the latter of which were anathema to Yeats, were also opposed by the more collaborative literary methodologies to which Wordsworth himself elsewhere lays claim. His earlier publication with Coleridge of *Lyrical Ballads* in 1798 defies, in particular, many of the legal and moral justifications put forward in the argument for an extended term of copyright, and accordingly triggers a restrained angst over the public signification of the dual signature that is worth considering in more detail.

Wordsworth's and Coleridge's now familiar joint publication, *Lyrical Ballads*, was originally published anonymously and Coleridge explains to their publisher, Joseph Cottle, that this is because his and Wordsworth's names have no public or commercial value: 'Wordsworth's name is nothing – to a large number of persons mine *stinks* [emphasis in original].'[54] Jack Stillinger's interrogation of the 'myth of solitary genius' highlights the volume's various methods of authorial self-effacement and notes the emphasis on an anonymous sole author: the several references to 'the author' (singular), 'his expressions', 'his personal observation', 'his friends', and 'the author's own person' in the prefatory 'Advertisment' clearly implied, and were taken to indicate, single authorship.[55] As Stephen Prickett further points out, the assumption of singular authorship which this anonymity subtly encourages is used to avoid the threat of aesthetic rupture by recognising that the collection's artistic unity would perhaps be lost on a public unable to believe in an individualistic dual style and schema.[56] Wordsworth and Coleridge's choice of authorial anonymity, therefore, is one which substantiates the cultural power of the solitary author in the literary marketplace.

Coleridge's preoccupation with the cultural and market worth of his and Wordsworth's proper names is further suggestive of a broader anxiety concerning literary origins and individual authority. The note to Cottle intimates recognition of the performative nature of authorial signatures through understanding that it is the social forces which surround them that designate cultural and literary authority. This authority is one which often bypasses the living person behind the signature. Hickey notes a similarly fraught obsession with proper names in Coleridge's earlier collaborative relationship with Robert Southey and the publication of their co-authored play, *The Fall of Robespierre* (1794), and suggests that Coleridge recognises that 'the authority of a "proper" name, rather than being the inalienable "property" of the person to whom it apparently belongs, is a collectively constructed fiction.'[57] The anonymous lone author of *Lyrical Ballads* thus volunteers a sanctioned and somewhat neutral male literary figure to its audience, one which deliberately obscures the collaborative partnership from which it emerged. In so doing, it subtly reveals at least one set of anxieties that the joint authorial stance creates in public and which is further exacerbated through Wordsworth's and Coleridge's editorial interventions in subsequent reprints of *Lyrical Ballads*.

Coleridge (if only privately) did indeed believe in the dual compositional authority of the collection and reasoned to Cottle that: 'We deem that the volumes offered to you are to a certain degree <u>one work</u>, in <u>kind tho' not in degree</u>, as an Ode is one work – & that our different poems are as stanzas, good relatively rather than absolutely: – Mark you, I say <u>in kind</u> tho' not in degree.'[58] Despite his later and very personal divergence from Wordsworth's poetic creed, Coleridge still maintains this collaborative unity in his description of the joint aesthetic and symbolic 'plan' of *Lyrical Ballads* in his autobiography, *Biographia Literaria* (1817):

> During the first year that Mr. Wordsworth and I were neighbours [1797], our conversations turned frequently on the two cardinal points of poetry ... The thought suggested itself (to which of us I do not recollect) that a series of poems might be composed of two sorts ... In this idea originated the plan of the 'Lyrical Ballads'.[59]

The fertile and generously collaborative environment that Coleridge, Wordsworth and the latter's sister, Dorothy, fostered during their walking tours of the late 1790s in Devon arguably framed the inception of the first edition of their experimental ballads. John Beer notes the 'considerable intellectual excitement' that surrounded both poets at this time, and concludes: '[a] whole range of ideas had come to the surface in their minds simultaneously, and were fermenting together – ideas which they were ready to explore further.'[60] Yet successive versions of the *Lyrical Ballads* significantly begin to erase these collaborative origins and reinsert in their place a more legally and aesthetically acceptable model of authorship and literary composition. This seems due, in large part, to the increasing personal and literary rift between Wordsworth and Coleridge, but is significantly fuelled by their individual anxieties about the poet as central origin of literary creation.

The process of separating and redefining the authorial lots played in composing *Lyrical Ballads* can be seen most clearly in Wordsworth's increasing authorial distance from the compositional role he played in 'The Rime of the Ancient Mariner'. In the Preface to the second edition, Wordsworth clearly distinguishes the individual authorship of each of the poems in the collection and divides his own from Coleridge's by individually listing and singly attributing the contributions of the latter. Elsewhere, Wordsworth's commentaries on 'The Ancient Mariner' further seek to distinguish his individual literary contributions and ideas from Coleridge's in ways that gradually obliterate the much more exulted moments of open collaboration that the authors shared:

> Much the greatest part of the story was Mr. Coleridge's invention; but certain parts I myself suggested, for example, some crime was to be committed which should bring upon the Old Navigator ... the spectral persecution, as a consequence of that crime, and his own wanderings ... I also suggested the navigation of the ship by the dead man ... I furnished two or three lines at the beginning of the poem, in particular:

And listened like a three years' child;
The Mariner hath his will.[61]

The poem's relegation to the back end of volume one in the later edition further discards the collaborative artistic unity Coleridge had described in *Biographia Literaria* as being at the heart of the book's formal structure and philosophical thematic. This is additionally compounded by Wordsworth's suggestion in the Preface that Coleridge's poems have only been included for the 'sake of variety' and through a 'consciousness' of Wordsworth's 'own weakness', rather than to consolidate the collaborative ideals which Coleridge hints were the original genesis of the collection.[62] Wordsworth finally puts the nail in the coffin of the collaboration by reprinting the second edition under his own name and referring to Coleridge as simply an unnamed 'Friend' who has liberally assisted him in furnishing the collection with a few additional poems, ones which offer the 'same tendency' in the 'colours of [their] style' to his own.[63]

Critics have usefully picked up on these and other important distinctions between the first (1798) and second (1800) editions of *Lyrical Ballads*. Prickett argues that the later edition 'is still a collaborative effort, but the nature of that collaboration was no longer spontaneous, unforced, and open-ended: capable of developing into something individually beyond the reach of either'; and Beer maintains that Wordsworth's 'staking out of his own territory of the human heart' for the second edition marked the 'end to a *concordat* that had seemed at times like the adoption of a dual identity'.[64] Neither critic, however, entertains the idea that the increasing split between the two poets lies outside of a predominantly aesthetic difference of opinion or, at the very least, that that split is aggravated by other influential factors. There is room to suggest, I would argue, that a certain authorial anxiety played a role in Wordsworth's and Coleridge's apparent inability to admit that their co-authored works could potentially supersede their individually executed ones. As this book will later go on to demonstrate, this is in complete contradiction to Somerville and Ross' more positive attitude towards collaboration and the superiority of their dual- over single-authored works.

Coleridge was certainly plagued by a very particular anxiety of authorship, one which acted as a burning catalyst in his almost obsessive need to continually redefine the philosophy behind literary composition and original genius. Writing in December 1811 to an unknown correspondent, Coleridge defends Walter Scott's use of his poem 'Christabel' against a charge of plagiarism by asserting that: 'I have ever held parallelisms adduced in proof of plagiarism or even of intentional imitation, in the utmost contempt ... It will not be [by]

Dates, that Posterity will judge of the originality of a Poem; but by the original spirit itself.'[65] Despite this reverence for the disclosure of tradition through the poetic act, this notion of 'parallelisms' in literature – the co-existence of several texts, voices and narratives within a single structure of ideas – was also a source of unease for Coleridge throughout his career. In describing the writing of 'Kubla Khan', for example, Coleridge remains uncertain as to the validity of his singular creative processes: 'if that indeed can be called composition in which all the images rose up before him as *things*, with a parallel production of the correspondent expressions' [emphasis in original].[66] In his now famous essay 'Tradition and the Individual Talent', Eliot would much later authenticate the individual cognitive and emotional processes which Coleridge here associates with creative thought. In so doing, he also dispels the latter's anxieties by confidently (and very similarly) claiming that 'the poet's mind is in fact a receptacle for seizing and storing up numberless feelings, phrases, images, which remain there until all the particles which can unite to form a new compound are present together'.[67] Whether collaboratively or singularly authored, these anxieties and ideas are all suggestive of the ways in which literary creativity is rarely a solitary process.

Contemporary theorists of artistic creativity still significantly uphold these earlier definitions of compositional practice, maintaining that 'creativity occurs in a portion of the mind where images and thoughts are combined without conscious manipulation'.[68] For Coleridge, however, this refraction of individual compositional authority into a diffused set of prior texts made known and new through an enabling poetic tradition rather than *ex nihilo* creation suggests the social nature of authorship upon which such theories rely. The poet here recognises, as he must do, the challenge socialised authorship represents to the solitary inspired artist so crucial to legally sanctioned concepts of authorship and originality and, hence, the discordance of his poetic creed with the kinds of public authorship to which he is wedded.

Jerome J. McGann rightly associates 'Kubla Khan' and its Romantic subject of 'loss and the threat of loss' with these wavering aesthetic and intellectual beliefs: 'even as Coleridge (like Hegel) saw real human history flow unselfconsciously out of the precedent idea, he lost his conviction that this pattern could be surely grasped, even unselfconsciously, in the single inspired individual.'[69] However, Coleridge's advocacy of Aristotle's general law of association in *Biographia Literaria* (heavily influenced by the German philosopher J. G. E. Maass) is implicated in these intellectual developments and also needs attention. Coleridge's understanding of Aristotle is concomitant with what McGann recognises as the poet's desire for unity and containment, as well as this aspiration's incompatibility with a belief in the 'determining primacy of the creative person'.[70] According to Coleridge, Aristotle's '*common condition* under which all exciting causes act' is founded on the power of recollection, or '*after-consciousness*', of an expressed idea [emphasis in original]. That is to say, 'every partial representation [single idea] awakes the total representation [linked ideas] of which it had been part' or, more pertinently, every idea continually recollects the 'total impressions' with which it had previously 'co-existed'.[71]

The affinities of associationism with the compositional rhetoric that surrounds 'Kubla Khan' are fairly obvious, as is the anxiety of Coleridge's position within such a philosophy, but what needs stressing here is the disjunction between these intellectual beliefs and Coleridge's earlier criticism of public distinctions between literary and other property: 'the natural, but not therefore the less partial and unjust distinction, made by the public itself between *literary* and all other property' [emphasis in original].[72] This criticism was similarly repeated by Southey, who drew even more directly on the previous century's legal analogies between literary and landed property put forward by Young, Blackstone and Hargraves in the argument for the protection of literary properties:

> My opinion is that literary property ought to be inheritable, like every other property; and that a law which should allow you the use of the trees upon your estate for eight-and-twenty years, and after that term make them over to the Carpenter's Company, would not be more unjust than that which takes from me and my heirs the property of my literary labours, and gives it to the Company of Booksellers.[73]

Recognising the way in which legal mechanisms conflate 'literary and all other property', and desiring (like Wordsworth and Southey) to publicly and rationally maintain this distinction in order to justify an extended term of copyright, Coleridge attempts to remove the disjunction he perceives between an unfair public perception of literary property and legal definitions of the same. He achieves this largely by subordinately pitting what he calls '*passive* fancy' (the state that Nature hath provided) against '*mechanical* memory' (the Labour of his body and the Work of his hands) [emphasis in original].[74] But his later philosophising on the origins of ideas and their expression validates, even if unintentionally, the 'unjust distinction' he is attempting to collapse.

In the case of literary property, eighteenth- and nineteenth-century copyright laws cannot protect an idea; they can only protect that idea's representation and, therein, according to the courts, lies the work's originality. If Coleridge (via Aristotle) is right and an idea is merely a partial fragment of a larger entity with which, at one point, it co-existed, and to which it perpetually re-enacts that co-existence, then the law (conceptually at least) is equally unable to protect that idea's representation. The latter will, in any textual format, always be expressive of the 'after-consciousness' of the idea it seeks to represent. 'Literary property', then, is not like 'other property' in this case and such a conceptual dilemma has very literal ramifications for how copyright law deals with collaborative authors and their works. The physically available evidence (identifiable labour) of legal ownership becomes much easier to demarcate in singly authored works (one idea) as opposed to collaboratively authored works (unity of ideas). Note, for instance, that Wordsworth attempted not only to distinguish his individual ideas in the 'Ancient Mariner' from Coleridge's, but also the 'representation' of those ideas, that is, the particular lines he composed (according to him) singly. In order to extricate his individual authorial identity from the poem, Wordsworth divides the poem into separately owned parts and individually enacted labours, thus relying on sanctioned notions of legally enforced property rights.

These anxieties over collaboration significantly link back to the question of poetic genius. As Jerome Christensen aptly puts it in his study of Coleridge's *Biographia Literaria*, such a question is ultimately 'the question of the poet's property in his works and in himself'.[75] The fact of genius for Coleridge, Christensen maintains, 'is the reality of a mind autonomous and whole', and it is this autonomy and wholeness that collaboration most endangers.[76] The potential subversion of authorial legitimacy which, to varying degrees Wordsworth and Coleridge attempt to thwart, is thus also an attempt to preserve their individual status as *bone fide* poets. Collaboratively or singly authored, then, literary works potentially remain subject to Coleridge's interpretation of Aristotle's general law of association and this feeds into Coleridge's broader concern with the loss of a personal individual identity and authority, as well as a specifically artistic one. His texts frequently expose the collaborative unity of ideas as well as the resultant refraction of the autonomous author, the latter of which has been culturally and legally constructed as the only valid method and sign of literary authorship and original genius. The contradictions between these positions (the reality of authorship and the construction of authorship) are allowed to remain, and legal mechanisms to operate as they do, largely because of the contrived simplicity on which copyright law subsequently relies and actively generates to clear the muddy waters surrounding the relationship between an idea and its expression, as well as originality and plagiarism. Such 'binarisms', Saint-Amour maintains, usefully appeal to the 'legislative need for categorisation', but they also do a grave 'violence to the inherently complex and ambiguous objects they govern'.[77] In terms of actual collaboration between two or more people, there is consequently an instinctive tendency to maintain these binary distinctions and view such a practice as a precise 'doubling' rather than an unmanageable 'dispersal' of authorial control. Literary authority is here viewed as always individualistic and inalienable and there is also, therefore, a propensity to disentangle rather than accept as a whole the products of such partnerships and collaborations. Within this body of thought, collective authority is always bypassed as an illegitimate or somehow suspect kind of authority.

Wordsworth and Coleridge waver between acknowledging the artistic benefits of collaboration and being consumed by an anxiety that collaborative authorship, and even collaborative systems of creativity that operate within singular authorship, are not *real* authorship. As a result, the outwardly schizophrenic attitude that Robert MacFarlane, among others, detects in Romantic pronouncements on literary originality and authorship here becomes an internalised conflict between the known realities of compositional poetic techniques and the pressures of the literary marketplace.[78] The financial and aesthetic posterity Wordsworth and Coleridge yearn for, however, significantly downplays the ferocity of this intellectual battle in public by the poets' more open and subsequently alleged favouring of individualistic notions of authorship and ownership on which such posterity relies. Collaborative methods of literary composition are gradually demoted within this easing into the public and legal consciousness of a Romantic ideal of original creativity – an unworkable ideal hallmarked by the 1842 Copyright Act and subsequently endorsed by the nineteenth century's ongoing efforts to professionalise the figure of the author.

The second half of the nineteenth century saw not only the establishment of the Society of Authors, but also the entrance of the literary agent, the introduction of a basic royalty system for authors, and the authorisation of international copyright regulations, all of which continued to favour the propertied and professional author figure. Moreover, the Royal Commissioners' Report on Copyright in 1878, albeit finally quashing the argument for perpetual copyright, solidified the conception of copyright as the best and most fair means by which the rewards for individual creativity and public interest can be impartially balanced. The subsequent history of copyright reform in Britain suggests a lack of influential resistance to the inexorable fact of copyright as guaranteed by the 1878 report and this history has thus proved a largely repetitive one: ever-increasing extensions to the length of authors' rights over their public works. The now ostensibly reserved fourteen-year term originally instituted by the Statute of Anne in 1709 has, two centuries later, become a life-of-the-author-plus-seventy-year term. The irony of the 1878 report has been, therefore, somewhat damaging. Despite failing to sanction perpetual copyright, its validation of copyright as both a 'proprietary right' and one which it would not be 'expedient to substitute' with any other form of legal right has simply allowed the proponents of copyright to move ever closer to that which the report attempted to deny: never-ending rights for authors.[79] In spite of its history of public and forceful detractors over the last two centuries then, and without wanting to gloss over the copyright battles of the twentieth and twenty-first centuries, copyright law arguably maintains its hegemony over definitions of authorship and literary properties and continues to underwrite the communal compositional techniques which conversely make possible the works it purports to protect.

While not disputing that there exists both historically and currently an underlying tide of subversive rhetoric against the often flawed logic of copyright, as well as the compositional techniques which defy the legal and literary marketplace, this book nonetheless maintains that the ontological and legal foundations for copyright were sanctified as a dominant discourse in the late nineteenth century. The inevitability of copyright was thus secured by the time Somerville and Ross entered the literary marketplace but, despite copyright's exclusion of their collaborative practice as professionally and legally valid, the literary duo determined to avail of the financial and cultural advantages which copyright had bestowed on the profession of authorship. The contradictions inherent in their position placed an enormous ideological pressure on their public self-fashioning of dual authorship and, combined with public resistance to their professional status on the grounds of their gender, further fuelled their sense of needing to navigate with skill and caution various public discourses in order to achieve the cultural and financial standing they both felt were rightly theirs. Several features of their collaborative stance, however, remained largely untouched by these contradictions throughout their careers: the duo's unfailing belief in literary partnership as culturally and socially equal to singular authorship; their repeated attempts to defy and exploit their marginal literary position; and the centrality of the dynamics of that marginality, as well as of their collaborative practice, to the political and cultural ideologies which governed their writing.

The dynamics of female collaboration: Somerville and Ross

Scholars of artistic collaboration have long noted the imaginative fertility of collaboration's dual linguistic roots, as well as its entrenchment in the literary and academic mind with regard to coauthorship. The *OED* defines collaboration as an act of working together, particularly in intellectual work, but also as an act of traitorous cooperation with the enemy and thus simultaneously friend and foe, partner and colluder, colleague and turncoat, teammate and mole. Despite their antithesis, however, both senses of the word 'collaboration' cluster together in their continual interrogation of identity, the self, and individual authority. Within this context, much was made of collaboration's dual definition in the early 1800s by critics of the Romantic poets and their collaborative circles, denouncing them as a 'sect of poets', and 'dissenters from the established systems in poetry and criticism', as well as for their 'most formidable conspiracy'.[80] Moreover, and contemporaneous with Somerville and Ross' coauthorship, the authorial anxieties that seem to govern collaboration and its twinned meaning can often be seen to explicitly manifest themselves in the texts produced by joint authors. Max Saunders, for example, recognises in the writings of Joseph Conrad and Ford Maddox Ford, both during and after their stint at coauthorship in the late 1890s, an anxiety 'produced by the ambivalences of conspiracy and collaboration':

> Both Ford and Conrad write often about the idea of leading a double life; and both used the phrase 'Homo Duplex' to express it ... All three of the Ford-Conrad collaborations are on the verge and sometimes over it, of hysteria: they teem with excess, terror, anxiety, scandal, impulse, neurasthenia.[81]

Conrad and Ford were part of a much larger collaborative literary circle, later known as the Rye Group, which initially came together in 1898 alongside Henry James, H. G. Wells and Stephen Crane, and lasted for over a decade. However, where the Ford-Conrad collaboration found a somewhat angst-ridden success out of the communal group dynamic, the other dyadic relationships which spawned from the Rye Group ultimately came to failure. James and Wells' tentative stabs at forming a literary partnership 'ended with a set of disastrous public attacks on one another's work', and the other possible pairings within the group never came to fruition.[82]

James' lack of success with Wells is particularly unsurprising given his decidedly ambivalent attitude towards artistic collaboration; an outlook which he indirectly expressed in the early 1890s with stories such as 'Greville Fane' and 'The Real Thing', and most explicitly demonstrated in 'Collaboration', published in *The English Illustrated Magazine* in 1892. The story was loosely inspired by the literary partnership between Rudyard Kipling and Charles Belastier and it openly evokes the dual signification of traitor and teammate implied in the word 'collaboration'. The story takes the Franco-Prussian War (1870–1) as its backdrop and, more generally, the wider imbalances of national power that swept over the European continent in the late nineteenth century and which would eventually erupt in 1914 and again in 1939. 'Collaboration' narrates the coming together of two male artists, a German composer and a French poet, in their joint ambition to write an opera, one which would defy in its compositional execution the hermetic 'terms on which nations have organised their discourse', and thus the 'hideous invention of patriotism'.[83]

Despite the story's oft-times sympathetic narrator, the act of cross-national artistic collaboration that he describes is repeatedly unable to free itself from the anxieties surrounding the more general essence and appeal of collaboration. The collaboration is described by its progenitors as the swearing of a 'tremendous oath' and the undertaking of a 'sacred engagement', one which fully acknowledges the personal and patriotic sacrifices that it will entail in its testimony for 'the religion of art ... the love for beauty'.[84] Nonetheless, it is generally perceived by nearly everyone else in the story as a 'monstrous collaboration', an 'unholy union', and an 'unnatural alliance'.[85] It is further cited as perverse and its executioners verging on insanity, a pairing born out of the narrator's Mephistophelian handing over of the French poet's 'pure spirit' to the German composer's 'literally German Faust'.[86] In spite of their detractors, however, the two artists choose to live and work in poverty on 'alien soil' in the Genoese Riviera, 'where sunshine is cheap and tobacco bad', in order to complete their 'musical revelation'.[87] As Duncan Aswell concludes in his larger study of James' fictional and actual collaborations, 'James could never have viewed collaboration as a feasible or healthy artistic possibility.'[88]

James' story analogously represents one extremity of the public's reaction to artistic collaboration and betrays the Romantic fear of singular authorship's dissolution into a shared artistic soul, one that potentially outranks in its literary products those of the individual hero-artist. The story also expresses a covert anxiety over the possibility of homosexual relations within artistic collaboration. Despite its crises of faith in both textual and sexual collaboration, however, the story can't help but admit to the revolutionary stance of the German-French pair and their 'epoch-making' work; a musical composition so far in advance of its time that it 'may very well be that [it] will not obtain any hearing at all for years'.[89] The work, therefore, has the approved Wordsworthian markings of artistic genius, antedating as it does the public's favour and taste. In so doing, however, James is also forced to recognise, albeit fleetingly, the collaborative authorial space as one which has the potential for a less pejoratively labelled subversion, particularly in the face of more mainstream literary communities. Not unlike the Rye Group, of which he was a part, James echoes the future sentiments of H. G. Wells when the latter characterised the group as 'a ring of foreign conspirators plotting against British letters'.[90] This self-conscious play on the dual signification of collaboration is not an isolated incident among the nineteenth century's literary collaborators. Somerville and Ross similarly described themselves as being on the 'outer skin' of the predominant Irish Revival movement of the late nineteenth and early twentieth centuries, and further positioned themselves as undercover agents for their own particular literary brand: 'Somerville and Ross Ltd'.[91] In 1901, for example, Ross figures herself as an infiltrator of Irish dramatic affairs during a performance at the Abbey Theatre ('I daresay the Irish Literary Revival was quite disastrously unaware of my presence in the shades at the back'), and Somerville would later feature herself as loyal scout in an excursion to Dundrum to observe the work of the Yeats sisters' Cuala Press: 'it will be interesting to see what they are doing'.[92]

In the hands of Wells, James, Somerville and Ross, therefore, there is a subtle change in emphasis and these otherwise treasonous acts of collaboration are treated as potential conduits for a favoured revolution in the arts, rather than as exclusively heinous literary crimes against the majority artistic establishment. As a result, the alienated or marginalised position of the collaborator becomes a significant position of power, one that achieves success through its collaborative mindset. If James' story sits, therefore, at the dystopic end of the collaborative spectrum, it nonetheless gestures towards the other end of that extreme, one that is candidly rendered in another fictional tale of the nineteenth century. In 1852, Anna Mary Howitt's serialised novella 'The Sisters in Art' appeared in *The Illustrated Exhibitor and Magazine of Art* expounding the utopian virtues of female artistic collaboration as a distinctly feminist mode of production, one which sanctified the process and products of collaborative work as a cut above the talent and output of the individual:

> the three friends ... brought together by circumstances had never separated. Time with them had effected no other change than to draw them together into a holier and truer communion of sympathy, taste, and pursuit, and to evolve from the unity of separate talents a result, of which singly they were not capable.[93]

In contrast with the 'unholy alliance' of James' literary-musical collaborators, Howitt's artistic sisters enjoy the intellectual and emotional profits of their celebrated and almost heavenly union. Howitt's fictional tale of three women artists who successfully come together to collaborate in their work and found a school of art was one based on personal experience and a lifetime of familial, social and artistic collaborations.[94]

Howitt collaborated on various literary and artistic projects with her parents throughout her life, and also forged strong collaborative ties in the 1850s with Bessie Raynor Parkes and Barbara Leigh Smith (founding members of the feminist and socially progressive Langham Place Group), finally moving on in the 1860s to collaborate with her father and husband in several automatic writing and drawing experiments. Linda Peterson argues that Howitt's mother, Mary, 'embodies the dominant early to mid-Victorian model of the professional woman author and ... articulated an ideology of collaborative work to support it':

> Mary Howitt viewed writing as a family business, as a professional endeavour pursued by father, mother, and children gifted with literary ability. This model of authorship emerged early in the century ... and rose to prominence at mid-century ... Their book prefaces and autobiographical writings explain this collaborative model not merely as useful or strategic for the woman of letters (though it was), but more provocatively as enabling a high quality of artistic production.[95]

The younger Howitt's professional life thus embodies an all-encompassing spectrum of successful collaborative endeavour: from the conservative and familial partnership with her mother, father and husband, to the more radically collaborative and feminist ambitions of the Langham Place Group. Moreover, her explanatory narratives of collaboration, as well as her fictional accounts of the same, continually reinstate the potential superiority of combined over individual talent and do not share in the anxieties that otherwise seem to prevail over coauthorship and its embrace of a shared artistic consciousness. Moreover, the patterning of attitudes towards collaboration in this period significantly coalesces along gendered lines and this appears to be more than coincidental.

In his study of James Joyce's collaboration with his younger brother, Stanislaus, James Cahalan argues that 'male styles of interaction' are 'completely antithetical to the collaborative, mutually supportive, feminist lives' of female writers such as Somerville and Ross.[96] Other significant studies of male literary collaborations offer similar findings and often suggest, in particular, that the dynamics of power and authority between male collaborators are distinctively hierarchical. Wayne Koestenbaum's comprehensive study of male writing partners in the late nineteenth and early twentieth centuries argues that such collaborations are an expression of a socially unacceptable homoeroticism. Moreover, Koestenbaum detects an overarching pattern of domination and subordination in the writing couples he analyses, suggesting that male collaboration is one where 'the active collaborator hypnotizes his passive mate'.[97] Several prominent male collaborators of this period exhibit both in private and in public exactly this kind of imbalance in power relations within their own collaborative efforts, a one-sidedness in levels of creativity which eventually render null and void the collaboration.

When Andrew Lang questioned Ross about her collaboration with Somerville, arguing that there had to be one dominant hand behind their literary productions, it was largely from his own personal experience that he was speaking. Lang collaborated with various scholars and editors on translations of classical literature, most famously with H. Rider Haggard, and also silently collaborated with fellow literary critic Edmund Gosse, in a multiplicity of supporting editorial roles. However, despite the success of many of his jointly published works, Lang professes to Ross that he can't comprehend 'how any two people could equally evolve characters etc – that he had tried, and it was always he or the other that did it all'.[98] Walter Besant was also a prominent and successful literary collaborator, publishing a succession of well-liked novels and short stories with James Rice throughout the 1870s, including the very popular *Ready-money Mortiboy* (1872) and *Golden Butterfly* (1876). Besant's comments on the process of collaboration, however, fall far short of seriously championing this particular style of literary production. Collaboration is dismissed as an amateur practice and one which merely holds an author back from plumbing the individual depths of the soul for true literary inspiration. He also echoes and hardens Lang's theory that one or other partner usually takes final control of the text during the collaboration: 'one of the two must be in authority ... absolutely must have the final revision of the work or the writing of the work'.[99] Besant's American counterpart, the collaborative writer and critic James Brander Matthews, who was also an advocate of authors' rights and a key organiser of the American Copyright League, had already made this point in 1890 when he maintained in an essay on dramatic collaborations that while no great art has been written collaboratively, 'collaboration has served the cause of periodical literature; a cause presumably less noble than that of great art'.[100] He also grants final importance to 'the part of each partner in the writing of the book' above all other considerations concerning the text.[101]

The downgrading of literary collaboration's products is here very evident. But more pressing is the insinuation of the mechanised processes that lie behind such collaborations in comparison to Romantic conceptions of 'great art' and the inspired individual, as well as the emphasis on legally definable components of a jointly authored text. All three critics associate collaboration with a clear-cut division of labour, and Besant and Matthews invoke Romantic literary ideals as a high point that collaborative authors will never reach. Lang further suggests to Ross that she must know a good deal about the 'science of bookmaking' and, in so doing, effectively assigns her collaborative practice with Somerville to the ranks of industrial labour, as opposed to artistic vocation.[102] Within this rhetoric are the seeds of collaboration's public demise and expulsion from a legal framework of copyright which recognises only one very particular type of author. Like Somerville and Ross' publisher and readers, as well as Wordsworth, Coleridge and Southey before them, all three male critics emphasise a process of divisible Lockean labour as key to understanding the collaborative method. In her memoir of her and Ross' literary partnership and friendship, *Irish Memories* (1916), however, Somerville mocks those who both trivialise literary collaboration as an amateur practice and mechanise its means and manners within a framework of quantifiable labours. Contemptuous and bored with the endless curiosity-seeking over her and Ross' collaborative practice, Somerville rails against those who falsely and disparagingly assume that the '*métier*' of the collaborative author is a kind of 'cross between the trades of cook and conjurer', believing that if 'the recipe of the mixture, or the trick of its production, can be extracted from those possessed of the secret, the desired result can be achieved as simply as a rice pudding, and forced like a card upon the publishers'.[103] Ross' dismissal of Lang's line of questioning, and Somerville's outright exasperation at her readers' assumptions, are in effect a blatant rejection of the underlying premise of collaboration as a mechanised labour process. As Chapters 2 and 3 will go on to detail, mine and thine in terms of textual and cerebral labour seem to play very little part in the two women's conception of collaboration. Indeed, texts which sometimes bear only the smallest legal imprint of labour from one or other collaborator are placed no less decisively under the dual signature in comparison to those texts which appear to be fought out between the two partners word for word. Collaboration here becomes much more than a textual or creative strategy and, as past and present female collaborators will testify, it is variously a support network, an affirmation of authorial professionalism, an intellectual friendship, and sometimes a physical passion.

Jill Ehnenn argues that in both contemporary and historical female literary collaborations, 'women come together to imagine utopia ... collaboration enables the woman writer to imagine and make concrete something – goals, ideas, desires – that her society deems unsuitable, perhaps even unthinkable'.[104] Howitt's 'The Sisters in Art' certainly pays testament to this argument, sacralising the artistic unity of the three collaborators and allowing them to create a space of creative refuge from disapproving social forces. Other nineteenth-century female collaborators also ground their literary partnerships and texts within sacrosanct and immortalised utopian spaces. The poetic duo of Katherine Bradley and Edith Cooper, publicly known under the pseudonym Michael Field and (alongside Somerville and Ross) one of the most prominent female literary partnerships working in the late nineteenth century, asserted: '[a]s to our work, let no man think he can put asunder what God has joined … The work is perfect mosaic: we cross and interlace like a company of dancing summer flies.'[105] Looking back on her partnership with Ross, Somerville similarly maintained in her essay, 'Two of a Trade', that: '[o]ur reliance on one another, whether on this plane or another, is what can never be explained … Sometimes the compelling creative urge would come on both, and we would try to reconcile the two impulses, searching for a form into which best to cast them … as two dancers will yield to the same impulse, given by the same strain of music, and the joy of shared success.'[106] Unlike their male contemporaries there is no attempt here to apportion textual or intellectual lots to each partner, the resultant text is a reconciliation of 'two impulses' and a 'perfect mosaic'. The image of partnered dancing jointly yielding to a common impulse suggests not a masculine hierarchy of authorial power, but a conjoined and equal process of creativity where both partners as individuals are nothing without their dancing mate. Bradley and Cooper make this explicit when Bradley writes of herself and her writing partner, '[we] make up a single individual, double stronger than each alone'.[107] This further belies the notion put forward by Lang, Besant and Matthews that the individual artist is somehow limited in his creativity in partnership and only excels *as* an individual, either singly or in a collaboration of unequal literary authority.

Moreover, Somerville's insistence on the mutual reliance that exists within literary partnerships and its unknown qualities is suggestive of an additional dismissal of the emphasis placed on the textual mechanics of coauthorship. Despite her advocacy of her and Ross' works above the senseless curiosity of who held the pen, Somerville also recognises and centralises the creative process and intellectual friendship behind those works, including the myriad non-textual benefits to each partner. Verification of authorship certainly seems to sit high up on the list of such possible advantages for women writers. Somerville and Ross' Irish predecessor, Maria Edgeworth, is much better known for her collaborative work with her father, but it is in her informal correspondences with her female circle of relatives that the real value of female collaborative processes can be found. Marilyn Butler's *Maria Edgeworth: A Literary Biography* (1972) remains one of the few texts that take seriously Edgeworth's letters to her female relatives. She even goes as far as arguing for Edgeworth's letters to Margaret and Sophy Ruxton as 'informal notes for the novels'.[108] Like Somerville and Ross many years after her, Edgeworth variously used her intimate circle of friends and family as editors, sources of local anecdotes, literary critics, and an enthusiastic audience on which to air her draft stories. Searching for material for her *Moral Tales*, for example, Edgeworth writes to Sophy Ruxton asking her for 'any good anecdotes from the age five to fifteen, good latitude and longitude will suit me'.[109] She later uses her correspondence with Charlotte Sneyd for both editorial assistance and literary ideas. Edgeworth's letters to familial members of what she called her 'Committee of Education and Criticism' further reveal that she often incorporated her extended family's suggestions for alterations into her final published texts and paid serious attention to their reactions when her draft stories were read aloud to them, as they often were during the family's evening entertainment.[110]

Edgeworth's epistolary relationship with the Ruxtons, however, goes beyond this very practical collaborative element of her authorship, whereby she begins to strongly rely (particularly on Margaret) for her sense of identity as a professional author. Butler points out that the Ruxtons knew of and participated in everything Edgeworth wrote between her early children's stories and *Ormond* in 1817, with perhaps the single exception of *Belinda*. More significantly, however, the Ruxtons aided Edgeworth in defining and maintaining a professional sense of her public identity as 'author'. Margaret insisted on being kept abreast of what she called Edgeworth's 'authorship Self', and both Sophy and Margaret accord that self with the level of professionalism which it merits, but which Edgeworth occasionally protests against in her anxiety over her own cultural authority: 'I beg [she writes to Sophy] that you will not call my little stories by the sublime title of "my works", I shall else be ashamed when the little mouse comes forth.'[111] These elements of deprecation in Edgeworth's authorial self-presentation are suggestive of the anxieties that surround her perception of her professional identity, as well as representative of her complex and gendered relationship to the public gaze. She nonetheless continues to utilise her epistolary relationships with these women to feed her desire to speak (if only privately) as a recognised author and, in so doing, to debate her literary ideas with them, take fortitude from their encouragement and praise, incorporate their editorial suggestions, and nurture a mutual intellectual relationship. It is perhaps no small coincidence that Somerville and Ross cherished Edgeworth's correspondence with their great-great- grandmother, Nancy Crampton, and saw in Edgeworth a literary predecessor.

Ross more than recognises the significance of what is fleetingly observed in Edgeworth's letters to the Ruxtons and amplifies this dynamic when she comments to Somerville on what she believes are the main reasons behind their successful literary partnership: 'I think the two Shockers have a very strange belief in each other, joined to a critical faculty.'[112] This 'strange belief in each other' becomes an essential component in the two women's ability to successfully pursue their literary ambitions amid a somewhat hostile commercial and familial environment. Despite the driving force of a utopian vision, the realities of the social and economic conditions of women's literary work in the nineteenth century continually tether their idealised mental pictures to an uncompromising and potentially destructive truth. Howitt's 'The Sisters in Art' narrates the rise of a numerously fortuitous artistic communion between three kindred female spirits, but it is also forced to expose the decline and eventual rupture of these women's collaborative practice. These women's belief in the superiority of collaboration, a belief validated in the story by the women's united success in a Belgian design competition, does not free the three 'sisters' from the conventional marriage plot of Victorian fiction. This belief only allows them to delay it: 'they agreed, indeed vowed, to lay aside all mere personal considerations till the great purpose of their study and life was accomplished, namely – the establishment of an advanced School of Female Art in their own country.'[113] Rather than a lifelong artistic commitment, the founding of the 'School of Female Art' becomes a concluding point in their collaborative feminist ambitions and signals a dispersal of the three women's shared life-work narrative into three individual stories of love, domesticity and marriage.

The mutual exclusivity of 'personal considerations' and collaborative intellectual ambition was certainly not lost on Somerville and Ross. In *Irish Memories*, Somerville stated that her literary collaboration with Ross was 'the beginning of a new era' for both of them: 'for most boys and girls, the varying, yet invariable, flirtations and emotional episodes of youth are resolved and composed by marriage. To Martin and to me was opened another way and the flowering of both our lives was when we met each other.'[114] Six years prior to meeting Ross, Somerville had already lost a former literary collaborator to marriage, her cousin and familial 'twin', Ethel Coghill: 'that unprincipled woman the Twin has been and gone and engaged herself to Jimmy Penrose.

She had to come up and 'fess to her injured Twin – She ought to be ashamed of herself.'[115] As the wedding day loomed, Somerville made a private declaration to herself to withstand the conventional outcomes prescribed for women beyond their youthful prime, and swore in her diary: 'I will paint. I will also work.'[116]

In part, Somerville and Ross' partnership followed a comparable trajectory to Howitt's and was similarly driven by an idyllic vision of the merits of female friendship and intellectual collaboration. This was something not only reflected in Somerville and Ross' commentaries on their own working relationship, but also keenly observed by others. Writing in 1916 on the death of Ross for *Country Life* magazine, for example, Somerville's friend, Jem Barlow, wrote that: '[f]ate never did me a kinder turn than when one gave me the opportunity of observing what a truly splendid thing friendship between women may be.'[117] Furthermore, not unlike Howitt's induction into collaborative working life through a family-centred practice, the genesis of the Somerville and Ross partnership stems from two less professional but nonetheless family-based projects which were both instigated and sanctioned by the authors' mothers. The projects largely consisted of compiling the 'Buddh Family Dictionary' alongside a genealogical history of the Somerville, Coghill and Martin clans, both of which effectively demarcate a self-important heritage for all three families and forge strong ancestral ties between them. Furthermore, the dictionary project arguably represents an elite and almost dynastic linguistic code that constitutes a united familial identity, cataloguing as it does the English-Irish paronyms and phrases that were peculiar to the inner circle of each family.

The overarching significance of these early projects is that they incorporated the *ennui*-laden siblings and cousins of the Somerville family home in Castletownshend into Somerville and Ross' works, and this was more in keeping with the communal values of the Somerville and Coghill clique. Working together and working on a family project of benefit and interest to all could be labelled as, and seen for, the harmless pastime from which it began. Friends and family were eager to contribute and Somerville and Ross were glad of their help, a dictionary project being an inherently and conceptually collaborative enterprise to begin with. The shift in family opinion is openly evident and obvious when Somerville and Ross decide to abandon their amateur and domestic ventures in favour of working in more professional and public authorial mediums:

> It was in October, 1887, that we began what was soon to be known to us as 'The Shocker,' ... to our family generally, as 'that nonsense of the girls,' and subsequently, to the general public, as 'An Irish Cousin'. Seldom have the young and ardent 'commenced author' under less conducive

circumstances. We were resented on so many grounds. Waste of time; the arrogance of having conceived such a project; and, chiefly, the abstention of two playmates.[118]

The divergence of Somerville and Ross' now professional status from their previous authorial work markedly severs the sense of that work as simply an extension of their familial roles, an extension which their earlier forays into authorship had unambiguously maintained. Howitt experiences a similar tension when her collaborative ideology shifts from the public to the private sphere, reneging on her working family commitments to pursue a collaborative mediumistic practice that produced only inner spiritual benefits. It has also been suggested that Howitt's husband, Alfred Alaric Watts, and his encouragement of this private mediumistic role, played a significant part in deterring Howitt from pursuing a public career as a painter – a situation which art historians now view as the loss of a potentially great female artist.[119]

These renegotiations between professional and domestic commitments reiterate Bette London's point that to study women's collaboration is 'to study the conditions of its erasure'.[120] Female professional work is consistently devalued within the nineteenth century's patriarchal approach to women's lives and work, and while literary collaboration was favoured for its ideological and intellectual benefits by women such as the Howitts, Bradley and Cooper, and Somerville and Ross, the public perception of collaboration as an amateur pursuit also significantly assisted in shielding as well as doubly limiting these women's artistic practice. The collaborative relations that existed between these women thus served as conduits and foundations for a working practice which otherwise may not have been able to bear artistic fruit. Moreover, and as the following chapter will go on to discuss, Somerville and Ross' configuration of their openly socialised working practice is also centrally motivated by a confluence of professional and explicitly personal ties.

CHAPTER TWO

The erotics and politics of female collaboration

Writing in 1917 in *Irish Memories*, just two years after Ross' premature death, Somerville reflected on the literary collaboration that had dominated the last 28 years of her life and concluded that the 'outstanding fact' of artistic and independent women 'who live by their brains, is friendship'. This was no less than a 'profound friendship' which extended to every 'phase and aspect of life', including all intellectual, social and economic activity.[1] A similar dynamic is celebrated in Howitt's 'The Sisters in Art', where the bonds of friendship between the three women artists become inextricably entwined with their collaborative working practice, each mutually sustaining the other. It was also via the tie of friendship between Barbara Leigh Smith and Elizabeth Raynor Parkes that the origins of the liberal feminist Langham Place Group, of which Howitt eventually became a part, are to be found. The significance of friendship in the lives and work of women which Somerville and Howitt here acknowledge in their own intellectual and artistic partnerships arguably recognises what Virginia Woolf would much later (and now famously) explore as the socio-cultural importance of women's friendships in 'A Room of One's Own' in 1928. Despite the overt lesbian implications of Chloe's liking for Olivia, 'A Room of One's Own' also directly addresses the complexity and diversity of women's relationships with each other, as well as the paucity of such relationships as represented in English literary history: 'I tried to remember any case in the course of my reading where two women are represented as friends.'[2] The imagined shining of light into that 'vast chamber' of women-oriented experience is as much about exploring and representing the secret intellectual and emotional lives of women as it is their taboo sexual relations with each other.

A significant part of feminist criticism in the mid- to late twentieth century has turned Woolf's imagined searchlight into a reality and has concerned itself with investigating and explicating women's relationships with each other in all their multiple contexts. Mary Daly, Janice Raymond, Lillian Faderman, Sharon Marcus and Philippa Levine, to name but a few, have all variously explored the homoerotic and sexual dimensions of current and historical female relationships; sought to elucidate the socio-cultural value and significance of female friendship for past suffrage and current feminist discourse; and argued for the interconnectedness of the intimate, intellectual and emotional aspects of female friendship. Feminism's historical and ongoing engagement with the issue of friendship, argues Sasha Roseneil, is one which affirms a shared belief in the necessity of women's affectionate attachments with each other in transforming gender relations: 'friendship is seen as political solidarity, as constitutive of feminist movements and the basis of collective identity, and it is seen as a mode of personal support, intimacy and care, and, as such, productive of self-identity'.[3] Elaine Showalter shares this belief in the significance of what she calls women's 'emotional friendships' with each other, particularly in the late nineteenth century, and further situates the personal 'bonds of the female subculture' as an active catalyst in women's desire to write 'in teams'.[4] Nearly a century after Somerville wrote about her collaboration with Ross and placed friendship at the heart of their dual authorship, female co-authors continue to centralise friendship as part of their working practice. The American literary critics and theorists Carey Caplan and Ellen Cronan Rose maintained in 1993 that '[w]ork and friendship' remained the bedrock of their collaboration: '[f]rom our first encounter, we have been unable to distinguish between the two.'[5] Janice Doan and Devon Hodges (also non-creative writing partners) similarly claim that their 'collaboration maintained a friendship' that helped them to jointly 'deal with' their 'economic and social position as women'.[6]

Historically, however, literary and intellectual couples have often suffered at the hands of critics from an overemphasis of the biographical over the textual, a critical approach which has underestimated the significance of women's personal relationships for both their professional partnerships and their writing. As touched on in the previous chapter, and like Somerville and Ross' own nineteenth-century audience, critics have often interrogated the partnership with a view to dismantling it, opposed to understanding the two women's bond as a realisation of a new type of authorship. More recently, critics have begun to explore the social dynamics of literary creativity in partnership, and have crucially demonstrated how coauthorship can complicate traditional concepts of authorship, textuality and writing. When repeatedly questioned about her collaboration with Ross, Somerville notably yearned for such a corrective process and lamented the reduction of her working relationship with Ross to the technicalities of the pen holder: 'it's the books that matter,' she privately wrote to her brother, 'not who held the wretched pen.'[7]

In the case of Somerville and Ross, the synergy between work and friendship has often been obscured in favour of an empirical and voyeuristic quest to determine the two women's sexual orientation. As Maryann Dever rightly points out more broadly, this kind of critical exercise is ultimately futile and simply locks the critic into seeking the 'kind of evidence seldom required to "prove" the assumed heterosexuality of other writers'.[8] Moreover, it ignores as irrelevant and purely domestic the element of friendship which foments and maintains the literary partnership, as well as that friendship's overtly erotic dimensions which exist within that friendship. At the other end of the spectrum, and in an effort to divert from a purely biographical approach, even critics such as London, who otherwise offer a wholly illuminating and necessary rethink of female collaboration as a theoretical subject, seem wary of conferring (or are unable to) any vestige of the domestic pleasures of friendship on Somerville and Ross' working practice. This is despite Somerville's repeated efforts in *Irish Memories* (1917) and her much later essay on collaboration, 'Two of a Trade' (1946), to assign her friendship with Ross its rightful and significant place within their joint authorship. On 'Two of a Trade', for example, London argues that the essay 'reverses the trajectory of the Somerville and Ross career, overwriting the life of two professional writers into a story of perfect female friendship. As such, it reconstructs the collaboration along lines more in keeping with conventional assumptions about gender.'[9] The 'life of two professional writers' here becomes entirely incompatible with 'a story of perfect female friendship' and this is partly, it seems, due to London's own assumptions about female friendship as purely private, domestic and conventional.

A similar trend can be found in other recent studies of women's collaborative writing. Lorraine York, for example, rightly asserts that there has been a tendency among critics of collaboration theory to 'celebrate women's collaborations unproblematically and idealistically', and as necessarily 'revolutionary, sisterly, or morally superior'.[10] Criticising the arguments of influential feminist theorists which are reliant on a universalising philosophy of relational ethics between women, such as Nancy Chodorow, Carol Gilligan and Mary Belenky, York argues that collaboration theory has too often given in to an 'idealistic brand of social history' which favours women's collaborations as sites of 'fusion, ... affirmative union, and monovocality'.[11] While York is right to dismiss these collective and romanticised versions of women's collaborative practice, particularly in view of the 'difficult negotiations of space', which she demonstrates have significantly made up women's literary and critical collaborations, her propensity to locate the origins of such thinking within critical discourses of female friendship and gender solidarity is perhaps equally problematic.[12] Like London, York rejects the fact that women collaborators have themselves characterised their partnerships as founded in friendship, arguing that such a strategy is simply an emotional indulgence or temptation, as well as a bid to harmonise (at least in public) the unity of the artistic bond.[13] However, this kind of thinking seems to be a result of segregating female friendship as a domestic or personal partnership, and classifying it as an uncomplicated marriage of two personalities, temperaments and intellects, rather than a tie that is also full of 'difficult negotiations'.

Much of this chapter will concern itself with redefining Somerville and Ross' friendship as an integral part of their collaborative working practice in order to combat such reductive readings of the two women's personal bond, as well as to understand the working friendship as a politicised 'framework of emotional connection', rather than as something indistinct from the relationship's professional concerns.[14] Janet Surrey offers this framework as a way of understanding the relational empowerment achieved when traditional models of authority and power are dispersed in what she calls 'mutual power' relationships: 'power or the ability to act does not have to be a scarce resource, nor based on zero-sum assumptions'.[15] Ross certainly recognises this dynamic when she tells Somerville that the success of their partnership lies in the fact that they 'do not fight their own hands all the time'.[16] And yet this is not to rewrite the partnership as an idyllic fusion of minds, bodies and texts, or to ignore its erotic impulses, but to recognise once again the process of Cixous' and Deleuze's 'working (in) the in-between', where 'struggle and expulsion' (the 'zero-sum assumption') is replaced by an incessant 'process of exchange'.

Such analogies can only be utilised, however, by also recognising the distinctiveness of Somerville and Ross' relationship, as well as the two authors' self-examination of their collaborative practice. Shortly after Ross' death, Somerville lamented that 'no one can ever know what we were to each other'.[17] Like Woolf several decades later, Somerville is here aware of the lack of representation in the public sphere of women's variegated relationships with each other and, as a result, knows that a full appreciation by others of her collaboration with Ross has been rendered inconceivable, as have the landscapes of creativity and experience which women's intellectual and artistic collaborations open up for each other. Somerville's point also endorses Holly Laird's argument that there can be no 'grand metanarrative or overarching theory' of women's collaborations, and that the diversity of such working relationships can only be found in 'discrete, plural, personal stories'.[18] This chapter will attempt to tease out some of the 'personal stories' of Somerville and Ross, as well as the plural discourse (both public and private) that they offer on their collaborative authorship, as a preface to redefining their literary partnership. It will also analyse the duo's third novel, *The Silver Fox* (1897), as a fictional representation of the power of female relationships in the face of both Ireland's political turmoil at the end of the nineteenth century, and socially prescribed gender roles.

The public face of female friendship

Ehnenn's study of late-Victorian female literary collaborators, including Somerville and Ross, is one of the first studies to concretise the idea that women's collaborations of this period were often both artistic and political. Such collaborations can offer, argues Ehnenn, a 'model for resistant social action' in their successful defiance of both 'gendered and heteronormative ideologies about femininity', as well as 'conventions about the creation and circulation' of literary texts.[19] In addition, and by simultaneously recognising the primary value of friendship for women involved in literary partnership, Ehnenn makes implicit what female collaborators have long recognised as the public and political dimensions of their friendship. In fact, Ehnenn goes as far as suggesting that beyond the textual product, 'the writing process becomes a conduit for relationship-building, pleasure, and desire', and it is these 'excesses of collaboration' that many female partners value most.[20] Couching the narrative of their collaboration in terms of 'perfect friendship', Somerville thus equally recognises the work-as-friendship dynamic in 'Two of a Trade' and, indeed, renders explicit the entwined personal and professional roots of her literary collaboration with Ross.

Somerville's essay was commissioned in 1946 for the opening number of an Irish literary magazine, *Irish Writing: the magazine of contemporary Irish literature* (1946–54), edited by the aspiring David Marcus and Terence Smith. Marcus proved to be a pivotal figure in the Irish literary landscape, fostering the work of writers such as Frank O'Connor, Flann O'Brien and James Stephens. Alongside Somerville, Patrick Kavanagh, Louis MacNeice and Sean O'Faolain all featured in *Irish Writing*'s first issue. However, Geraldine Cummins' biography of Somerville gives an account of the latter's disinclination towards the essay she had been asked to write, as well as the commercial astuteness of Marcus in commissioning the piece, which he used as advertising for the launch of his magazine:

The Editors were anxious to obtain this contribution from her for their first number as the many readers of the Somerville and Ross books were keenly interested in the mystery of two people so harmoniously working together 'with one pen'. Edith had always avoided discussing this subject, and after commencing the Essay, wasted the short time which she had for its composition by writing and, to the Editor's dismay, offering them a short essay on 'Quarterlies', a subject that bore no relation whatever to the already advertised article 'Two of a Trade'. But her tormentors remained firm in the demand for the completion of the latter, and on the eve of *Irish Writing* going to press it arrived.[21]

In asking for 'Two of a Trade' Marcus identifies the commercialisation of the Somerville and Ross signature in the literary marketplace and what Somerville refers to in the essay as the 'eternal youth' of the curiosity-seeker, both of which will act as a sure-fire draw in securing a general first-time readership for Marcus' new publication.[22] Long used to her audience's attitude towards collaboration and their desire to understand the perceived mechanistic and unsolved processes of literary production, Somerville engineers a narrative perfectly attuned to meet the needs of Marcus' magazine. Cummins unceremoniously rebukes the essay as a 'thoroughly Irish masterpiece of evasion' that pokes fun at Somerville and Ross' inquisitive audience and gives away 'nothing of the least importance'. Somerville retorts that '"there are only two good sentences in it. I won't tell you which they are ... Nor will I tell the reader. He can select at his own pleasure."'[23] Her remarks are suggestive of the public ownership of the Somerville and Ross literary brand, and these comments hark back to Coleridge's anxiety over proper names in the public domain in their recognition that the Somerville and Ross signature is an alienable property subject to the collectively constructed fictions of that signature's audience. More pertinently, Somerville maintains that there is nothing to tell in terms of her collaborative practice with Ross, or at least no more than can be summed up in two sentences, but also simultaneously hints at a supposed hidden truth which keeps the public interested and guessing.

The essay itself operates on similar lines, oscillating between the author's protestations of complete inadequacy in attempting to disseminate the mystery of collaboration, and surprisingly detailed and insightful passages on the practicalities and history of Somerville and Ross' joint methodology. Somerville argues that on the question as to 'how two people can write together', she can offer no satisfactory answer, that as much as she would 'enjoy giving away a secret, there is none to tell'.[24] Instead, she proposes an 'explanation or two', but then finally concludes that 'it seems to me that I have done little or nothing in elucidating this difficulty of two minds, and two hands, and only one pen'.[25] Somerville thus consciously invites further conjecture upon the subject by hinting that there is a deeper difficulty to be understood about the collaboration and, in her indubitable professional and commercial mindedness, joint authorship and a dual signature are here recognised for the profit-making commodities they eventually became for Somerville and Ross. In appealing to and nurturing the public's insatiable curiosity, Somerville and Ross opened themselves up to commercial possibilities that acted as free advertising for their works, such as personal interviews in literary magazines and periodicals during their working lives together. A constant, ongoing point of interest and discussion gave critics reason to turn again and again to the works of Somerville and Ross.

Despite this overt commercial exploitation of the partnership, however, Somerville maintains in *Irish Memories* that as to the question of 'which of us held the pen', it was 'a point that never entered our minds to consider'.[26] 'Two of a Trade' may attempt to play a subtle commercial game with its readership, but it too insists on this point and, like *Irish Memories*, attempts to foreground the 'excesses of collaboration' as key to Somerville and Ross' success as literary partners. Both texts are written after Ross' death and, as Gifford Lewis has pointed out, *Irish Memories* in particular occasionally amends historical fact to suit Somerville's purposes and is often inflected by Somerville's nostalgic view of the recently deceased Ross. 'Two of a Trade' is also a conscious fashioning of the partnership into a very specific narrative. Despite its playfulness with the reader, however, it has less of the idealism written into *Irish Memories* and gives an insight into the longer-term retrospective thoughts of Somerville on her partnership with Ross. The holder of the pen, argues Somerville in 'Two of a Trade', was 'wholly fortuitous'.[27] In the essay, Somerville traces the origins of her collaboration with Ross back to the 'Buddh Family Dictionary', their first collaborative effort, and she significantly situates their blossoming friendship as a precursor to their ensuing detachment from the 'gay and idle ... pack of lads and lasses ... with nothing whatever to do but amuse themselves' in Castletownshend.[28] The collaboration is also given its ancestral roots in the marital partnership of Charles Kendal Bushe, Lord Chief Justice of Ireland, and his wife Nancy Crampton. It is the Bushe–Crampton marriage that links the respective Somerville and Ross family trees and creates the two women's familial bond, subsequently facilitating the two women's friendship. Bushe and Crampton are also cited as inspirational artistic and intellectual figures:

> Charles Kendal Bushe, Lord Chief Justice of Ireland ... brilliant wit and
> orator ... and his wife, Nancy Crampton ... a lovely creature in whom
> there burnt a flame of Art, whether glowing in Literature, Music, or
> Painting, so intense and so determined that even for three succeeding
> generations it has touched some of her descendants with something of
> her bright spirit.[29]

Somerville finally suggests that her and Ross' 'early Johnsonian efforts' were a response to 'ancestral stabs from the Chief Justice and his Nancy', ones which 'were well directed and went deep'.[30] Somerville thus situates the origins of her collaborative life and work with Ross in the social, literary, intellectual and professional traditions of their Anglo-Irish heritage, but it is also clear that the two women's friendship plays a catalysing role in their working relations, as well as ringing a discordant note within that heritage. The patriarchal institution of marriage that it invokes arguably has no place for two female friends determined on a life of professional writing, potentially at the cost of marriage and the perpetuation of the Anglo-Irish race.

Somerville's alignment of the duo's friendship with the Bushe–Crampton marriage segues into her earlier belief that instead of a traditional marital union, 'another way' was opened up for her and Ross.[31] Indeed, Somerville suggests that despite the devotedness of her husband, 'marriage had subdued the artist' in Nancy Crampton and she had been 'immured inexorably within the padded cell of the amateur', as were many other 'young ladies of quality' in 'those days'.[32] Somerville's genealogical positioning of her and Ross' collaboration and friendship alongside the Bushe–Crampton marriage is fiercely loyal to her Anglo-Irish roots and interest in her family's heritage. However, it also significantly gestures towards the professional and intimate possibilities of personal and social partnerships between women, and leaves open the question of, and potential for, same-sex desire. In so doing, it attempts to confer the same kind of public status on female friendship that is usually only reserved for public heterosexual relations, and explores the opportunities of an alternative gender dynamic to traditional male–female unions. The nineteenth-century laws, ceremonies and rituals that institutionalise and make public relations between heterosexual couples gives to them socio-political legitimacy, recognition and protection. Somerville comprehends in her friendship with Ross, as well as in the literary work they carry out together, a similar but unauthenticated socio-political reality that enables the writing couple to traverse both the social dictates of their class and the familial conventions proscribed for most of their female peers, including what had been proscribed for her great-grandmother.

In *Irish Memories*, Somerville recalls the friendship between Nancy Crampton and Irish author, Maria Edgeworth, and cites Edgeworth's desire to meet again with Crampton in the knowledge that their 'minds would open and join immediately'.[33] Somerville and Ross' friendship and collaboration is thus carefully positioned in the text as something Somerville recognises and reframes as both a type of civic, intimate and professional bond, and the blossoming of what was only an unfulfilled professional and personal desire for women like Edgeworth and Crampton.

This positioning of female friendship as a form of public union recalls Janice Raymond's theoretical study of female affection, where certain types of women's friendships are viewed as a 'social trust', one which is continually renewed, revitalised, and entered into by two or more political beings 'who claim social or political status for their Selves and others like their Selves'.[34] Somerville outlines with both brutal clarity and humour in *Irish Memories* the hostility with which her professional writing with Ross was initially greeted by their respective families: 'when not actually reviled, we were treated with much the same disapproving sufferance that is shown to an outside dog who sneaks into the house on a wet day. We ... hid and fled about the house, with the knowledge that every man's hand was against us.'[35] Somerville and Ross' friendship is, therefore, a bond of 'social trust' in its ability to fortify against familial disapproval of their increasingly professional ambitions and, like Edgeworth and her network of female relatives before them, provide necessary intellectual stimulation and encouragement to pursue an otherwise censured writing career.

In so doing, Somerville and Ross' friendship has the potential to induce beneficial social change for women. When Somerville recalled that in their early attempts at joint authorship the two budding writers were 'hunted from place to place like the Vaudois, seeking in vain a cave wherein we could hold our services unmolested', she once again reifies her collaboration with Ross as a sacrosanct activity, but also significantly distinguishes it as one which exists, like the minority religious group she invokes, in heretical defiance of Anglo-Irish authority and tradition, as well as broader nineteenth-century gender norms.[36] Female friendship here becomes the kind of civic tie which has for centuries been utilised as a model for public relations more widely, but which has almost exclusively relied on friendships between men as its foundation. The socially defined purpose of friendship which Aristotle first outlined in *Nichomachean Ethics*, and on which much modern theorising of friendship still depends, argued that male friendship provided an exemplary type of relationship that had the ability to unify a political community for the benefit of a shared recognition of and pursuit of the good, as well as a common project of creating and sustaining the life of the *polis*. Somerville recognises and challenges this foundation in *Irish Memories*: 'The doctrine that sincere friendship is only possible between men dies hard.'[37] In Somerville and Ross' case, however, the common good is one of their own feminist making and it dictates and sustains an alternative *polis*: a female minority community fostering an unconventional but nonetheless favourable emotional and intellectual network of support for the broadening of women's professional and social life choices.

Marilyn Friedman's feminist study of personal relationships and moral theory recognises and explores this social dynamic amid women's friendships across varying historical periods. She argues that communities of women founded on friendship have not only been the 'cement' of various historical waves of feminism, but have enabled women to move out of their given communities 'into new attachments with other women by their own choice … motivated by their own needs, desires, attractions, and fears', and often in opposition to 'the expectations and ascribed roles of their found communities'.[38] The influential forces for social transformation that Friedman cites as arising from women living unconventionally in their friendships, both professionally and personally, are not merely a useful corollary to collaborative life and work, but a key to founding and sustaining what is otherwise considered a deviant creativity, particularly for women in the nineteenth century.

It is interesting to note, for example, that Somerville's and Howitt's separate attempts to pursue individual artistic careers as professional painters represented a much more contentious and eventually unrealised ambition compared to their collaborative literary efforts. Howitt's attempts to make inroads into the largely masculine domain of historical art were dramatically and unfairly scorned by the likes of John Ruskin and further dampened by her husband's patriarchal attitude towards women and professional work. This hardening rhetoric against Howitt's artistic aspirations eventually derailed her labours in this field and she relinquished her interest in professional painting. Somerville, in turn, fought her family's sense of female propriety in order to train professionally in Paris' *ateliers* for female art students, but her individualistic and professional desires were never fully accepted by her family and she repeatedly gave in to the enforced domestic duties which continually called her back home to Ireland. In an agonised letter written from the Académie Délécluse in Paris in 1895 to her brother Cameron, Somerville laments but acquiesces to the fact that she is not to be given the chance to 'make the most' of her talent:

if only I could stick to it – I suppose, for me, this is out of the question – I suppose I can never hope really to find out what I am good for – it is too difficult and seems too selfish to give up being at home, where I am more or less wanted, for the sake of getting myself on. I have money enough now – and have more coming in – to stick to it for a good bit, but I know it can't be done for other reasons. You know how hard it is at home to make people understand this: they don't know what it is to want to make the most of your talent – (whether small or great). They are awfully good but I think they all think that I can draw 'quite well enough' and that it is waste of money and hard on them that I should stay away to work when it isn't necessary – If they only knew! However, this is all very egotistical.[39]

For both Somerville and Howitt, individual want gives way to a gendered ideology of socially accepted norms of female conduct and even though the social space exists (in Somerville's case the Parisian studios that accept women artists for training), the corresponding desire to use that space is thwarted by external social prescriptions.

As Chapter 3 will go on to explore, issues of genre and reception certainly play their part in such behaviour, but a lack of female social support, intellectual encouragement, and shared affection (all on which Somerville and Howitt have previously thrived) also have a bearing on the failure of these professional and individual pursuits. Both Somerville and Howitt succeed in partnership (and friendship) where they notably struggle as artistic individuals. In part, such a dynamic suggests that the public status afforded female friendship, through recognition of friendship's potential political muscle in the face of social and familial disapprobation, is one of significant practical import. This trend appears not just in the lives of Somerville and Ross, but also in their texts. The duo's fourth novel, *The Silver Fox* (1897), is set amid the political and cultural tension between nineteenth-century English imperial ambition and the private and social traditions of the native Irish. Flanked on either side by these opposing groups is the novel's Anglo-Irish protagonist, Slaney Morris, whose personal and socio-political isolation is repeatedly emphasised throughout the narrative through the metaphoric use of the fox hunt: 'she was soon out of sight and hearing of the group on the road, and passed on through the loneliness of the barren hills, a tired figure on a tired horse, forgotten by all'.[40] Her want of intellectual companionship and female friendship is heightened when her brother's English wife, Lady Susan French, visits Ireland with her husband and resides in Slaney's home, French Court. Despite Lady Susan's initial waspish conceit, coupled with her predilection to label all women as either opponents or 'non combatants' (50) in the all-consuming battle for male attention, Slaney can't help but admit that she is 'fond of Lady Susan' (140): 'it was against all theories of womankind, yet the fact remained that Slaney liked Lady Susan' (112). In their depiction of the two women, Somerville and Ross recognise the patriarchal forces that often work to pit one woman against another and, like their protagonist, express much regret over the lost opportunities for the blossoming of female friendship. It is with a 'pang to Slaney's heart', for example, that Lady Susan turns in her distress at the sight of an Irish peasant's drowned body to a male figure rather than to her, expecting (as Slaney rightly assumes) 'no quarter from a girl' (135).

The tentative fellowship that forms between the two women at the end of the novel is largely a result of Slaney's refusal to yield to the same social impulses which have thus far governed Lady Susan's attitude towards her female circle of acquaintances. Slaney's character and behaviour frustrate the English industrial contractor, Wilfred Glasgow, to the point where he is forced to conclude that Slaney does not fit into his 'cast-iron theories of women' and is, as a result, 'abnormal' (138). Slaney's attempts to safeguard Lady Susan's reputation in her 'daring and careless' (180) flirtation with Glasgow is both an indication of her care for Lady Susan and her sense of female solidarity against the predatory attentions of men like Glasgow. Slaney, too, has past understanding of the beguiling and false attentions of Glasgow, and in this shared experience grow the seeds of her empathy and feeling for Lady Susan. This sisterly bond significantly replaces the earlier posturing of Lady Susan in her attempts to portray herself as a feminist figure. With her bicycle, cigarettes and Parisian hair dye, Lady Susan is offered up in the novel as a *Punch* caricature of the New Woman figure of the 1890s, the 'young modern woman and her bicycle' (138) so excoriated by Glasgow until he is charmed by the becoming curves of Lady Susan's waist. The portrayal of Lady Susan in the novel appears to be consciously situated in the public media debates of the period over the 'Woman Question' and, in particular, on the emergence of the New Woman figure. Lady Susan's character is suggestive of Elizabeth Lynn Linton's 'Girl of the Period', the nineteenth-century nemesis of the English 'ideal of womanhood' and an increasing menace to England's national and moral character:

> The Girl of the Period is a creature who dyes her hair and paints her face, as the first articles of her personal religion – a creature whose sole idea of life is fun; whose sole aim is unbounded luxury; and whose dress is the chief object of such thought and intellect as she possesses ... the Girl of the Period has done away with such moral muffishness as consideration

for others, or regard to counsel and rebuke ... she is far too fast and flourishing to be stopped in mid-career by these slow old morals; and as she lives to please herself, she does not care if she displeases everyone else.[41]

Linton published her essay in 1868 in the *Saturday Review*, and it both stoked public debate on the changing role of women in society and was the cause of much controversy. Linton continued her journalistic campaign against this new type of woman throughout her career and, in 1891, published 'The Wild Women as Social Insurgents' in *The Nineteenth Century*, once again upbraiding those women she perceived as 'obliterating the finer traits of civilisation': 'She smokes after dinner with the men; in railway carriages; in public rooms – when she is allowed. She thinks she is thereby vindicating her independence and honouring her emancipated womanhood. Heaven bless her!'[42]

The opening scene of *The Silver Fox*, which has been read as a tirade against English manners and customs and which reverses the common stereotypes of England and Ireland, takes on an added context here.[43] The emphasis on Lady Susan's modern appearance and selfish behaviour is set not just in contrast to a more provincial but less vulgar Ireland, but also against the 'ideal of womanhood' reflected in the more modest, innocent and civilised Slaney Morris. Like the women described in Linton's articles, Lady Susan's defiance of gender traditions and conventional female behaviour is viewed in the novel as 'artificial' (3), an almost superficial mimicry of the more serious and intellectual work of public female emancipation. Lady Susan's feminist stance thus clearly only exists on a superficial level and it is only in the female relationships she begins to cultivate at the close of the novel that any true feminist feeling and attempts at social change become evident. The coming together of Slaney and Lady Susan moves to one side the national divisions that dominate the rest of the novel and its tragedies, foregrounding instead female friendship as the site of political healing. Like their authors working in partnership, Slaney and Lady Susan finally reject the 'zero-sum assumption' and create their own shared female values for an alternative socio-political community, one where women have come to know themselves through 'bitter experience' (92) and come together to overcome those experiences. Rather than, like Linton, uncomplicatedly rebuking female behaviour like Lady Susan's, *The Silver Fox* thus explores the gendered social conditions that create such behavioural types and suggests ways in which these conditions can be challenged. The emasculation and, indeed, feminisation of Hugh as he attempts to come to terms with the trauma of his horsing accident also locates the novel's male characters within these gendered concerns. Lady Susan's transformation of character at the close of the novel, for example, is one which significantly improves her marital relations, and releases her husband from his 'consciousness of failure' (57).

Such ideas are further cemented in Lady Susan's encounter with the much-beleaguered Irish peasant, Maria Quin, who suffers the loss of her father and brother in the novel due to the industrial exploits of Glasgow and the superstitions of her local community. Upon witnessing Lady Susan fall from her horse to her near-death, Maria is initially convinced that such an act is 'terrific and just retribution' for the deaths her family have suffered at the hands of Glasgow and his friends, but upon her acknowledgement that 'Mother of Our Lord! – the rider was a woman', Maria moves to save Lady Susan's life: 'the peasant heart struggled in the grave-clothes of hatred and superstition, and burst forth with its native impetuousness and warmth' (166). Maria's saving of Lady Susan is emblematic of the female solidarity Slaney has throughout the novel exhibited towards Hugh's wife. Moreover, Maria's gesture temporarily discards the national and class issues at the heart of the novel's tragedies and, like the budding partnership between Lady Susan and Slaney, finds common ground in the social plight of women. Risking her own reputation, Maria shares with Lady Susan the impropriety of Glasgow's former behaviour towards her and warns Lady Susan against him:

> 'Mind yerself!' she said in a whisper; 'that fella would throw ye on the roadside whin he'd be tired o' ye ... I can tell ye of the day I wint to Glashgow to the office, axing him to take back the price o' the land, and he put a hand on me to kiss me; he thought that was all he had to do to humour me. He remembers that day agin me yet' ... Neither the straining misfit of the black dress, nor the atrocious pretensions of the cheap boots, could impute vulgarity to the speaker. (173–4)

Recognising the import of Maria's revelation, the two women end their encounter on equal ground and with a handshake that reinforces the social and emotional impact of their meeting. It is also a pact which elicits the only reasoned political agreement and understanding of the novel in Lady Susan's promise to no longer hunt the silver fox of the novel's title, who (it is believed) has brought such ill omens upon the Quin family. The shedding of Maria's hatred and superstition, as well as Lady Susan's recounting of and admittance to her ignorance of the local situation, also leads to Maria's concession that Lady Susan's behaviour has thus far been one of an uninformed stranger, opposed to the machinations of one 'wanting to desthroy us', and this further frames the new political understanding between the two women (173).

Both women share their past experiences in order to develop a new social and emotional understanding of each other and, in so doing, they begin to disrupt the novel's fated political trajectory. In this light, Maria's uninhibited conversation with Lady Susan can be seen to bypass class conventions in order to establish the grounds for friendship and allow an ethic of female solidarity and care to emerge. Maria's and Lady Susan's concluding self-reflections on their joint situation with regard to Glasgow, as well as the broader English–Irish political relations, which damagingly govern their respective communities, also hints at their own individual socio-political maturation. Their outspoken conversation leads both women away from unthinking acceptance of the superstitions, opinions and politics of their friends, families and respective communities, and instead encourages independence of thought.

All three women have, in one way or another, suffered at the hands of Glasgow and it is initially this misery that unites them. Out of their collective maltreatment, however, and the sharing between them of their individual circumstances, derives the kind of mutual interest, trust, concern, intimacy and benevolence that is characteristic of the bonds of friendship, and it is this bond that eventually empowers the three women to make alternative social and political choices. Such relationships, argues Raymond, force the sharing of different perspectives and moral values and, in turn, foster 'vicarious participation in the very experience of moral alternatives'.[44] As a result, the kind of friendships between women Somerville and Ross depict in *The Silver Fox* are ones which have the capability of broadening and enriching the 'empirical base for evaluating both the abstract moral guidelines we already hold and alternatives we might consider'.[45] Female friendship for Somerville and Ross is, therefore, more than just a private and emotional bond. It is a political tie engendering a relational sense of self that has the potential to transform social and gender relations through its support of unconventional values, as well as stimulate moral growth and act as an egalitarian model for citizens of an alternative polity. Mary Wollstonecraft had much earlier elucidated this power of friendship's sociality and command over ethical behaviour when she wrote in *A Vindication of the Rights of Woman* (1792) that 'the most holy bond of society is friendship'.[46] Wollstonecraft further maintained that friendship was 'the most sublime of all affections' and in this recognition lie the entwined emotional and intellectual intensities that also mark the Somerville and Ross partnership as an affection of the heart as well as the mind.[47]

The affections of the heart between female friends in *The Silver Fox* are, however, also determined by an intimate and sometimes explicitly erotic context. Slaney's private emotional and increasingly intellectual admiration for Lady Susan, for example, is aroused and most openly admitted during a scene in which Slaney is also drawn to acknowledge Lady's Susan's physical attractiveness: 'Slaney had never thought her so handsome; her eyes seemed to look out of her heart and into a remote place unseen of others, instead of summing up things around her with her wonted practical glance … the fact remained that Slaney liked Lady Susan' (112). Slaney's growing sense of moral care for the latter thus frames itself within an intimate context, one which highlights Slaney's admittance and appreciation of Lady Susan's physical attractiveness. Lady Susan and Maria Quin also share a similarly tense moment of heightened physicality as they shake hands in friendship and with a new-found sense of female solidarity and cultural understanding. After the hunting accident, Lady Susan faces Maria in a dishevelled and physically exposed state, which is charged with an erotic subtext. Drawing hard breaths after her fall, Lady Susan's hat dangles by its guard and her bare shoulder is revealed by the burst sleeve of her riding habit (168). Maria stares at her 'as if taking in her good looks' and issues her warning about Glasgow (173). The two women shake hands in silence 'but some thrill ran horns to Maria's heart at the meeting of the palms, and sent the dew to her hot eyes … Lady Susan … walked uncertainly, and once or twice her hand went up to her eyes' (175). The touching of the two women's palms brings tears to both their eyes, a recognised sign of female sexual arousal. A layer of physical intimacy is thus added to the temporary moment of care and trust which the two women engender in their brief encounter, and this intimacy is marked by both an erotic thrill and the triumph of female political and emotional cohesion.

The gains in self-knowledge, as well as the accompanying individual spiritual and intellectual growth, which Slaney, Lady Susan and Maria Quin exhibit by the end of the novel become, therefore, reliant on the erotics and politics of these female ties. The possibilities of same-sex desire are acknowledged and cautiously explored in *The Silver Fox* but never come to fruition. By the end of the novel, Lady Susan has reconciled with Hugh, who has regained his lost confidence and masculinity; Slaney is married to Major Bunbury, her intellectual equal; and they all learn that Glasgow, after returning to England with his wife, has died on an engineering project in a mine shaft accident in Argentina. Like Howitt's 'The Sisters in Art', then, traditional heterosexual marriage eventually overrides the female unions which have been tentatively explored in the story. Glasgow's death, however, rings a note of unease at the end of *The Silver Fox*, and this temporarily disrupts the otherwise conventional quartet of Slaney and Bunbury, and Lady Susan and Hugh. The closing scene of the novel is reminiscent of Lady Susan's earlier sexually daring exploits with

Glasgow, as well as the political rift in Irish–English relations, and the story refuses to conform to a conventional happy ending.

The final chapter of *The Silver Fox* is removed from the rural demesne of French Court, with its dangerous but exhilarating landscape and hunting, and is instead set in Dublin during 'Horse Show week' amidst a game of polo in which Hugh is applauded for his horsemanship and sporting success (189). Slaney and Lady Susan remain friends, but there is a lack of authenticity marking both Lady Susan's reconciliation with Hugh and her bond with Slaney. As she was with Glasgow, Lady Susan is tempted by the attentions of Captain Onslow as they both watch Hugh playing polo, and the reader is reminded of Lady Susan's potential for infidelity in the 'charming' glance of recognition she offers Onslow in response to his flirtatious questions (191). Lady Susan's ride back to her hotel with Slaney in 'the Dublin outside car', with its 'exhilarating swing and swiftness', also bears comparison with her improper and near-fatal journey with Glasgow in the brake van engine (191) earlier in the novel. Furthermore, Lady Susan's friendship with Slaney is marked by their recent shopping expedition in the city and rings a superficial note. Here the admiring gaze is reversed between Slaney and Lady Susan, but the erotic and political frisson of Slaney's earlier feelings for Lady Susan are altogether forgotten: '"I never saw you look as well as you do to-day. I'm awfully glad I made you get that hat. It makes your eyes just the right colour"' (193). Hugh's sharing of Glasgow's death, which he reads in the newspaper at the polo club, also brings back memories for all of them of '"all that time – and what they said of the bad luck, and everything"' (195). The silver fox thus significantly rears its head again, even if only in memory, to haunt the final pages of the novel.

Maureen O'Connor's study of fox hunting in Somerville and Ross' fiction argues that the figure of the fox is 'elusive and wily, a trickster and sorcerer', but also an underprivileged figure that is hunted for the 'pleasure of killing' and expressive of 'sectarian and class tensions that are sometimes resolved, but just as often complicated by gender allegiances'.[48] The briefly felt female solidarity of Lady Susan, Maria Quin and Slaney Morris certainly conforms to this reading and the ending of the novel recalls the power of that female bond but also the complexities of class and race relations in late nineteenth-century Ireland that threaten to pull that bond apart. The fox's disruption of the novel's closing heterosexual unions also reminds of the alternative same-sex possibilities for women and this erotic element is intertwined with the colonial politics of the novel. Glasgow's railway project in Ireland is thwarted by Irish superstition and the unyielding geography of the landscape long before his wife sends him home and, as Roz Cowman has argued, that same landscape is 'described with an intimate detailed passion' and is 'profoundly eroticized'.[49] If Glasgow is representative in the story of masculine colonial power, then that power is metaphorically overcome by an erotic female authority that eventually kills him in a subsequent colonial context in the Argentine Republic.

In their essay on collaboration as feminist practice, Leonardi and Pope consider whether collaboration can be figured as erotic regardless of the sexual self-identifications of the collaborators, as well as how an 'erotic energy' might be registered in the texts of such collaborators who clearly acknowledge that part of the pleasure of joint composition resides in the 'composing of the couple'.[50] Female friendship and socio-political collaboration between *The Silver Fox*'s female protagonists certainly seem to be influenced by Somerville and Ross' lived collaborative experiences, as well as their accompanying ideologies of authorship and literary partnership. As the following sections of this chapter attempt to demonstrate, the bonds of work and friendship between the writing couple are evidenced in the mechanics of their collaborative practice and the private letters which facilitated that practice. This further eschews any purely sentimental understanding of female friendship and reveals the complex intellectual motivations and personal pleasures of Somerville and Ross' collaborative dynamic.

The conventions of Victorian letter-writing and female desire

With the unexpected commercial success of their first novel, coupled with the financial self-sustenance that it granted, Somerville and Ross began to imagine and plan for the future of their professional writing career, as elucidated to Somerville's brother, Cameron, in 1888: 'I trust we will get our first £25 in Feb. or thereabouts, as Martin and I have a deeplaid scheme ... of going together to Paris. I would paint in the morning and we would write together in the afternoon, and possibly pitch the plot in Paris and give true local colour – it would be too enchanting.'[51] This utopian vision, however, did indeed prove 'too enchanting' for Ascendancy reality to bear and the couple were forced to carry out a large proportion of their collaborative work amid the demands of their social and domestic lives, as well as across county boundaries in Ireland. With Somerville positioned in Cork, and Ross in Galway, much of the collaboration was carried out via a prolific correspondence which spanned the two women's working partnership. The letters and draft manuscripts ferried between Ross House and Drishane reveal some of the practical mechanics behind the textual collaboration, as well as the varying shades of intimacy which comingle with

Somerville and Ross' intellectual endeavours. Moreover, they also play a central and crucial role in the nurturance of the two women's blossoming friendship and professional ambitions, and this arguably foregrounds these documents as not merely historical artefacts but as sites of socio-cultural transgression that push against the conventional genre boundaries of private female epistolarity.

The eighteenth century, an era aptly known as the Age of Letters, has long been recognised as a high point for the popular publication of private letters, the epistolary novel, and the letter-writing manual. Many of the cultural and commercial contexts which surrounded these publications went on to considerably influence and overlap with the concerns of both the nineteenth-century literary marketplace and the corresponding attitudes which governed the role of female letter-writers. After conducting his rather conformist and unadventurous 'enquiry into the duties of the female sex' in the late 1790s, the Anglican priest, poet and abolitionist, Thomas Gisborne, concluded that women are 'ambitious to be distinguished for writing ... good letters', and that though a lady ought not to be discouraged from writing a good letter, those who make it their 'study' to do so commonly produce 'a composition to which a very different epithet ought to be applied': '[t]hose letters are only good, which contain the natural effusions of the heart, expressed in an unaffected language. Tinsel and glitter, and laboured phrases dismiss the friend and introduce the authoress.'[52] Gisborne here reflects the prevailing cultural mindset of the late eighteenth century both in his insistence on the sentimental and natural rhetorical strategies of the female letter-writer, and his recognition of the increasing number of women who defied these narrative strictures. For Gisborne, the intrusion of the egocentric female writer into the familiar letter elevates both the text and its creator onto unacceptable levels of cultural authority and professional authorship, and is far removed from the usual categories ('sentimental, non-literary and private') socially proscribed for women's letters.[53]

Barbara Zaczek's study of the limitations imposed upon the female epistolary voice in the late seventeenth and early eighteenth centuries argues that such categorising designates women's epistolary texts as 'dictates of the heart' and a 'spontaneous flow of emotion', and this reduces their output to 'a love letter *sensu strictu*, or a letter expressing familiar sentiments, those of a mother, a daughter, a wife'.[54] This type of private and sentimental writing for women was an acknowledged and encouraged form of textual communication within the context of the familiar letter throughout the eighteenth century, and the later decades of the nineteenth century emphasised the social and utilitarian aspects of women's epistolary activities by subtly formalising such textual communications as part of a woman's necessary domestic duties. In her study of Emily Dickinson's private letters and the conventions of Victorian letter-writing for women, Stephanie Tingley outlines the politicised alignment of the female letter-writer with the role of nurturer: '[s]ince letter writing provided one way for a Victorian woman to follow her culture's dictates to subordinate her own needs to the needs of others, it became one of a myriad of household tasks and responsibilities regularly assigned to the female realm because it was ... private, and an essential means by which women could fulfil their duty to nurture relationships and strengthen familial bonds.'[55] Modern cultural and literary theorists continue to imagine the social letter as a feminised textual space, most notably in Lacan's and Derrida's critical dialogue on the role the letter plays in Edgar Allen Poe's short story, *The Purloined Letter*, as well as in that text's own alignment of the letter with a royal female character. However, as Mary A. Favret points out, these critical discourses have erroneously encouraged a 'fiction of letters', which literally disarms the female letter-writer and, like her Victorian forebears, denies her a public voice.[56] Such critics, argues Favret, 'rely on an identification between literature and letters which does not acknowledge the woman who writes letters', and offers us instead a fiction 'which gives the letter the figure of the woman'.[57]

This modern theorising also ignores the kind of historical reality Gisborne warns against in his diatribe on the ambitions of female letter-writers. Bridget Glaser confirms that, far from accepting the purely functional and household aspects of letter-writing, women had been using the 'means of correspondence networks and manuscript exchanges' as early as the seventeenth century to 'share their ideas with other people and receive some critical response'.[58] Letter-writing as a form of acceptable social practice for women, as well as an increasingly necessary domestic responsibility, thus offered a sanctioned and shielded textual space in which women could begin to assert a much more public and critical voice and, in so doing, pursue literary and other artistic career paths which might otherwise have remained closed to them. In this critical reconfiguration of the female letter-writer, letter-writing comes to symbolise both domestic refinement and the potential for domestic rebellion for women. Opposed to simply an empty signifier of woman, the familial letter is more appropriately a sign of female desire (in all its professional and personal manifestations) as penned by a female hand and represents, at its most fundamental level, a conscious effort at self-representation, as well as cultural recognition and validation of female experience.

Had Woolf looked to women's private epistolary writing, opposed to what she eventually found in English fiction, 'A Room of One's Own' might have taken a slightly different critical curve. Indeed, the issues of female sexuality with which that essay is concerned are arguably far more entangled and explicated in women's letter-writing than in any other textual format. This has its corollary in the fiction of the eighteenth and nineteenth century, whereby female desire becomes the generative and actual life force of the private letter and the latter is consciously utilised as a familiar plot device in the period's fiction. In so doing, of course, the physical letters of these novels then also become representative of that most dangerous of female desires: sexual need, longing and aspiration. Nicola Watson suggests that, like the female physical desire for which they stand, 'letters in the novels of the post-revolutionary years are always liable to go astray, to engage in duplicity and deception, or to circulate out of control', and even Somerville and Ross' *The Silver Fox* avails of these well-worn narrative devices.[59] Lady Susan's sexual attraction to and desire for Glasgow is revealed in an anonymous letter to her husband Hugh, which Lady Susan finds by chance in Hugh's jacket pocket. Also, the marital relations of Glasgow, hitherto unknown to his friends in Ireland, are discovered in the leaves of a book by Slaney in a letter written to him by his wife. Elizabeth Cook concludes that the letter comes to signify female sexuality itself, 'that folded, secret place which is always open to violent intrusion ... There is always within the letter's decorously covered body that crevice or fissured place where the stirrings of desire can be felt.'[60] Foucault's arguments in the first volume of *The History of Sexuality* similarly located the self-fashioning of sexual truth in the confessional format of the private letter, arguing that such documents became key sites for the expression of homosexuality in the nineteenth century.[61]

Such critical thinking has rightly accorded sexuality a central place in the development and subsequent expression of the self and, within the historical context of the nineteenth century, understands the illicit nature of such textual expression, whether that expression takes the form of unchecked female sexual desire and pleasure or the homoerotic passions of same-sex relations, or indeed both. More subtly, however, the textuality of female correspondence can also be representative of a shared erotics which defines both the writing and female self and exists outside the sexual self-identifications of the correspondents, mirroring Leonardi and Pope's suggestion that there is 'an erotic pleasure' in the activity of joint composition which derives from the pleasure associated with the 'composing of the couple'.[62] Somerville and Ross partake in this kind of existential composition, defining their lives as joint authors and passionate friends through their correspondence with each other. As Glaser notes, the '"I" of a letter does not have a life of its own – it is dependent on the "you" of the addressee'.[63] As such, Somerville's and Ross' individual identities as both authors and intimate friends is defined within a specific relationship, and their joint authorial status is finally subject to the success or otherwise of that human bond. In terms of both work and friendship, the 'composing of the couple' is evident throughout their correspondence and, in fact, the two women's friendship is partially instigated via Ross' attraction to Somerville's writerly self.

Ross met Somerville for the first time in 1886 during an extended visit to Castletownshend and she was much enamoured of Somerville and her sister Hildegarde. On Somerville's subsequent departure for Paris, Ross endeavoured to initiate a more permanent acquaintance than her original visit had allowed and twice wrote to Somerville in the following few months. Both these letters make mention of her 'enthusiasm' and enjoyment at hearing Somerville's letters to her mother read aloud to the family in Drishane, and her second letter both admonishes Somerville for not replying to her original missive, and once again underscores the charm and fascination for Ross of Somerville's epistolary character: '[y]ou know and should blush to know that there is no reason in the world why I should write to you – but there are people to whom it interests one to write ... As I have heard each of your letters declaimed I have felt that I should like to make merry with you over many things therein.'[64] Ross' persistence in capturing Somerville's attention amid the latter's 'many correspondents' exhibits the communal ground that Ross intimates from Somerville's familial letters will exist between them as a pleasurable foundation and justification for their further acquaintance.[65]

Somerville and Ross' friendship is thus partly founded on the attraction of the self as composed and dramatised in epistolary exchange, and the development of their ongoing relationship would remain, in many ways, dependent on this form of oscillatory communication. In part, the letters replaced the live conversations which the two women viewed as integral to both their friendship and authorship, and the letters also reveal the extent to which their personal affection bore a physically intimate dimension both common to their wider circle of female friends and relatives, and indistinct to themselves. In a letter to Somerville, for example, Ross expresses missing the physical presence and warmth of her writing partner in bed, and both Somerville's and Ross' diaries reveal that the two women also unremarkably shared their beds with Somerville's sister Hildegarde and cousin Ethel. As Gifford Lewis has noted, bed-sharing between women in the nineteenth century was quite common practice.[66] Moreover, the expression of affection and intimacy between the two writers repeatedly surfaces in their correspondence, particularly through the less reserved Ross, and range from Ross' self-conscious declarations of 'foolishness' in missing Somerville when the two are apart, to the former's desire to share her life's passions with her writing partner: 'I have the wish for travel in my blood now – I looked up into the blue Connemara hills and could have cried that I wasn't in among them with you.'[67] Somerville and Ross' different biographers have variously tried to categorise such behaviour within both an explicitly lesbian context and a socio-cultural framework of normative nineteenth-century female friendship. However, despite the differing conclusions, the critical motivations for both these types of discussion repeatedly converge on the desire to know and understand the sexual nature of the two women's relationship and how far the passions of their friendship did or did not extend to physical sexual activity and homoerotic longing. The letters here become documents of empirical investigation and, more often than not, these biographers rely on inventive conjecture where empirical fact is lacking. Any conclusions drawn in this way, however, simply seem to leave the question of sexual practice open to debate. More damagingly, this kind of reading obfuscates the ways in which women's letter-writing enabled other radical forms of self-expression and, indeed, facilitated a relational and ongoing development of the self on a personal, professional and erotic level.

Female professional literary aspiration and desire is categorised by Gisborne as an unnecessary 'duty of the female sex', and such rhetoric had a powerful influence over even the most determined artistic women. In her frustrated letter to Cameron at not being able to pursue a professional artistic vocation, for example, Somerville employs the language of necessity and duty, bemoaning her family's opinion that her ambition 'isn't necessary', but equally admitting that she is being 'selfish' and 'egotistical'. Duty thus drives Somerville's compliance with her family's wishes that she spend less time in Paris developing her skills as a professional artist. This practical effect of her family's disapproval, however, is perhaps far less damaging than the ideological consequences of their displeasure, which indoctrinate in the young Somerville a sense of wrongdoing over the general pursuit of individual desire and ambition. Her collaborative writing with Ross initially suffers from the same sense of disapprobation from family quarters, and this is additionally coupled with both a belittling of their joint literary efforts ('that nonsense of the girls'), and physical attempts to distract the writing duo from their work, who found themselves to be the victims of an 'inverted Boycott': 'a determination to pursue them to any retreat in order to compel participation in the sport of the moment'.[68] But the mutual support, encouragement and belief that derives from the collaboration allows Somerville and Ross to recreate in their letters and friendship (both of which are sanctioned activities) the artistic freedom, spirit and professionalism Somerville recognised in the female-only Parisian salons.

Somerville and Ross' letters to each other are, therefore, sites of mutinous female desire, but they are characterised not just by the passions of their friendship but by an accompanying intellectual aspiration which marks all aspects of their literary collaboration. This, in turn, engenders its own kind of erotic encounter. The contemporary American writer and activist, Sandra Butler, reveals the zenith of such erotic dynamics when she aligns the sexual and the textual in her former literary collaboration and personal partnership with Barbara Rosenblum:

> Each morning we would … sit beside each other, one of us at the keyboard, the other sitting closely alongside. We typed, interrupted, criticized, added, paced, drank coffee, laughed, then grew thoughtful, intense, or joyous with relief when just the right word or image emerged. It was a making of love. An honouring of our bond. Lovemaking. The work we did had the focus, the passion, the sense of completion our lovemaking once had. I often felt similarly spent when a work session ended. But so loved. So known. So deeply connected to this woman.[69]

Butler's recognition of the erotic play behind the intellectual dialogue and debate of her work with Rosenblum allows for a tangible sexualisation of the textual encounter which, despite its contemporary mindset and explicitly lesbian context, offers a useful way of framing the intellectual and emotional connections engendered by the Somerville and Ross partnership and the development of their joint authorial bond. Friendship here acknowledges and is open to the prospects of same-sex desire, but it is also an attachment which is defined and generated by a woman-centred and 'thoughtful passion', which retains the possibility of heteronormativity.[70] Drawing on the classical Greek tradition of friendship, Raymond argues that the ideal of female friendship resides in its understanding of the 'friendship union as a primary passion associated with thinking'.[71] Whether or not the friends are lovers, a thoughtfully passionate friendship is 'passion at its most active':

> It keeps passion active and does not allow it to degenerate into its more passive modes. More concretely, it helps two women to become their own person. There is a dynamic integrity of existence in a thoughtful passion that is missing in a more sentimental friendship. Friendship that is characterized by thoughtful passion ensures that a friend does not lose her Self in the heightened awareness of and attachment to another woman.[72]

This seems to offer a much more constructive framework for interrogating and understanding Somerville and Ross' personal and professional partnership. It neither denies nor promotes the possibilities of lesbian attachment, and thus avoids the empirical investigations of sexuality which have consistently marred critical attempts to explicate the nature of Somerville and Ross' authorial and sentimental bond. Most significantly, it foregrounds friendship as an intellectual passion, and as a relationship characterised by the intermix of its cerebral and erotic encounters, a dialogue between the Self and its Other, and this reflects Somerville and Ross' own dialogic practice.

Such a practice is explicitly evidenced in the two women's private correspondence, the latter of which plays a crucial part in the methodologies of joint literary creation. Somerville and Ross' letters to each other become sites for the plotting and composition of their novels, short stories and essays, as well as the provision of raw real-life material which was cribbed for dialogue, plots, character and descriptive narratives.[73] In so doing, the daily trials of dealing with publishers, agents, editors, booksellers and the general reading public are also thrashed out in their letters to each other. Such letters have obvious historical relevance as rhetorical documents of women's entry into the nineteenth-century literary marketplace, and they are also vital to understanding the often difficult negotiations that had to be made with regard to women's public roles within the professional (and largely male-dominated) arena of professional writing. The final section of this chapter offers a reading of these compositional strategies as outlined in Somerville's and Ross' letters and other private manuscripts, particularly with regard to the legalities of what Somerville and Ross called their 'respective shares' in the collaboration. The final section of this chapter, however, will precede this discussion with an analysis of the textual mode of Somerville and Ross' letters to each other, and the dialogic space these letters afforded the writing duo in which to offer and receive criticism, debate literary ideas, and share in the joys and difficulties of the writing process more generally, as well as encourage and define a specific authorial identity for each partner. Thoughtful passion is here manifested in the 'composing of the couple' and its erotic dynamics, as well as the revelation of self through dialogue, and the gradual teasing out of an intellectual and communal feminist vision.

'A tooth and naily fight': Somerville and Ross' epistolary relations

In 1888, towards the end of the final copying of the manuscript which would become *An Irish Cousin*, Ross wrote to Somerville to let her know that she intended to 'burn the lot of Shocker things':

headings mottos and so forth and feel a faint sentiment in doing so. Any period of good work has a nice honest romance about it. I do not think much of the Shocker all round I am bound to say. It has its points but it is indifferently written – with awkwardness and effort. However the tone is very sound and the sentiment is genuine and it is sincere and unusual. That is my opinion. You once said a little thing about it and what the writing of it did for us – if you don't remember it I do – that is good enough. Anyhow it was a nice little thing.[74]

Ross here pledges to toss the textual by-products of her and Somerville's shared literary production into the fire, and admits to her mediocre opinion of their debut novel. Nonetheless, their shared literary activities are still prized by Ross as a 'period of good work' and a 'nice honest romance'. Her letter to Somerville repeatedly reflects on the personal gains of their literary collaboration, the 'nice little thing' that it did for the two women, as opposed to simply the physical product of their partnership. Ross returns to this idea in a later letter which, giddy with pride and disbelief at seeing *An Irish Cousin* 'heading Bentley's list', divulges to Somerville that alongside all that it 'taught' them in a 'literary way', Somerville was above all 'a nice woman to write with'.[75] Again, what Ehnenn calls the 'excesses of collaboration' come to the fore in Ross' thoughts on her and Somerville's original literary collaboration, and it is repeatedly the personal pleasures of collaboration and the joyful experiences of joint composition that Ross highlights in her retrospective thinking on the literary partnership. As the commercial and critical success of *An Irish Cousin* gradually becomes evident in 1889, Ross also encourages Somerville to write with her again for both professional and personal reasons: '[i]t would be too bad to let go such an opening as we have now, and I am not man enough for a story by myself.'[76] Having entered the literary marketplace under male pseudonyms, Ross playfully situates their female doubling up as a means of equalling masculine strength in the literary marketplace, but she also subtly invokes the felt potency of her and Somerville's personal and intellectual bond. This is further evidenced in the duo's forward looks to accepting the remunerative offers from publishers which began to be made after the publication of *An Irish Cousin*: 'we might be very glad of the £15 ... by the time we got it – I know *I* should – and I should much enjoy writing with you'.[77] Ross reiterates this point in a later letter concerning the same publisher's offer and, conceding to the lower than desired rate of pay, declares that: 'I shall write it with you with pleasure and profit to myself – if you want me.'[78]

Ross thus repeatedly circles back to the idea that it is the act of writing and the pleasures that derive from this practice (both personal and intellectual) that drive her ambition to continue and further her professional partnership with Somerville. Both the end literary product and the need to make money, though obviously compelling and guiding forces in their professional deliberation, are continually accorded second place. As the duo's commercial and critical success increases and the friendship develops further, the two ambitions become increasingly intertwined; literary partnership becomes a mode of being which encompasses all facets of life. Moreover, the letters the couple write to each other during their time apart become an important part of their compositional practice, as well as their affectionate relations. Writing about the mechanics of their literary collaboration, Kaplan and Cronan Rose reveal that (even in the twentieth century) letter-writing forms an important part of exercising their joint authorship: 'we learned to prepare for our time together by stimulating each other with ideas and hints in letters. Indeed, we now write diary letters to one another each week, letters that include gossip and dailiness as well as intellectual exchange.'[79] Over a century before them, Somerville and Ross utilised the letter form in a decidedly similar manner and for astonishingly like-minded purposes, as did many other women of the same period. Recent research into nineteenth-century women's letters affirms that Somerville and Ross were not alone in their exploitation of epistolary writing to further (and indeed catalyse) their artistic career. In their introduction to an edited collection of British and American women's letters, Jennifer Cognard-Black and Elizabeth MacLeod Walls argue that such letters constitute no less than 'evidence of women's authorial revolution'.[80] They go on to suggest that letter-writing for artistic and intellectual women of the nineteenth century provided both a way of verbalising 'what it meant to be an author', and a crucial outlet that would otherwise have been 'restricted by their domestic responsibilities and various other social strictures': 'letter writing as both an expedient communication tool and a testing ground for female artistry confirms that women authors throughout the Victorian and modern periods used letters to create, enhance, publicize, and defend their writing'.[81]

The seething intersection of domestic life and the demands of professional authorship are just as deliberately evident in the letters of Somerville and Ross as they are in the letters of Kaplan and Cronan Rose. Indeed, it is in Somerville and Ross' letters to each other that the grinding of Carbery's bones for literary fodder becomes unashamedly candid. This is largely due to the way in which the letters were composed, read, annotated, categorised and filed away by their authors as literary documents to be recycled into their published fiction, often over a decade after the original idea had been captured and formulated in a letter. In this way, the letters became part of a purposeful and almost business-like system of joint literary creativity that served multiple objectives. As historical documents, the letters were stored as a working repository of Somerville's and Ross' lived experiences in Ireland and further abroad, and as ongoing lines of vital communication, these same letters were used as a textual space within which the two authors could debate their literary ideas, formulate their conceptions of joint authorship, and express their hardening friendship.

Somerville and Ross were certainly more than aware of the professional intent their own letters to each other fulfilled and, in part, the letters duplicated the role of the working notebooks the cousins used to collect an array of raw material for their fiction, including recorded instances of local dialects, stories, and tales told to the authors by others, and records of domestic events at Drishane and Ross. All four of the extant notebooks are currently held as part of the Somerville and Ross papers at Queen's University Belfast. This collection includes the earliest and most significant of the notebooks, which was begun by the cousins in 1886 and was later thematically indexed and entitled 'Irish Memories. Collected and Compiled by E.Œ. Somerville and Martin Ross'. The title page further includes a complete list of their published works. Somerville and Ross appear to have used this notebook as a comprehensive and organised repository for all their hastily scribbled snatches of dialogue, as well as local tales and events, which would otherwise have been lost in the back pages of diaries and pocket notebooks. Each entry was transcribed under an appropriate heading, which ranged from 'Hunting &c &c Foxes' to 'The Supernatural', and was then marked off with a cross once it had been used in a published work. The crossed-out entry was often then further annotated with the name of the short story or novel into which the particular phrase or tale had been incorporated.

The extent of and exactness with which Somerville and Ross employed these notebooks and their contents is quite staggering. Over half (if not three quarters) of the several hundreds of pages of raw material in the notebooks have been marked as used, and much of the recorded dialogue was reproduced either verbatim or with only slight alterations in their published fiction. For example, studies of the comic short story 'Poisson d'Avril' (1908) alongside the notebook demonstrate that the story is actually a combination of two factual stories the cousins heard and recorded in their notebooks – one concerning a man whose parcel of fish gets lost on a train journey, and one relating to a man whose train is delayed because the train driver decides to stop off mid-journey and have a game of cards with an *en route* stationmaster. Both incidents are fairly closely reproduced from the notebook in which they were originally recorded, and much of the dialogue spoken by varying characters is also garnered from recorded dialogue the authors had heard spoken locally. The dialogue, for example, between the stationmaster and an impatient English passenger trying to get to Belfast is borrowed from the notebook, as are selected outbursts of the 'seven shawled and cloaked countrywomen' with whom the principal character finds himself unexpectedly interred in his train carriage.[82]

'Poisson d'Avril' is a common example of the way in which both the plot and dialogue of their fiction originated in Somerville and Ross' working notebooks, but it also situates the story's textual history within an ideological framework in keeping with the cousins' dual authorship. Just as the mechanical image of two hands working as one disrupts the singular authority of the cerebral writing figure, the exposure of Somerville and Ross' literary methods unbalances traditional ideas of genius by accenting the manifold textual origins of their published works. It was in the transformation, rearrangement and new combination of original oral sources that Somerville and Ross found most of their inspiration for their published writing, and such literary strategies remained a key creative process throughout their joint authorship. Spontaneous inspiration in their dual working practice gives way to authorial effort and labour, and the assumed organic structures of a literary work are superseded by the conditionality of that work to its compound origins. This once again gives the lie to Romantic ideals of authorship and creativity, and further renders what Walter Ong has called the '*de facto* intertextuality' of print culture explicit: '[m]anuscript culture ... deliberately created texts out of other texts, borrowing, adapting, sharing the common, originally oral, formulas and themes.'[83] The modern anxieties of influence which Ong refers to, as well as the earlier cited anxieties of Wordsworth and Coleridge, however, are largely unfelt by Somerville and Ross and, in fact, the preservation and formal labelling of their main working notebook as an intentional compilation of 'Irish Memories' is duly signed off with the joint authorial signature, 'E.Œ. Somerville and Martin Ross'.

Albeit unpublished, the notebook is thus physically documented as an authored work, one which Somerville and Ross were no less proud of than the list of published titles which adorns its cover. It also unashamedly allows their authorship and works to become part of the increasingly industrial world in which they lived. The indebtedness of the authors to the published titles on the cover of the notebook is reverently acknowledged in these titles formal listing, and this additionally pays testament to the authorial effort and manufacture of raw material which went into their production. Such creative activities have their mass corollary in the scrapbook culture of the nineteenth century. Roger

MacFarlane argues that the scrapbook, or commonplace book, of the nineteenth century provided a 'liminal zone' in which 'proprietorial distinctions between texts were confounded' and subordinated to the practice of 'arrangement, juxtaposition, and connection': '[i]n the medium of the scrapbook, source was of less importance than context, and selection was valued beneath generation.'[84] Nineteenth-century author and dramatist, Charles Reade (1814–84), was possibly one of the most prolific and professional scrapbook collectors of his time and, like Somerville and Ross, he formally indexed his literary notebooks and consciously utilised the medium of the scrapbook as a repository of textual sources for his fiction. He spent at least one day a week cutting and pasting a variety of newspaper articles and illustrations into his scrapbooks and formally dubbed his working practice as the 'great system.'[85] Like Reade, Somerville and Ross' 'great system' pushed the boundaries of documentary realism and was largely based on transcriptions of real-life oral narratives, including stories the duo heard in the local petty sessions court in Skibbereen, County Cork, and which formed the mainstay of many of the Irish R.M. tales. Furthermore, Somerville and Ross' creative system also utilised their epistolary exchanges as an additional 'liminal' textual space in which to forge their fiction.

Further to the material gleaned from their notebooks, for example, 'Poisson d'Avril' contains a short phrase borrowed from a letter written almost ten years before the composition and publication of the story. In the almighty squash of the train carriage, the seven country women declare that 'we're as throng as three in a bed this minute!', which tallies with Ross' declaration in a letter of 1888 that '[t]hrong as three in a bed will Drishane be – literally perhaps.'[86] This letter was obviously used several times for different publications, as Ross' recollection of an Irish countrywoman mourning her sons' emigration to America had earlier been used as a model for Norry the Boat in *The Real Charlotte*, who is made to repeat the woman's lament as recorded in Ross' letter:

> I think often of a thing that a country woman here said to me the other day – apropos of her sons going away from her to America. 'But what use is it to cry, even if ye dhragged the hair out o' yer head – ye might as well be singin' and dancin'. She was crying when she said it – and was a wild looking creature whom you would like to paint and the thing altogether stays in my mind.[87]

Like the notebooks, passages in Somerville and Ross' correspondence are frequently marked out by the authors with either a cross, or a line running down the margin, to indicate where material has been used in their published fiction. Furthermore, they kept, labelled, annotated and filed these letters away in meticulous fashion to be retrieved as primary data in what Somerville would much later term the 'Somerville and Ross ... Limited Company'.[88] Letters were also often labelled with similar titles to those indexed in the 1886 notebook. Many envelopes are marked with titles such as 'Hunting', 'Hunt Ball' and 'Agric. [ultural] Show – Races' and, in addition, the content of particular parts of some letters has also been given thematic headings.[89] Again, like the notebooks, some letters further contain annotations denoting which published work became the destination for certain events or dialogues recounted in personal letters. Somerville, for example, has clearly marked a fragment of a letter written to her by Ross (*c.*1893) with the title 'Jack Buckley's Horse', and she has also added a note in the top left-hand corner indicating the story's use in *Wheel-Tracks*.[90]

Like the notebooks, then, the letters became a source of plot, characterisation and authentic dialogue, and were handled as such. Emily Herbert was possibly the most famous example of the cousins' poaching from real-life when she was closely and unabashedly used as the inspiration for Charlotte Mullen in *The Real Charlotte* and initially described by Ross in a letter to Somerville in May 1886.[91] Even the most fleeting of second-hand characters often made it into Somerville and Ross' works, such as the 'Morris girls', who were described to Ross by Somerville's cousins and then worked into the short story 'A Conspiracy of Silence' in 1908, after having been originally described in a letter by Ross to Somerville in 1895.[92] Within the text of the letters, Somerville and Ross would also often highlight the potential of a story or event being relayed and acknowledge the 'precious things' that they were recounting.[93] A fragment of a letter survives, for example, from Ross to Somerville in which the early genesis for the first of the Irish R.M. tales, 'Great-Uncle McCarthy', is to be found. Ross evidently realised the literary potential of the story she was transcribing and ends the letter hoping to find a 'better account' of it.[94] The letter was also marked for later use at the time of writing and the story of the sweep which Ross had heard and recorded was eventually transposed in minute detail to the second half of 'Great-Uncle McCarthy'. This was a common tactic and the two women would often suggest to the other that 'this has the makings of a story', or request that a letter was 'saved' so that it could be used 'later' in their fiction.[95] One of Ross' last surviving letters to Somerville, for example, contains a long narrative of her visit to Tyrone House and the illicit inter-racial and inter-religious relations of that house's inhabitants. In that same letter, she wonders if she and Somerville 'dare to write up that subject' and Somerville eventually used the letter after Ross' death to compose *The Big House of Inver*.[96] Additionally, it was often the recipient and not the sender of a letter who realised the merit and promise of what had been received, and this mirror process was well-served by the vacillating nature of their textual communication: 'and by the way, (since I am a sympathetic reader,) I would like to tell you how very well I realise that bonfire, and Thady Connor – and – I say it seriously – you ought to make a sonnet, if only for the sake of bringing in the phrase "a welcome killed by memories". It seemed to give me the feeling of the whole thing.'[97]

One of the lengthiest and most extensively used plots derived from a combination of material contained in the notebooks and the letters was an incident at Ross House concerning the suicide of a local boy in the bogs of Pouleen-a-Fearla in December 1893. Ross originally wrote up the incident verbatim, as told to her by a local Irish man who worked on the Ross estate, Mat Kenealy, and from this transcript she composed two letters to Somerville recounting the event in her own narrative. The cousins finally adapted this story into *The Silver Fox*, and the fate of Tom Quin in the novel is largely an extended dramatisation of the tragic life and drowning of the boy at Ross, as well as Ross' interpretation of this real-life event: '[n]ever was a more bitter comment on a parish feud, and never was there a more innocent and godly life turned to active insanity by bad treatment.'[98] The process from notebook and letter to novel exhibits a gradual teasing out of the ideas which had begun to significantly impress themselves on Ross' mind, and her letters to Somerville slowly and perhaps quite unconsciously identify the passages and phrases provided by Mat's dialogue that would eventually be used in their novel. Passages from *The Silver Fox* show the minute details Somerville and Ross borrowed from Mat's retelling of the tale and explicitly reveal the creative and collaborative movement from the original source, in which Ross intimates that the event has 'the making of a story almost', to the final published text.[99] The letters also reveal Ross' reliance on Somerville to assist her in 'talking' the incident into a more appropriate 'shape' for a publishable story.[100] Her letters to Somerville in this instance, therefore, pinpoint the way in which their private correspondence opened up a space for the nurturing of literary ideas. A story that may eventually have been lost or forgotten is given new life and cultivation through its recounting in familial letters.

Criticism and debate were also crucial elements in the collaboration and, once more, the letters generate an authorial seat from which the two writers could afford to discuss and fine-tune their work. Lengthy critiques of each other's writing and on shared collaborative projects comprise another valuable facet of the Somerville and Ross correspondence. It was arguably the minute critical details they shared with each other that provided the artistic 'backbone' and intellectual encouragement that was so essential to their collaboration, and it is this type of critical dialogue that can so often be found in their letters.[101] Their criticism to each other ranged from detailed suggestions of alterations to phrasing and ideas, through more complex plot changes and notes on characterisation, and finally even to thoughts on where best to attempt placing an article or story for publication. Selections of Somerville's letter to Ross in 1888, which concern a newspaper article on which Ross had been working, give a good range of examples showing the different kinds of criticism they applied to each other's work and the detail they went into:

> I have read your paper twice ... and – as you want my candid opinion I think it is *awfully* good – full of ideas and originally-applied adjectives, and the real feeling and sense of and for things. What struck me when I first read it, was a certain tightness and want of the ideas being expanded. It read too strong. Like over-strong tea. It felt a little crowded and compressed in style, and *perhaps* now and then ... a superfluously ingenious adjective – entirely expressive and well applied, but still its very ingenuity tending to load the sense, and task the reader's strength of appreciation ... On page 5 ought the third paragraph to begin 'startled question', or 'a startled etc' or 'questions'? ... On page six the suggestion of the old man's tragedy is very artistic, but would I think, bear expansion ... On page 8 would you say 'to see tomorrow's *day* dying' etc instead of merely the possessive? ... I think for *Temple Bar* you might want to pad and pan more ... Constance Bushe told me, she heard Saxons openly discussing the natives as if they were Central Africans who knew no word of English. Could you work a parallel case ... It now reads like a sympathetic news article and not a magazine one. Would the <u>Saint James Gazette</u>? or even the <u>Saturday</u>? with a few more deep questions of life and death thrown in? ... I agree that it is not at all the <u>World</u>'s form: too serious, and not bitter enough.[102]

Another letter from Ross to Somerville in the same year, regarding a poem Somerville had written, exhibits a very similar tone of criticism, and also provides ideas for publishers, showing that the critical impetus was very much a supportive two-way process.[103]

The letters further presented an opportunity to air and debate the changes they were separately making on working manuscripts for collaborative projects. There are several surviving letters written between the two women composed during the final creative toiling of *An Irish Cousin*, and which were sent alongside altered manuscripts explaining the modifications that had been made, or praising/negating the adjustments that had been received:

> for pity's sake try and write by return of post to say if you like pages 71 and 72. I have always felt something like that there – *don't* say it is premature – it isn't – and I do think it is the kind of thing that seems to me probable … I know you must loathe my sticking in these putrid things and then fighting for them … Please goodness we will have many a tooth and naily fight next month – but don't let us combat by post; it is too wearing.[104]

The discordant nature evident here of Somerville and Ross's literary haggling is not an isolated example, but something that repeatedly governs the collaborative compositional process between the two women. In an essay on the creative origins of the Irish R.M. stories, 'Étaples: where the Irish R.M. began', Somerville explains that 'we talked and argued into existence one after another of the little group of men and women who were destined to become for us … intimate friends'.[105] This brings us back to York's argument that harmonious portraits of female collaborators are a fallacy generated by uninformed public opinion and, occasionally, the duplicitous rhetoric of collaborators themselves. York argues, instead, for the idea that all successful collaborations are, of necessity, relationships both motivated and enhanced by discordance: 'difference and disagreement strengthen rather than disable collaboration'.[106]

The fact of Somerville and Ross' literary skirmishes is in no doubt and crops up early in their correspondence. A letter written by Ross to Somerville shortly after the completion of *An Irish Cousin* verifies the often dissonant process of literary collaboration and two imaginations trying to work as one, as Ross reflects on 'the long time that we fought over' the novel.[107] Several years later the duo were busy working together on *The Real Charlotte* and their collaborative working practices seem to have undergone little change in this respect. Ross' diary reports that the two collaborators had 'arrived at a violent collision with regard to final course of the plot'.[108] The language of collision, violence, combat, and a 'tooth and naily fight' repeatedly characterise the duo's self-reflections on their writing practice. Such violence, however, is recognised as a crucial ingredient in Somerville and Ross' creative process and Somerville makes this explicit in *Irish Memories* in her attempt to offer a technical explanation of how she jointly put pen to paper with Ross:

One or the other – not infrequently both, simultaneously – would state a proposition. This would be argued, combated perhaps, approved, or modified; it would then be written down by the (wholly fortuitous) holder of the pen, would be scratched out, scribbled in again; before it found itself finally transferred into decorous MS. would probably have suffered many things, but it would, at all events, have had the advantage of having been well aired.[109]

Moreover, Somerville and Ross appear to look forward to and cherish their moments of live oral debate, and the obvious desire and pleasure marking this textual jousting is not unlike the erotic dimensions of their friendship: '[p]lease goodness we will have many a tooth and naily fight next month.' Indeed, as Chapter 5 will go on to demonstrate, it was precisely this element of their dual authorship that Somerville would miss most after Ross's death. Recognition of this dynamic further deflates the presumption of critics who have argued that the two women's imaginations easily became one during the writing process, and that their joint authorship proceeded at all times with 'equal harmony'.[110] Significantly, Ross' comments on *An Irish Cousin* in 1889 usefully distinguish her and Somerville's proclivity for argument and debate from the mechanism of struggle and expulsion, once again advocating 'working (in) the in between':

> We have proved that we can do it, and we shall go on. The reason few people can, is because they have separate minds upon most subjects, and fight their own hands all the time.[111]

Faith in each other as professional authors, women, feminists and friends is the tie that holds the collaboration together, allowing the critical faculty full exertion in often highly combative dialogue, but always without rupture. Somerville and Ross' personal and writing relationship exists as an ongoing conversation, sometimes a violent one, which informs both the texts that they produce, as well as their individual senses of self.

Somerville and Ross' correspondence fuses the two women's varying forms of communication and collaboration: their letters act as both text and speech. Lewis informs us that both women frequently refer to their letters as 'talking' and an example of this can be found in Somerville's letter to Ross written on the night of her mother's funeral: 'I can't go to sleep, I have tried but it is no use, so I have lighted my candle and will try to think that I am talking to you.'[112] The writing of this letter actively manifests itself as an imagined conversation between Somerville and Ross in Somerville's hand and, by focusing her attention on the imagined Other that is Ross, Somerville simultaneously produces both a monologic and dialogic text. This level of imitative artifice was arguably an essential quality to two collaborative writers who were often forced to collaborate apart, and it was a skill that Somerville and Ross gradually honed in their dual authorship, no doubt aided and sustained by their extensive correspondence. The critical level of debate and finely tuned oral communication that hallmarked their joint compositional practice also then infected their individual creative efforts. Writing to Somerville in 1889 on an essay on education, which would eventually become the singly authored 'Cheops in Connemara', Ross recognises and relishes the imagined Somerville at her side in lively debate with her on the piece in hand: 'I got a sort of grip of the "Education" thing today, and I hope it may continue – but I am a fraud in the way of writing ... I feel you saying "Well, but I don't see" – and then I don't see either. But it is good for me.'[113] Ross' sense of self as a writer here becomes embroiled in her relationship with Somerville and, even when writing alone, her creative thinking is dominated by the processes of exchange and dialogue which characterise her collaboration.

Like the friendship from which the collaboration derives, then, the professional facets of the relationship between Somerville and Ross take pleasure in the composition of the couple and this, in turn, becomes part of each individual's personal make-up. This chapter has attempted to demonstrate the ways in which friendship and collaboration become almost indistinguishable in Somerville and Ross' writing career and, in so doing, defy the type of authorship sanctioned in legal and aesthetic discourses of the nineteenth century. Somerville and Ross' profound belief in each other, however, was continually challenged by a public audience which made suspect collaborative modes of creativity. In addition, issues of gender and genre begin to affect the couple's resistance to legal narratives of literary property and the next chapter attempts to tease out some of the complexities of Somerville and Ross' collaborative stance in the public domain.

CHAPTER THREE

Women's popular literature in the commercial marketplace

I n her late-life essay 'The Gentle Art of Collaboration', the Australian writer Marjorie Barnard gave an insight into the workings of her literary collaboration with Flora Eldershaw, and explained of their writing practice in the 1930s: '[w]e worked it up together and our thoughts and ideas became inextricably blended into a whole. There was no mine and thine but ours. This not only excluded proprietary rights on either side but gave the book its unity.'[1] Somerville offers a similar public explanation in 1901 of her and Ross' joint style and the blending of their 'thoughts and ideas', arguing that 'their styles were as distinct as blue and yellow on the mixing palette and that the resultant green was a style also and more than the two styles apart'.[2] The monogram Somerville devised for the frontispiece of their books further reflects this intermingling of two distinctive styles into a larger whole. Based on traditional Celtic knot work, Somerville combines in a single graphic her and Ross' initials so that they remain apart and distinct on the page, but are connected by the design's Celtic interlacing motif. After Ross' premature death, Somerville also designed a mosaic floor as a memorial for her now deceased collaborator and, again, she utilised traditional Celtic knot-work patterns, basing the design on a page from the Book of Kells.

These images of merging and fluidity are also common to other nineteenth-century female collaborators and Somerville's memorial to Ross is visually reminiscent of Michael Field's description of collaboration as a 'perfect mosaic', one which crosses and interlaces 'like a company of dancing flies'.[3] However, while the memorial and the authors' logos both insist on Somerville and Ross' Irish heritage, as well as repeat images of merging and unity which reflect their collaborative ideologies, they also explicitly belie some of the known practicalities of the duo's joint authorial labour and practice. Ehnenn argues that the public narratives offered by female collaborators on their dual writing practice are not 'straightforward documentation', but a kind of textual performance of 'their identity as female and joint authors, a performance that works both with and against existing notions of authorship and authorial labour'.[4] 'Metaphors of merging and boundlessness' operate as a means of asserting female authority as joint authors, as well as signalling awareness that 'writing as a couple subverts what is considered to be the authorial norm'.[5] As already demonstrated in Chapters 1 and 2, the sharing of textual spaces, and the dispersal of authorial ownership and control, defies literary models of authorship that favour Romantic ideals of the solitary author. The rhetorical and visual assertions of unity demonstrated by women co-authors arguably gesture towards recognising authorial difference, as well as legitimising joint authorship in the wake of these more traditional precedents. As Yopie Prins points out in her study of 'Victorian Sappho' and Michael Field: 'the intertextuality of their relationship, the very possibility of crossing and interlacing, depends on difference between the two'.[6] Somerville and Ross are certainly aware of the ways in which collaborative authorship is understood by the general reading public, as well as the nineteenth-century's literary critics and reviewers, and they enact their own distinctive textual performance which, in turn, often creates a disjunction between their public united front and the practicalities of their private writing selves.

As the next chapter will go on to explore, the public tropes of merging and fluidity which characterise women's coauthorship sometimes seem to go against the grain of the more physical and pragmatic arrangements for joint composition that enable those same partnerships, but they are seen to be less a covert strategy in denying or covering up the mechanics of dual authorship, and more an attempt to argue for alternative modes of thinking about unitary selfhood. As a prelude to this discussion, this chapter will focus on the ways in which the 'harmony' of Somerville and Ross' writing also had to fare in an increasingly professionalised literary marketplace where the women's dual signature had to withstand the pressures of public opinion and perception. This chapter will begin to detail Somerville and Ross' professional status as both women and joint authors and explore the ways in which they navigated the material conditions of their writing. It will also explore how the two authors engaged in a critical self-fashioning of their collaboration. In the public domain, Somerville and Ross' collaborative persona assumes a new and very professional outlook where, as Bette London argues, they tested 'the limits for granting collaboration credibility' and 'availed themselves of all authorship's new institutional structures': 'if we take Somerville and Ross as representative, collaboration assumes a new professional dimension: a site where women

could acknowledge and protect their business interests'.[7] Proprietary rights
may have been diminished in private, but Somerville and Ross maintained
their professional authorial rights in public, hiring a literary agent early on in
their careers and securing membership of the Society of Authors. The personal
pleasures and intellectual benefits of collaboration, which are so highly prized
by the two authors, also do not diminish the economic necessities of their
Ascendancy positions. Both women eventually took financial and managerial
responsibility for their large family estates and, as spinsters, also had to
support their independence and, often, each other's. In 1890, Ross declared to
Somerville: 'I <u>must</u> make money, so must you'.[8] It was, thus, with an eye to the
burgeoning commercial and professional possibilities of the late nineteenth-
century publishing world, as well as the intellectual and emotional pleasures of
joint authorship, that Somerville and Ross embarked on their writing careers.

An 'Egyptian taskmaster': editors and agents

In her essay on the origins of the Irish R.M. tales, 'Étaples', published in *Happy
Days* in 1946, Somerville remembers how her and Ross' French excursion
in the summer of 1898 was interrupted by reminders of work that they had
both committed to that year: '[i]nto this time of blessed irresponsibility and
freedom from all worldly cares, came a sudden reminder that so far from being
free we were practically only at liberty on parole ... we had a taskmaster, a little
man of iron determination, a Literary Agent (which is the modern equivalent
for an Egyptian taskmaster) and he did not forget.'[9] In 1897, Somerville and
Ross hired James B. Pinker as their agent and Somerville had a successful initial
meeting with Pinker in London that year, where she met with editors and
publishers keen to commission further work from the duo in the style of some
of their already successful comic hunting stories, like 'A Grand Filly' (1896) and
'Fanny Fitz's Gamble' (1896), published in *The Badminton Magazine*: '[t]hey
... all ... swore we had got hold of a very good thing in this serio-comic hunting
business.'[10] Alongside A. P. Watt, Pinker was one of the leading literary agents
in London, the former of whom had been recommended as a possible agent
to Ross following the critical success of *The Real Charlotte* in 1895 by Andrew
Lang: '[h]e said we ought to employ Watts the agent to work with publishers,
adding that he was only a man for people whose position was assured.'[11] In her
book-length study of the professional literary agent in Britain at the turn of
the nineteenth century, Mary Ann Gillies demonstrates the crucial role the
literary agent played in the late nineteenth century in challenging existing
practices in the publishing world, arguing that they were 'important players

in the transformation of literary culture in the period 1880–1920'.[12] Gillies utilises Somerville and Ross as a case study for exploring Pinker's professional relationship with his clients, as well as his particular championing of female authors and younger writers. If Watt was the only man for those 'whose position was assured', Pinker actively sought out what he termed in an interview for the *Bookman* in 1898 'the unknown man' and 'the youngster struggling for reputation and bread and butter'.[13] His advert in *The Literary Yearbook* for 1901 reiterates this point: 'Mr. Pinker has always made a special point of helping young authors in the early stages of their career, when they need most the aid of an adviser with a thorough knowledge of the literary world and the publishing trade.'[14] Pinker thus distinguished himself from the model of agenting established by Watt in the 1870s by pursuing a different type of client. He also firmly situated his agency as one which was directed towards authors and the protection of an author's rights, as opposed to Watt, who acted as an agent for both authors and publishers.[15]

There is little evidence to help explain Somerville and Ross' choice of agent. Whether or not they pursued Lang's recommendation is unknown, and how far Pinker's fresh approach to literary agenting and promotion of new writers influenced their decision in choosing an agent is also only something that can be surmised. What is certain, however, is that Pinker 'set out to attract women writers as clients' and his attitude towards women's suffrage was something that Somerville and Ross would go on to both appreciate and discuss with him.[16] Alice Williamson, Rebecca West, Katherine Mansfield, Dorothy Richardson and George Egerton were also on Pinker's client list and, in the case of Somerville and Ross, Pinker managed to secure some of their most lucrative publishing deals. It is also evident from their early experiences of dealing with publishers and editors that they were increasingly in need of an agent.

Prior to Pinker's involvement, Somerville and Ross had largely relied on their own inner circle of acquaintances and literary networks to help promote their work and get it into print. This took up a lot of their time, and though many of their marketing strategies met with some success, they also fell foul of rogue middlemen, as well as editors and publishers who were tardy with their payments. Ross' familial contacts and string of literary connections in London – including her journalist brother, Robert, and editor and founder of *The World*, Edmund Yates – helped both women launch their literary careers. Ross was particularly instrumental in pushing their first novel, *An Irish Cousin*, into the hands of literary reviewers and critics through her own and her friends' contacts. Her letter to Somerville in August 1889 illuminates the 'energy' she put into securing the book's success:

Mama did not come home today, but she shall at once be set to work tomorrow. I go into Oughterard to fetch Rose out in the afternoon and shall set Molly and Edmund on the trail. In fact everyone I meet or can think of shall not be ignorant of the Shocker [*An Irish Cousin*] ... You will have to take to getting up early & religiously writing a certain number of letters before breakfast. I am afraid this is a baddish time for books to come out, but we must make up for that by energy. What about Egerton's man on the *Saturday* [*Review*]? I incensed Edith about Willie Wilde and Desart [journalists for *The Daily Telegraph* and *Vanity Fair*], and must concoct a discreet line or two to Edmund Yates – Edith is going up to the Horse Show, and accordingly will see everyone she knows in Ireland, and can go round the book shops – and the Gays are trusty people of large acquaintance.[17]

She follows up this letter a few days later with good news from Carnegie Libraries, who have agreed to subscribe to and circulate *An Irish Cousin*, as well as recommend the book to the booksellers Eason and Son. Ross continues to corral family and friends in helping to promote the book:

Molly Helps has been very kind about it – and said at once that she would write to Charlie Graves, who reviews the light literature for the *Spectator*, to give us a good word ... now let us collect our newspaper friends – the *Saturday*, the *Spectator*, the *World* (?), the *Sunday Times*, *Vanity Fair* (Desart) and Willie Wilde who is I think the *Daily Telegraph*. I wrote the best letter I could to Edmund Yates today. Indeed I write letters all the time and Rose is very good about it too – Mama of course ploughs away, but her eyes come against her. I should make Aylmer ask about it at every station on the Underground if I were you. I am sure that your mother is magnificent in the way of letters, and if the family really put their shoulders to a wheel they could do a great deal.[18]

Somerville also utilised her brother Cameron in like-minded fashion, employing him as a go-between with editors and publishers, and exploiting his military contacts in advertising and requesting her and Ross' books both nationally and internationally in libraries and book stores across the globe. Early in 1889, Somerville wrote to Cameron asking him how well he knew the editor of *The Universal Review*: 'do you think you could sloother him into writing a kind critique [of *An Irish Cousin*] for us?'[19] In the same year, Somerville also asks Cameron if he knows, or if 'any of the company know – how to get at the Service Papers' in order to 'get us a paragraph' on *The Kerry*

Recruit, an illustrated edition by Somerville of the traditional Irish song of the same name.[20] The following year, she requests that Cameron urge the 'faithful company' to write to their 'soldiering friends' in different regiments and request *The Kerry Recruit* at 'military bookstalls' across the UK.[21] Somerville also discusses with Cameron the possibility of approaching Eason to act as an agent for the book and laments that 'without a professional touter we are done'.[22]

Somerville and Ross' self-promotion and self-advertising for their works was largely the result of perceived neglect on behalf of their publishers, and they frequently felt that their publications were suffering at the hands of printers and publishers who did little to sufficiently advertise and promote them. In 1894, Somerville writes in frustration to Cameron about the lack of advertising for *The Real Charlotte* by their publishers, Ward and Downey: '[i]t is sickening that Ward and Downey never try to push it, but just leave it to chance to be found.'[23] Other editors and publishers also noticed this neglect. In 1904, the editor of the Australian colonial paper *The Book Lover*, who republished some of Somerville and Ross' Irish R.M. tales, wrote to Somerville to exclaim that: 'I must say that I am surprised to see that "Some Experiences" was only now in its 25th thousand! Can't you get a publisher who is really interested in the books to take up your next attempt.'[24] Earlier, in 1891, Somerville similarly complained about the poor marketing and low print run of *The Kerry Recruit* by their publisher, Perry and Son, as well as a delayed cheque from the editor of the *Lady's Pictorial*, Alfred Gibbons, for her and Ross' travel text of Connemara: 'I suppose the odious little Gibbons is still sporting about the continent as he hasn't sent us our cheque. I have written again to Perry re. the Kerry Recruit.'[25] Before this, Somerville had complained to Cameron about the poor handling of *The Kerry Recruit* and her regret in placing it with Perry: 'numbers of people had asked for it in the big London shops but had found it had never been heard of ... Perry ought to have placed copies in all the big shops and on the underground railway bookstalls ... I have said most of this to Day [lithographer] but if you could stuff it again down his throat it would be well ... I am now beginning to think that he [Perry] is nothing but a pen maker and has no facilities for putting books out.'[26] Here, as elsewhere, Somerville recruits male members of the family to intervene with publishing and marketing issues on her and Ross' behalf. In 1893, Ross' brother, Robert, is drafted in to assist with an overdue payment from Ward and Downey for *The Real Charlotte*: '[w]e are in howlts with Ward and Downey just now – they are backing out of paying their 2nd instalment of the Real Charlotte, and Robert is now applying force, in the shape of a solicitor.'[27]

Throughout the 1880s and 1890s, Somerville's letters to Cameron offer numerous examples of the difficulties Somerville and Ross encountered with a variety of editors, publishers, printers and literary middlemen, and the majority of these issues revolve around poor marketing of their works, as well as poor or delayed payment for those works. In 1893, Somerville writes of the editor of *Black and White* that though he said of her recent submission, 'it was the best hunting story he had ever read … he hasn't yet paid me for it'.[28] Some of Somerville and Ross' worst cases of underpayment and poor marketing derive from placing their work with dishonest middlemen. With regard to the dealings over *The Kerry Recruit*, Somerville calls Day, for example, 'not a publisher – only a jackal who collects for big men'.[29] The publisher William Heinemann would write of the 'middleman' in 1893 that 'he is generally a parasite'.[30] Though Heinemann's comments derive largely from his own professional position, and the general fear over the changing relations between authors and publishers as a result of the appearance of the literary agent, his point about the parasitic nature of literary agency is not wholly unfounded. In 1890, Somerville and Ross sold all rights to their second novel, *Naboth's Vineyard*, for £20 to a rogue middleman, Mr Langbridge, who sold it on at a profit to the London publishing firm of Spencer Blackett. Somerville writes to Cameron in July 1890:

> We have just got the miserable little 20 guineas for 'Naboth's Vineyard'. We should never have got it only that we ourselves went to Spencer Blackett's and asked about it. His manager was most civil and I think little Langbridge must have got a lot more than £20 from him for the story, as he volunteered the remark that 20 was very low pay. I must say that we had sold Mr. L. the ms. to publish and take his chance with, not to sell, like a sweater, to another publisher. He had the audacity to ask us if we would like him to find us a publisher for our next book! And probably illicitly pocket half the money – not very much.[31]

Somerville and Ross continue to lose out financially on the book as it is published in subsequent editions and formats. In 1893, the publishers Griffith and Farran produce a cheap paperback edition of the novel to which Somerville and Ross can make no financial claim:

> 'Naboth's Vineyard' has come out in 2/- form and is doing rather well. Mr. O'K. (of Griffith and Farran's) spoke with guarded loathing of little Langbridge and held up his hands when he heard that we had been given £20 for the book – 'you might as well have taken nothing at all' he said.

He didn't say what littlerednoseandeyes had got for it, but he said that only the other day they had made him another payment and bought out his final rights in it. I should like to know what he made out of it.[32]

It is perhaps no surprise, then, that when Somerville and Ross finally employed Pinker in 1897 to handle their publishing contracts, one of his first tasks for the authors was to attempt to recover a debt owed to them by the London periodical, *The Minute*.[33]

The two authors' employment of Pinker, however, also symbolises their own sense of themselves as professional authors, a designation that they repeatedly note is unfairly denied to them by family and friends, as well as publishers and editors. Somerville's family largely viewed the two women's literary efforts as 'nonsense' and both women complain of the 'feeling that interruptions incessantly impend', as well as the need for 'mental tranquillity'.[34] Siblings and cousins at Castletownshend frequently sought the duo out and attempted to derail their writing efforts, dismissing their work as a mere interruption to the social life and activities at Drishane House. In a letter to her sister Hildegarde in 1893, Somerville protests against her cousin and unsuccessful suitor, Herbert Greene, and his insistent engagement of her time socially, as well as his 'persistently ignoring that I have any work to do'.[35]

While keen to commission work from the two authors, publishers and editors also often treated Somerville and Ross as amateurs, despite the quality and success of their artistic and literary work. In 1886, Somerville relates to her sister Hildegarde her treatment at the hands of the sub-editor to an illustrated magazine, *The Graphic*, who was in the process of taking for publication Somerville's pictorial strip 'A Mule Ride in Trinidad'. In his discussion with Somerville over pay, the sub-editor tells her that 'thirty shillings a page is the usual amateur price', to which she retorts 'with dignity', 'But I am a Professional.'[36] Even after the two women had become well-established and successful writers, they still encountered these same attitudes over their professionalism. In 1905, Ross' brother, Robert, passed away after suffering a variety of serious illnesses the previous year and Ross was invited to contribute to a memoir which was being compiled and edited by Robert's political friends, including David Plunket (1838–1919), retired MP and former solicitor general for Ireland under Benjamin Disraeli, and Sir Henniker Heaton (1848–1914), Conservative MP, fellow journalist and member of the Royal Society of Literature. Ross travelled to London in 1906 to discuss her input to the memoir with Heaton, and subsequently related her frustration and fury to Somerville over her treatment there:

my part is to be about 15000 words! He said 'about twelve columns of *The Times* – but you write all you like, and we can select what is wanted' – I at once said that I was too busy to write stuff that might not be wanted, and he seemed quite surprised – I don't think he at all realises the position, or that I am a professional writer. I shall not put you in a passion by telling more of his recommendations and advice.[37]

Heaton's officious and condescending paternalism is a familiar rhetoric that Somerville and Ross are also forced to endure at the hands of some of their editors and publishers, as well as in a more diluted form from some of their admirers and Anglo-Irish peers.

Ross' cousin, dramatist, and leading Revival figure, Lady Augusta Gregory, applauded and encouraged Ross' artistic endeavours with Somerville. On the publication of *An Irish Cousin*, Ross asked Gregory to advertise the book to the latter's social and literary circle of friends and Gregory predicted 'great fame and popularity' for the duo after reading the book.[38] Gregory also urged Ross to reap a 'fine harvest' by writing about her experiences of 'Dublin life' and, in turn, she sought Ross' commentary on her own and her Revival colleagues' works.[39] In 1905, for example, Gregory sent Ross a copy of John Millington Synge's *Well of the Saints* for her to read and on which to offer criticism.[40] Over the years, Ross continued to communicate intermittently with Gregory about her and Somerville's joint literary projects, and she spent time at Gregory's home, Coole Park, in 1901. In April 1905, during a trip to Dublin with her mother, where both attended plays at the Abbey Theatre at Gregory's and Yeats' behest, Ross wrote to Somerville to tell her that Gregory was absolutely 'rampant' that her and Somerville write a 'Shoneen play' for the 'Abbey Street Theatre'.[41] Ross' letters to Somerville at this time suggest that she was wary of both the attempt by Gregory to 'rope in the upper classes, and to drop politics', and Gregory's suggested involvement in the writing process of the play.[42] Gregory initially dismisses Ross' pleas of 'want of time' due to her and Somerville's other artistic commitments, and additionally offers to 'write a scenario for you': '[w]hen I divulged the fact that you had faint aspirations towards a play ... Augusta was enraptured – "A week at Coole would do it. We could give you all the hints necessary for stage effects etc – even write a scenario for you – the characters and plot picked from your books – I will look through them at once". I gave no further encouragement of any sort – and said we were full up.'[43] While a far cry from the 'abhorrent' Heaton's condescension, and despite her wholehearted enthusiasm, Gregory's proposed authorial control over the project generates an equally frustrated response from Ross, who swiftly puts an end to the idea of any kind of collaboration at Coole Park under the patronage of Gregory.[44] Somerville and Ross' position as professional authors, once again, seems not to have been realised.

This argument finds further credence in Gregory's last letter to Ross, written in July 1915, just four months before Ross' death. In that letter, Gregory divulges her and Yeats' 'uninterrupted enjoyment' of Somerville and Ross' latest and final instalment of the Irish R.M. tales, *In Mr. Knox's Country*: 'I love the "old Mrs. Aure" bits, there is so much of your mother in them ... I think one ought to be grateful for the laughter-calling gift. Your book will help heavy hearts to put by their trouble for a while. I have felt rather guilty during the war because I can't knit stockings ... and my sort of fighting is not wanted.'[45] While, no doubt, consciously unintended, Gregory's conflation of the stories with lighthearted relief, local biographical reminiscence, and the domestic war effort reduces the serious nature of those stories and their explicit engagement with the darker undercurrents of a slowly declining Ascendancy class in early twentieth-century Ireland. Gregory was certainly not alone in her reading or interpretation of the tales. Soldiers in the Boer War and the First World War did, indeed, read Somerville and Ross' comic short stories, and *The Times* newspaper chose the Irish R.M. tales for their 'cheering qualities' to include in their broadsheets of popular literature sent out to the men in the trenches during the First World War.[46] For Somerville and Ross, however, even the comic nature or tone of their short fiction was not something they saw as removing those tales from the ranks of more serious literary work; in fact the opposite is the case. During her stay with Gregory at Coole Park in 1901, for example, where 'high literary conversation raged', Ross defends humour against a disapproving Yeats and tells Somerville: 'Miss Martin said beautiful things about humour being a high art.'[47]

This attitude towards the type of fiction that Somerville and Ross often wrote certainly seems to contribute to their categorisation as amateur authors. The casual way in which even editors and publishers would make significant editorial changes to the two authors' texts without prior consultation with them also seems to fit in with this disregard of their professional status. Concerned over public propriety, for example, the editors of both *The Strand* and *The Badminton Magazine* made alterations to the dialogue used in several of Somerville and Ross' comic short stories, amending 'phrases they think improper'.[48] Somerville and Ross' subsequent ire is twofold. On the one hand, they fear being made a 'laughing stock to all Ireland' with the 'imbecilities' introduced by their editors: substituted words and phrases which, they fear, dent the authenticity of dialogue so central to their stories.[49] They are, however, equally outraged at not being given 'the option of altering phrases' for themselves. 'It is rather trying,' Somerville comments in 1904, 'to be Bowlderised in this meaningless way.'[50] In 1898, the then editor of *The Badminton Magazine*, Alfred Watson, went as far as significantly altering the content of one of the Irish R.M. stories without consultation with the authors. Fearing a 'storm of criticism' over a 'spirit writing incident' Somerville and Ross had introduced into the story, Watson requested the authors make amendments, to which they agreed, but the altered version was never published: 'imagine our fury on getting a letter from him ... that he had changed it himself! We are in agonies ... and altogether we are angry.'[51] Again, it is less the rationale for the alterations that rankles (Watson pleads potential controversy and shortness of time) than the fact of Watson's lack of consultation with the authors and his assumed capability of altering the story himself.

Like Heaton, Watson's arrogance in interfering with the writing process without any discussion with the authors, and subsequent, even if only indirect, insinuation of the amateur level of their work, feeds back into the discourses which delegitimise coauthorship as both a professional and high aesthetic creative practice. The attitude of Somerville and Ross' editors, publishers and literary colleagues clearly echoes the comments cited earlier in this book by Besant and Matthews on the literary products of joint authors in the assumption that such authors are 'first and foremost, and always, storytellers' and have no recourse to the 'work of pure and lofty imagination.'[52] Moreover, while these jointly authored works have clearly 'served the cause of periodical literature', it is a cause notably 'less noble than that of great art.'[53] Women writers appear to be doubly damned in this respect by virtue of their gender and, within this aesthetic hierarchy which removes collaborative work from the realms of 'great art', female collaborators are further demoted amid their male counterparts.

Before collaborating with Somerville, for example, Ross was in frequent correspondence with her cousin and playwright, Willie Wills, who she also visited several times in London between 1885 and 1890. His letters to her are familiar and affectionate and suggest that they were exchanging ideas for stage plots as well as considering a more formal collaboration, one which clearly exposes Ross as the presumed inferior partner. Reminiscent of Ross' exchange with Gregory over a play for the Abbey Theatre, Wills suggests to Ross that they should write a story together 'under my supervision and inspiration' and he refers to Ross not as his partner, but as his 'amanuensis.'[54] His domestication of the collaboration as mere literary 'chats' further diminishes Ross' role in the partnership: 'I am swarming with plots and should so like to talk one or two over with you ... I have a great deal to chat with you about in the old fashion – my work and plans.'[55] Julie Anne Stevens argues that, despite Wills' downplaying of her contributions as mere literary conversation, it appears that Ross 'worked with him in some capacity' and he both paid her for her work and attempted to get her more work with other playwrights and directors.[56] Stevens also concurs, however, with the one-sidedness of the correspondence and collaboration: '[o]ne gets the impression that the Wills/Martin correspondence devoted itself entirely to Willie Wills' genius.'[57] Wills takes little interest in Ross' other work and is deeply surprised on learning of the publication and success of *An Irish Cousin*, the latter of which he proceeds to claim as his own: 'I am sincerely delighted and proud of you, because it was I who reared you. Loftus has been here talking of your novel ... I spoke & claimed the praise for myself – I formed her, I said, I developed her nascent qualities, in fact I am the author of that book.'[58]

With Ross' commencement as professional novelist with Somerville, the collaboration with Wills largely comes to an end, but its gendered dynamics are not untypical of nineteenth-century attitudes towards women writers, or how women were perceived in mixed-sex collaborations. Writing in *The New Review* in 1892, Besant advises the 'young literary man' to find among his friends 'a girl, intelligent, sympathetic, and quick; a girl who will lend her ear, listen to his plot, and discuss his characters', and further suggests that, though just a minor 'detail', it might not hurt the collaboration if the young man decided to get engaged to her.[59] 'Woman does not create,' Besant concludes, 'but she receives, moulds, and develops', and the young man's literary figures will return to him 'distinct and clear, no longer shivering, unclothed, but made up and dressed for the stage': '[a]s in everyday life, so in imaginative work, woman should be man's best partner – the most generous – the least exacting – the most certain never to quarrel over her share of the work, her share of the kudos, her share of the pay.'[60] The female partner is here reduced to a passive helpmate and her intellectual and imaginative abilities are severely curtailed by the limited role she is allotted within the collaboration. Somerville was particularly concerned with this type of reductionism and viewed, more generally, the ongoing debasement of 'women's intellectual character' within society as an especial threat to female emancipation.[61]

In her suffragette address to the MWFL in 1912, Somerville comments on the 'Ladies' Papers' of her time, and warns that the 'arbitrary estimate of women's intelligence' that these magazines assume not only narrows down the topics contained in such publications to columns on fashion and cookery, but 'narrow[s] down women's intelligence to the contemptible level of their topics'.[62] This has had, she maintains, a 'stultifying effect' on the intellectual character and capabilities of women and it is sustained by the removal of women from 'all practical politics' and 'the big issues of government that signify'.[63] 'It is my conviction,' maintains Somerville, 'that as soon as women are given their lawful, natural share in the real business of the world, the editors will find that no special column of twaddle will be needed to interest the ladies.'[64] Towards the end of her life, Somerville explicitly blamed such attitudes towards women for her and Ross having to 'take a permanent backseat as writers' in spite of the success of their works: 'the fatal admission that Martin and I were women has been our ruin – in Literature and Art'.[65] In 1913, these views towards collaboration and female writers had a very material impact on Somerville and Ross' work as the duo attempted to take a stand against the authors of a collection of short stories, *By the Brown Bog*, which Somerville and Ross claimed was plagiarised from their Irish R.M. tales. The final section of this chapter will attempt to trace the legal, aesthetic and gendered discourses that come together in Somerville and Ross' appeal against Honor Urse and Owen Roe's book, as well as the coalescence of this dispute around the perceived literary value of Somerville and Ross' jointly authored short stories.

'Shameless thieves': cribbers and plagiarists

'I foresee that we shall soon have to give up Irish stories,' writes Somerville to Cameron in 1914, 'the plagiarists are getting too thick on the ground.'[66] Somerville goes on to console herself by arguing that 'Rudyard K. was similarly driven out of India', but there had certainly been no legal consolation in 1913 when, with the assistance of the legal team at the Society of Authors, Somerville and Ross attempted to take to court the authors of what they perceived to be a heavily plagiarised version of *Some Experiences of an Irish R.M.*[67] Owen Roe and Honor Urse's *By the Brown Bog* (1913) was only one example of the imitation stories engendered by the overwhelming popularity of the Irish R.M. tales. In the 1900s and 1910s, Somerville frequently reports to Cameron the instances of 'deliberate ... piracy' and 'barefaced imitation' of the Irish R.M. tales that she and Ross continually stumble upon in the press, very often in the same periodicals publishing their own work, including *The Badminton Magazine* ('shameless thieves that they are'), the original publisher of the first R.M. tales.[68] *By the Brown Bog* was published by Somerville and Ross' long-standing publishing firm, Longmans.

Using the trademark parallel columns of the nineteenth century's 'amateur literary detective', Somerville and Ross laboriously collocated passages from their original text alongside Roe and Urse's to substantiate their claim and highlight the direct instances of plagiarism in Roe and Urse's book.[69] While it seemed abundantly clear to Somerville and Ross that Roe and Urse had not only borrowed plot, incident and characters from the Irish R.M. tales but had also directly lifted passages of text and dialogue from their stories, the solicitors working on the case on behalf of the Society of Authors eventually concluded that there was not enough evidence to make a claim in court against the authors of *By the Brown Bog*. Indeed, Andrew J. Strahan, the leading legal reader in the case, forcefully concluded that '[n]o sane judge could hold that the later book constitutes in any way a breach of the copyright of the earlier one.'[70]

Somerville and Ross also found little support in the matter from their agent, Pinker, though his reasoning seems to have lain with more commercial and personal concerns rather than with any dispute over Somerville and Ross' charges against Roe and Urse. Somerville reports to Cameron in August 1913: 'if we don't go and hustle a bit nothing is done. Pinker is afraid, and the Society of Authors are dilatory.'[71] Their agent's fear was twofold. First, the impact of Somerville and Ross' legal claims would not only be felt by Roe and Urse, but also by Longmans, who were the publishers of both the Irish R.M. books and *By the Brown Bog*. By 1913, Longmans held Somerville and Ross' most profitable publishing contracts and to deliberately cause the firm professional and public difficulties wasn't necessarily in Somerville and Ross', or Pinker's, financial and commercial interests. Second, Pinker was well aware of the consequences if the claim of plagiarism was not upheld: '[i]f we make charges against these people which cannot be established in a court of law, they might haul us all up for libel.'[72] In the face of this reluctance on the part of both Pinker and the Society of Authors to pursue the case to court, Somerville and Ross eventually gave up their claims and settled for an amended edition of *By the Brown Bog* that revised the most glaring instances of direct plagiarism.

Part of the collapse of Somerville and Ross's case seems to have derived from its timing, which was particularly inauspicious for what Roger MacFarlane calls the 'plagiarism hunter'.[73] While the moral disrepute of plagiarism still held sway in the later nineteenth century, changing definitions of what constituted plagiarism, particularly in the light of a growing and robust defence of legitimate appropriation and imitation, began to turn the tide against those who declaimed charges of literary theft. Michael Wiley argues that the only 'essential differences between authorised appropriation and plagiarism' is that authorised appropriation is treated as a type of 'textual re-use validated by a dominant cultural, economic, and legal community', while plagiarism is treated as a 're-use invalidated by such a community'.[74] Towards the end of the nineteenth century, and in the wake of successive and ever more frequent cries of plagiarism, public debate was ignited over what constituted 'authorised appropriation' and, in the course of this debate, plagiarism was gradually redefined. What had seemed valid plagiarism earlier in the century was now disavowed by increasing sectors of the reading public, and various types of textual re-use were rebranded as culturally, economically and legally valid. This had a very public and real impact on the thus-far sanctioned impunity of the 'plagiarism hunter'. In his essay on the 'ethics of plagiarism' in 1886, Matthews champions and foresees what Pinker fears in 1913, namely that the 'man who makes the charge of plagiarism' should 'pay the penalty of having opened fire' if the charges prove false: '[t]he accuser should be put under bonds ... to make his charge good, and if he loses his case he should be cast in damages.'[75]

Matthews was well supported by other essayists, journalists, poets, and novelists of the later nineteenth and early twentieth centuries, including Andrew Lang, E. F. Benson, Edward Wright, W. H. Davenport-Adams, Fred Ford, William S. Walsh, J. Cuthbert Hadden, among others. Saint-Amour groups these writers together as 'plagiarism apologists' who 'defended or redefined plagiarism', not as a coherent group with a deliberate agenda, but as 'scattered purveyors of an emerging critique of original genius and literary property, brought to their critique by disparate ideological motivations'.[76] MacFarlane reinforces this viewpoint in *Original Copy* and argues that from the 1860s and 1870s onwards, a backlash occurred against plagiarism hunters, which was 'part of a more widespread literary-critical antagonism towards the hypervaluation of originality':

> For much of the nineteenth century in Britain, the plagiarism hunter thrived, buoyed up in public opinion by the high rating of literary originality. In its closing three decades, however, a counter-movement concerning originality and plagiarism emerged, which contested the aesthetic and ethical logic of the plagiarism hunter.[77]

This counterattack, however, doesn't seem to have affected the 'hypervaluation of originality' written into the nineteenth century's copyright laws. The redefinition of plagiarism and originality here advocated goes some way in, conversely, reinforcing the rhetoric of Romantic genius, even as it subtly loosens some of the extreme discourses on originality on which copyright laws relied. The goalposts are shifted somewhat, but the playing field is still one that excludes and does damage to collaborative writers, as well as hardens the hierarchical lines between popular literature and high-brow art, all of which seems to have contributed to Somerville and Ross' lack of success in taking Roe and Urse to court.

The central claims of the plagiarism apologists all seem to coalesce around the same set of key points. There is, first and foremost, a concern with what constitutes original or new literature, and the broad argument was made that there is nothing in literature that is purely original. All literature imitates, borrows and appropriates in some form or another. Matthews points out that it was the 'original owner of King Solomon's mines who asserted that there was nothing new under the sun ... the first discovery of a student of letters is that the history of literature is little more than a list of curious coincidences'.[78] Moreover, it is in the act and skill of appropriating existing material that true literary genius lies. In the pages of *The Contemporary Review* in 1887, Andrew Lang reminded his readers that 'the whole idea of a visit to Hell, and a record of it, was a stock topic in early mediaeval literature' and not the original outpourings of Dante, though the latter clearly did most justice to the subject.[79] 'Not the matter,' claimed Lang, 'but the casting of the matter; not the stuff, but the form given to the stuff, makes the novel, the novelty, and the success':

> The success or failure lies not in the materials, but in the making of the brooms, and no dullard can make anything, even if he steals all his materials. On the other hand, genius, or even considerable talent, can make a great deal, if it chooses, even out of stolen material.[80]

It is this positive and improving transformation of existing literary material that the plagiarism apologists focus on most, and the language they use to describe the supposed literary masters of this type of appropriation emulates Romantic discourses of genius and authorship. W. H. Davenport-Adams describes the process as one akin to 'rough ore' being turned to gold, a 'rude prosaic' sketch transformed into 'noble poetic creations'.[81] Edward Wright takes this one step further in his essay 'The Art of Plagiarism' and views this intertextuality as the perfecting of inferior men's labour and 'an act of infinite grace' by the man of genius who rescues such work from 'condign oblivion'.[82] Homer, Wright continues, 'with his better art', fashioned the tale of Troy from the 'lays sung by the first rude minstrels of the Latin races'; Shakespeare equally ennobled 'the base offspring of other men's minds'.[83] In his consideration of the borrowings of Homer from Virgil, Shakespeare from Marlowe, and Wordsworth from Milton, Wright finally claims such acts of supposed plagiarism as the 'sweetest and most noble' exploits of love and deeds of 'honour' by the 'true poet' towards the 'friend of his soul': '[i]t is a sign of communion, a sign of the spiritual bond uniting the singers in different tongues, of distant times, into the highest of earthly fellowships.'[84]

This deification of the 'true poet' is redolent of existing Romantic discourses on literary genius, and the individual talent, as such, of the man of genius is still the guiding force in the success or failure of a piece of art, the difference between greatness and posterity, and mere mediocrity or short-lived fame in the literary marketplace. In this context, the 'plagiarism' of Wordsworth, Shakespeare and Homer is simply 'appreciation in the grand style' and an augmentation, or amplification, of the original work, a loving recreation which deepens the 'magical significance' of the original text.[85] What is also noticeable in these critical essays is the emphasis on masculine and patrilineal modes of imitation and appreciation, which endorse and re-emphasise male canons of Western literature. They are also far more concerned with defending the work of the West's male-authored classic texts against charges of plagiarism, than more popular forms of published writing. What is at stake in these essays is the literary reputations and literary integrity of what are considered men of genius and their published works, but not particularly the writings of those who do not sit within this exclusive literary coterie. Davenport-Adams, for example, concerns himself with the borrowings of Racine, Moliere and Voltaire, and argues that they acted 'by the right of divine genius'; Matthews focuses on Shakespeare, Dickens, Hawthorne and Poe, among others of that ilk, and restates Jonson and Dumas by writing that 'genius does not steal, it conquers'.[86] Matthews also echoes the Lockean rhetoric that underpins copyright law, maintaining that 'genius takes by right of eminent domain and rectifies its frontier by annexing outlying territory, making fruitful that which was before a barren waste'.[87] This concept of labour and literary property is then modified and extended to Matthews' defence of certain types of plagiarism, the latter of which he wants to defend. The 'garden is not large', writes Matthews, and we often (sometimes unconsciously) re-cultivate land which has already been ploughed before and, in doing so, we make our own 'a nosegay of the same flowers of speech', or even 'pluck the same passion-flower'.[88] 'In literature,' Matthews concludes, 'that is his at last who makes best use of it': '[i]f the second comer can improve on the work of the first comer, if he makes it over and makes it better, and makes it his own, we accept the result and ask no questions.'[89]

Legitimate appropriation is, in these essays, cast unequivocally as the especial territory of those men already classified as genius; indeed, these men's high literary talents in the realm of critical appreciation and imitation become part of their 'divine genius'.[90] The ability to make new, to amplify, to make original and his own, is the ability and mark of genius. In fact, one of the few authors to feature in these essays who did publish in a more popular mode and who didn't classify amongst the literary greats of Shakespeare, Wordsworth and Milton is Charles Reade. Reade was publicly charged with accounts of plagiarism but, unsurprisingly perhaps, both Matthews and Lang find him partially guilty. Lang argues that Reade's use of Swift was 'appropriated ready-made' and that he acted with 'very great rashness': '[a] lump of such a brilliant manufactured article as a poem by Swift would be apt to look incongruous even in a true inventor's prose.'[91] Matthews concurs that 'Mr. Reade did not always remain within his rights.'[92] The reasoning behind this thinking isn't always clearcut but, on the whole, both Matthews and Lang find Reade's appropriation of other writers' works invalid on the grounds of what is perceived as Reade's deficient literary talent. Reade is not a man of genius in the eyes of either essayist and his textual re-use of earlier works is simply an incongruity in his writing, or something which pales in the face of the ingenious original. What is clear is that plagiarism is here being remoulded along subjective lines of literary merit, on whether the second comer has improved on, or amplified, the first comer. Lang argues that raw plagiarism is the unadorned appropriation of something 'ready-made', but it seems that this cannot be measured simply in terms of empirical observation and the number of lines in a text which have been appropriated from elsewhere. Rather, it is the form into which these lines have been cast. It seems not to matter if Shakespeare borrowed more lines, character and dramatic structure from Marlowe than Reade ever did from Swift; the judgement of plagiarism is made on the literary use to which that material is subjected. In the hands of Shakespeare, Barbarus' transformation into Shylock is an act of genius, but in the hands of Reade, Swift's brilliance only outshines and highlights more clearly Reade's own deficiencies as a writer and, it seems, the type, or class, of writer that Reade is perceived to be.

Equally, the man who cries false plagiarism is increasingly demonised within this new understanding of authorised appropriation. He is figured as base and uncouth in his accusations, 'feeble-minded' and 'irresponsible', 'lynx-eyed' and motivated by the 'delicate veiled passion of Envy'.[93] Charges of plagiarism have, laments Matthews, become a 'disease which bids fair to become epidemic in literary journalism'.[94] Davenport-Adams is possibly the most damning in his condemnation of those who cry '"Stop thief!"' to a 'great writer': 'a cry so often raised in the world of letters by the hangers-on of literature, simply to gratify feelings of vindictiveness and spite; a cry which usually originates in the consciousness of inferiority, and is sustained by the malignancy of envy'.[95] Somerville and Ross' bid to take Roe and Urse to court thus took place at a time when public conceptions of plagiarism were changing and these changes did little to support those writers who existed on the margins of an elite and largely male group of authors whose works, according to their critics, exemplified a type of literary greatness. Somerville and Ross' actions during their negotiations with the Society of Authors suggest that they were aware of these discourses and, even if they could not be included among their distinguished male literary predecessors, they were determined to both pursue what they deemed a rather brazen act of plagiarism, and disassociate themselves from a work they clearly saw as inferior to their own.

One of Somerville and Ross' first public responses to the publication of *By the Brown Bog* was to quash public speculation that the book had been authored by the now well-known dual signature of 'E.Œ. Somerville and Martin Ross'. Readers and reviewers had immediately discerned the similarities between Roe and Urse's book and the Irish R.M. tales, as well as the common publisher of both books and the advertisement for the latter stories at the back of the frontispiece of *By the Brown Bog*. Ross wrote to their publisher, Longmans, complaining that the advertisement was 'distasteful', and the duo additionally sent out a public notice to at least eight newspapers asking that they be allowed to 'state in your columns that we are not the authors of this work'.[96] Somerville wrote privately to Pinker about the 'injury inflicted' upon her and Ross by the sale of Roe and Urse's book but also, and more significantly, railed against the public and private 'humiliation' and 'annoyance' of having the book attributed to them.[97] In these reactions and the language that Somerville and Ross use, there is a clear repudiation of a work they obviously judge as vastly inferior to their own publication in terms of literary merit. However, the responses that Somerville and Ross received from both Longmans and the legal team at the Society of Authors mostly disagreed with their conviction.

Early on in the case, and based on the excessive likenesses between the first story in the Brown Bog series and the first Irish R.M. tale, G. Herbert Thring, secretary of the Society of Authors, believed that it was clear that 'the accumulative evidence will probably amount to an infringement'.[98] Somerville and Ross, and the legal team at the Society of Authors, spent much time attempting to accumulate this evidence and collated the most obvious instances of verbatim passages and borrowed literary ideas and characters between the two books. The goalposts for this 'accumulated evidence', in terms of an actual figure or quantifiable amount, however, seemed to be continually changing and other, more ideological and aesthetic arguments began to dominate the correspondence between Somerville and Ross and the Society of Authors, as well as their publisher. Longman wrote to Somerville in defence of his decision to publish *By the Brown Bog* and explained that '[i]t was obvious that they [Roe and Urse] were following in your footsteps, that they were writing a class of story which you had invented and popularised.'[99] Longman maintained that he thought the stories 'original' and further argued that they would 'be better in our hands than in those of some other publisher who would use them directly as rivals to the R.M. series'.[100] Thring made a similar point about the 'class of story' that the Irish R.M. tales supposedly fall into and additionally contended that he thought it 'quite possible that any sporting writer dealing with somewhat the same subject, might come near the descriptive phrases in Miss Somerville's book'.[101] The chief legal reader working on the case on behalf of the Society of Authors, Andrew J. Strahan, made these points unalterably plain in his concluding report:

> The chief resemblance between the two is that they both purport to be the life and adventures of two ex-military officers who have official appointments in a hunting county in the South West of Ireland. The life is naturally much the same but the adventures are very different. There is also naturally some likeness between the characters they encounter ... As for certain similarities of expression ... most of these are either expressions habitually used in Ireland or expressions descriptive of precisely the same acts.[102]

His closing remarks were definitive and not in support of the society pursuing the case to court: '[n]o sane judge could hold that the later book constitutes in any way a breach of the copyright of the earlier ones.'[103]

Somerville and Ross, however, particularly disliked 'being spoken of as pioneers' of a sporting genre of writing.[104] The generic taxonomy that was repeatedly applied to the Irish R.M. tales patently reduced the literary quality and distinction of those tales. Moreover, the establishment of Roe and Urse's work as equal in merit to the Irish R.M. tales, or even exceeding in merit, by Strahan, Thring and Longmans defeats the charge of plagiarism. In line with many of the contemporaneous debates over plagiarism and originality, the successful amplification of the first work by the second would, arguably, detract from a charge of plagiarism. It also fits in with earlier legal definitions of plagiarism and the founding motivations for copyright. In his examination of the laws governing literary property in England, *Laws of Literary Property* (1883), Thomas Scrutton points out that, 'with respect to literary productions', the 'interests of the state [are to] obtain *good* literary work'.[105] Moreover, he argues, the legal protection afforded by the state should be such that it induces the 'best men' to produce the 'best books'.[106] Forty years earlier, and as demonstrated in Chapter 1, Wordsworth had appealed to this same perceived interest of the state in his argument for extending and transforming the term of copyright to a perpetual right of the author. 'What we want in these times,' Wordsworth publicly argued in the *Kendal Mercury*, 'is not the circulation of books, but of good books', as well as the publication of works 'the authors of which look beyond the passing day, and are desirous of pleasing and instructing future generations'.[107]

Before the enforcement of copyright, the royal patronage system acted in a similar manner, granting protection and affording to authors economic privileges where those authors' texts were seen to align with moral law and order. The system governed the dissemination of and control over an author's published works, as well as acted as a kind of royal censor: 'if the work be not innocent in its nature, there is no property in it which law will enforce or protect ... no copyright exists in a work subversive of good order, morality, or religion.'[108] Crown censorship was gradually abolished after the introduction of copyright law in 1709, but there are significant overlaps in how those later laws dictated a kind of aesthetic marker against which texts would have to be measured in terms of what the law was willing to protect, and the ways in which the patronage system effected a kind of moral marker which played the same role.

Pinker believed that much of this legal thinking was part of Roe and Urse's defence against the original charges when a notice appeared in *Country Life* magazine in response to Somerville and Ross' public disclaimers of authorship of *By the Brown Bog*:

> It appears that we made a wrong guess at the authorship of *By the Brown Bog*. Miss Somerville and Martin Ross have had nothing to do with it. The authors, in a very courteous, and, indeed, cordial letter, write to say that the story was 'entirely founded on incidents which occurred within our own knowledge and are original'. At the same time, they agree that 'it is not surprising that the advertisement of their (Miss Somerville and Martin Ross) works which appeared on the first page misled you'.[109]

Forewarned that the notice was to be published, Pinker wrote to Ross musing that 'either these two people are very astute, or they have a very clever solicitor advising them'.[110] Roe and Urse's defence is two-pronged here. On the one hand, the notice makes it unambiguous that *By the Brown Bog* is believed to be 'original' and based on the two authors' personal knowledge. The advertisement on the first page for the R.M. tales further and subtly implies that the stories, however, do clearly bear a relation to those earlier publications by Longmans, and are consistent with that type of publication. Originality, but also augmentation of an earlier series of work, is reiterated in this public notice and it thus works as a kind of defence against Somerville and Ross' charges of plagiarism. Posited as a new and welcome iteration of an existing form of short fiction, it is surely the obligation of copyright law and the state to protect and encourage, not block, this type of writing. As Strahan points out in his report, the 'threats of an action' against Roe and Urse seem, in his opinion, to be mistakenly based on the notion that 'nobody else is entitled to enter the same field … [James Barrie] might as well insist that nobody should be able to write Kale-yard stories but himself'.[111] The notice also indirectly restates Longmans point that, by virtue of the advertisement, in the hands of the same publisher as Somerville and Ross, *By the Brown Bog* does not injuriously compete with the Irish R.M. tales. Scrutton's *Laws of Property* make clear that protection of an author's lawful remuneration is paramount in deciding whether a violation of copyright has taken place: 'if a work is published of such a character as to interfere with the sale of the original work, and directly indebted for that character to that work … such resort should constitute an infringement.'[112] J. B. Richardson's *The Law of Copyright* (1913) confirms that this legal thinking is still relevant at the time Somerville and Ross are attempting to take Roe and Urse to court. Richardson demonstrates that the question of '[w]ill the new work compete with the old?', and the consideration of how much 'original thought and labour' has gone into the new work, act as an influence, or a kind of applied test, in legal decision-making over copyright cases.[113] Roe and Urse's response to the charges made by Somerville and Ross are, therefore, certainly informed by the laws surrounding copyright in the early twentieth century.

The language used by Strahan, Thring and Longmans works within these myriad legal frameworks to gradually defeat Somerville and Ross' claims, and is also suggestive of a further denigration of the duo's works. Somerville and Ross' detractors in the case observe on the one hand that Roe and Urse's collection of stories are a kind of valid spin-off from the Irish R.M. stories. Implied in the categorisation of those stories as a particular 'class' of writing, however, there also appears to be a suggestion that the Irish R.M. tales cannot (in the first instance) be categorised as 'good' literature and that the state, therefore, is unlikely to be particularly concerned with protecting them. These arguments intimate that there is nothing distinctive about the tales, 'any sporting writer' might have written them, and they certainly don't rank as the type of literature that will 'instruct' future generations; they are not the 'best books' written by the 'best men'. There is, therefore, in the minds of these literary and legal men, nothing legally or aesthetically original about the Irish R.M. books for the state to protect and this is predominantly because of the *kind* of stories they are publicly perceived to be. In a bizarre reversal of fortune, where Wordsworth is able to construct and then claim the originality and aesthetic merit of his poetry via their commercial unpopularity, Somerville and Ross are forced to suffer the 'humiliation' and 'injury' of having the popularity of their Irish short stories signify a lack of professional and aesthetic credence. No one, it is assumed, can reproduce the genius of 'Tintern Abbey', but anyone, it seems, can write some allegedly lighthearted stories about a bunch of Irish folk getting up to mischief in a generic western corner of Ireland.

Somerville and Ross are well aware of these aesthetic markers and distinctions and while they ardently defended 'humour as a high art' and the serious import, if not external trappings, of the Irish R.M. tales (a viewpoint more recent critics of the tales also now readily concur with), they also recognised that it was in the more identifiably 'serious work' of their novels that critical legitimation as professional writers was to be found.[114] Financial circumstances, as well as the public's literary appetites, however, often deterred them from their novel-writing ambitions where their engagement with the sombre currents of Irish politics and culture was far more explicit. The R.M. tales brought in a steady stream of income for the two women and Somerville admits to Cameron in 1898 that the stories are 'such a good business that we can't afford to fall out with them'.[115] Even when the strain of writing to constant deadlines begins to take its toll the following year, Somerville confesses that 'only that we both want money so badly we would chuck them for the present'.[116] Despite these difficulties, and the desire to pursue more 'serious work', the two authors cannot deny that the stories have 'served us well, and got us more fame and kudos than anything we have yet written!'[117] Pinker was also in favour of the stories and writes in reply to Somerville and Ross' request to look for potential publishers for a more serious line of articles on which they are working, potentially a new novel, that 'I think your happiest work is in this semi-sporting vein, and, moreover, there is, so far as I know, no one who can touch you ... I should say from all points of view, that is the work to do.'[118] Pinker goes on to affirm that 'I am very enthusiastic about the <u>Badminton</u> stories' and that there has been nothing like them 'since Lever died': 'I am sure that I shall communicate some, at any rate, of my enthusiasm to the editors.'[119]

Pinker was not the only one who encouraged Somerville and Ross to develop their more humorous articles and stories over their novels, and the eagerness of the public for this type of Irish literary fare had arguably remained unchanged since the earliest days of Somerville and Ross' joint careers. Ten years prior to these conversations with Pinker, the effusively admiring Edmund Yates, then editor of *The World*, wrote to Ross in reply to an article she had submitted for publication on Home Rule in Ireland: '[i]f you can choose a subject with which a little more sunshine can find its way, or, say, a little of the proverbial Irish humour for your next contribution, it will, I think be deliverable. This sketch is excellent but from its subject is necessarily a little heavy.'[120] In 1887, a sub-editor on the *London Illustrated News* despondently replied to one of Ross' political articles with: '[w]e have had an overdose of Ireland.'[121] Prior to her formal collaboration with Somerville, Ross had been regularly working on these political pieces for *The World* and other newspapers and journals and was becoming increasingly aware of the changing publishing tide, as was Somerville. Somerville and Ross were not the only writers in the 1880s and 1890s who were being bombarded with more and more frequent requests for Irish humour; Somerville wrote of her and Ross' recorded instances of 'thoroughbred Irish shorthand' as being 'worth millions in the English market'.[122] This had a direct impact on the direction of Somerville and Ross' literary output and Lewis states that it was Ross who encouraged Somerville to maintain her position as Master of the West Carbery Hunt to enhance their 'status and authority' as sporting writers; she 'saw that their hunting stories, with their practical and life-like detail and uproarious humour, were marketable in a way that serious studies of Irish life were not'.[123] This ability to 'quarry coin out of the public', as Somerville put it, was thus both a hindrance and a benefit to Somerville and Ross' literary ambitions, particularly when it came to being taken seriously as professional writers.[124]

While Somerville and Ross thus wholeheartedly believed in the personal and professional value of their collaboration, public, legal and critical thinking on joint authorship, women writers and conceptions of high art in the late nineteenth century variously worked against the two authors' literary ambitions and, repeatedly, influenced the direction that those ambitions would take. Even the institution to which their profession was wedded, and to which they were admitted through their membership of the Society of Authors, was one founded on principles wholly repugnant to the duo's ethos of collaboration, not only in its valorisation of a particular type of author, but even in its structural format. Besant's attitude towards collaboration as a partnership of unequal ground (genius and subordinated helpmate), and one which will eventually rupture to allow a single partner to rise above collaboration's amateur status, extends to his vision of how the society ought to be managed. 'In every new society,' he claimed, 'it is one man, and one man alone, who at

the outset determines the success and the future of the association': 'it is this
one man who rules, infuses spirit, collects ideas, orders the line of march, lays
down the policy, and thinks for the society.'[125] Gender-based attitudes towards
the two women's work from their families also hampered their careers, both
ideologically and in a more practical sense. Shortly after having *An Irish Cousin*
accepted for publication by Bentley, with generous pay, Somerville admits
to Cameron that 'it so <u>far</u> exceeds our wildest hopes'. The briefly proffered
chance to write together – Somerville spending three months at Ross House
followed by a three-month stint at Castletownshend by Ross – proved too
difficult to arrange, however, in the face of their familial and social duties, as
well as what they termed their families' general 'persecution' of their literary
efforts.[127] Despite these hindrances, however, the collaboration prevailed
and even 'deepened somewhat tepid effort into enthusiasm'.[128] Like their first
novel, which quickly moved from being 'an insincere ambition of the "Penny
Dreadful"' to a 'genuine literary impulse', Somerville and Ross' subsequent work
maintained that 'thrill of genuineness' and was suffused with 'an ideal of Art' in
all the textual and artistic mediums in which they would go on to work.[129] As
the following chapter will go on to explore, Somerville and Ross exploited early
on in their career many of the publishing outlets which dictated their amateur
status to their own advantage, and continued to defy legal notions of authorial
proprietorship in their experimentation with the dual authorial voice.

CHAPTER FOUR

Through Connemara and beyond

W hile Somerville and Ross were keen to assert their proprietorial rights in the plagiarism case against the authors of *By the Brown Bog*, such individualistic legal concepts of authorial ownership were much less welcome within the partnership itself. Like Bradley and Cooper, and Barnard and Eldershaw, Somerville and Ross' successful literary partnership relies on Ross' observation that the duo do 'not fight their own hands all the time'.[1] Moreover, these writing partners appear to consciously share in 'the giving and receiving of authority' by provisionally ceding individual rights in their writing.[2] Anne Gere recognises this dynamic at work in historical and current autonomous writing groups and argues that such groups 'depend upon members who are willing to give away, temporarily at least, authority over their own writing, indicating that they respect and trust one another to surrender their language to one another's critical scrutiny'.[3] Both Somerville and Ross, and Bradley and Cooper, demonstrate this point in their explanations to others of their joint writing practice. In 'Two of a Trade', Somerville elucidates on her joint compositional style with Ross, describing the coming together of their ideas as a reciprocal exchange of authority through which individual creative impulses are reconciled: 'one releasing it, perhaps as a cloudy suggestion, to be caught up by the other, and given form or colour, then to float away in a flash of certainty, a completed sentence'.[4] Bradley and Cooper are even more explicit and forceful in terms of surrendering their authorial power to each other: 'if one begins a character, his companion seizes and possesses it; if one conceives a situation, the other corrects, completes, or murderously cuts away'.[5]

Like Barnard and Eldershaw, then, each of these writing couples eschews individual 'proprietary rights'. The 'resultant green', which emblematises the final products of Somerville and Ross' joint efforts, obscures the individual colours that went into its composition and thus defies any untangling of the two hands involved.[6] It also chimes with Somerville's later exasperation in 'Two

of a Trade' at the fallacious belief in 'that autocratic, commanding pen, which
has ... so much in its power'.[7] Somerville had earlier complained to her brother
Cameron in the months following Ross' death that 'various journalists [had]
been tearing' at her to write about the mechanics of her collaboration with
Ross. She maintains to Cameron that 'it is impossible to apportion general
responsibility' in her and Ross' writings, and laments the media's attempt to
stoke senseless public curiosity, as well as 'try and make money' out of what was
to Somerville 'a sacred thing'.[8] She ends by berating Cameron for furnishing the
media with an 'exaggeration' of their writing process, and yielding to a division
of labour as explanation: 'even to have said "hardly" a "paragraph, a phrase etc."
was written single-handed by either of us would have been an exaggeration'.[9]

'[G]eneral responsibility' in Somerville and Ross's writing, however, is
something that can be gleaned from their working manuscripts, but it is clear
that this authorial responsibility becomes something that is never understood
between the two writers in an individualistic or possessive way. The wielder of
the pen bears little relation to the public and private unity of the Somerville
and Ross dual signature and the two writers defy the public emphasis placed
on what Somerville referred to as their 'respective shares' in their writing.[10]
Legalised divisions of labour are often discernible in the unpublished
manuscripts of the duo's writing, particularly when Somerville and Ross were
working apart on joint texts. In *Irish Memories*, Somerville explains their shared
compositional method:

> One or the other – not infrequently both, simultaneously – would state
> a proposition. This would be argued, combated perhaps, approved, or
> modified; it would then be written down by the (wholly fortuitous)
> holder of the pen, would be scratched out, scribbled in again; before it
> found itself finally transferred into decorous MS. would probably have
> suffered many things, but it would, at all events, have had the advantage
> of having been well aired.[11]

When not working together in the Drishane studio, however, their methods
are, of necessity, radically different. Their short story 'A Patrick's Day Hunt'
(1902), for example, was plotted together but largely written by Ross and
wholly illustrated by Somerville. In the working drafts for their short story
'Boon Companions' (1902), written with Ross stationed in Galway and
Somerville in Cork, the two hands writing as one are again easily identified.
Commissioned by the Northern Newspaper Syndicate to write six humorous
Irish stories, Somerville embarked on a short story about pets 'for Martin' in

mid-December 1901, and promptly sent her idea to Galway. Ross returned the manuscript in early February 1902 complete with her original comments and her own draft of the now completed story. Somerville made a 'clean copy' of the story to send to the publishers, including a few adjustments and a more comprehensive ending that utilised both manuscripts. The final published version is, excepting these minor adjustments, Ross' manuscript in full, the last five pages being heavily based and cribbed from Somerville's original draft, followed by the last two pages of Somerville's manuscript and, finally, a short cobbled selection of both writers' work compiled during Somerville's clean copying. Works put together in this fashion were far from uncommon and were considered no less collaborative than those written and debated word for word, face to face, in the Drishane studio at Castletownshend.

This is all indicative of the permissible shifting boundaries of Somerville and Ross' 'shares' in their collaboration. Those 'shares' were, and still are, conspicuously more wide-ranging than allowed by their critics. The working draft manuscripts of stories like 'Boon Companions' and 'A Patrick's Day Hunt' appear to suggest that regardless of the ratio of quantifiable input into a text, the broader collaborative ethic was the thing that mattered and which accounts for the complexities of a Somerville and Ross dual authored text. All of Somerville and Ross' works arguably insist and rely on the friendship's profound and liberating faith and certainty in each author's abilities. Indeed, it is only the publishing modes through which Somerville and Ross operate that finally close off the otherwise ceaseless exchange of manuscripts and conversations that generate their writing. Somerville and Ross were notorious revisers of their work and the printers at Bentley finally 'rebelled' at the additions and alterations Somerville and Ross kept making to the proofs of *An Irish Cousin* until, 'with fear and trembling', the duo finally 'finished the proofs' off at the printer's vehement behest.[12] Parsing the collaboration into its measurable textual parts is, thus, clearly misleading. Such calculations cannot inform that element of collaboration which Somerville claims has no explication: 'our reliance on one another, whether on this plane or another, is what can never be explained'.[13] It is this 'fundamental sympathy' with each other that withstands the 'practical difficulties' and 'inevitable divergences of opinion' and achieves 'the overall harmony of our work', creating a unity out of two (sometimes discordant) voices.[14]

This chapter seeks to understand and demonstrate how such attitudes towards authorship have an impact on the two writers' thinking about Ireland and its politics in the late nineteenth century. Like *The Silver Fox*, Somerville and Ross' early travel texts witness a surfacing of the two writers' female collaborative ethic and, especially in their travel writing about Ireland, this principle is mapped onto the divided landscape of their native country. Moreover, travel texts like *Through Connemara in a Governess Cart* (1893), which will form the main subject of this chapter, demonstrate some of the most explicit moments in Somerville and Ross' writing of a deliberate playfulness with the dual authorial voice, exploiting its potential to interrogate both issues of gender and Irish politics.

The commercial industrialisation of travel in the 1880s and 1890s had opened the door for a soon-thriving market in tourist literature and, though it meant reluctantly pausing on their work on *The Real Charlotte*, the numerous practical and intellectual attractions of the genre appealed to the two women. Somerville and Ross' initial interest was prompted by Ross' English friend, Edmund Helps, and was spurred on by what Ross termed the 'vulgar' travel guides that were being published about Ireland in the late nineteenth century.[15] Like Emily Lawless before her, who writes in her 1882 sketch of Connemara that she 'does not believe in the possibility of exploring an entire tract of country, and plucking out the whole heart of its mystery within a space of twenty-four hours', Ross laments the factual inaccuracies of such guides and argues with Helps that 'two holiday visits to Ireland [are] not enough to learn the Irish character in'.[16] Like their short stories, Somerville and Ross' serialised travel pieces for periodicals also brought in a steady income and were more easily managed than their novel writing. As Somerville reveals to Cameron: '[i]t [*The Real Charlotte*] is an awful lot of work, more than anyone who hasn't tried it would believe ... I don't think we shall embark on 3 vols again in a hurry. Two people necessarily work slower than one; there is much more care and discussion of motive etc and it is too troublesome arranging ways and means.'[17]

Through Connemara is a carefully studied foray into the travel writing genre for the two women and, as Lewis notes, led to 'something of an industry' for them in the 1890s.[18] During the period between 1890 and 1893, Somerville and Ross made at least four significant tours, through Connemara (1890), Bordeaux (1891), Wales (1893) and Denmark (1893). They subsequently published accounts of these journeys in various periodicals and at least three of them eventually ended up in book form. Ross also separately published a series of short articles for *Black and White* on the Parisian Latin Quarter, 'Quartier Latinities' (1894–5). The articles were based on a visit she had made to Somerville in 1894. They both later made a tour of the Aran Islands in 1895, which Ross originally wrote up for *Harper's* magazine and then republished as 'An Outpost of Ireland' in *Some Irish Yesterdays* (1906). Somerville made two more significant tours after Ross' death in 1915, one to Sicily (1920) and one to the United States (1928). In 1930 she published a somewhat refined tour memoir of her American travels, *The States Through Irish Eyes*, and a description of her Sicilian tour was published in *Happy Days! Essays of Sorts* in 1946. All of these travel articles include illustrations by Somerville. As with their short stories, Somerville and Ross were forced to negotiate between the generic expectations of this particular industry's publishing outlets, and their own cultural, political and collaborative agendas. Writing about Connemara also pushed to the surface a consideration of their own position within Ireland as both tourist and native which, coupled with the dual authorial voice, evolves into a complex rhetoric on both gender and the nation in late-nineteenth-century Ireland.

Narrating the west of Ireland

In her study of the west of Ireland and Irish identity, Catherine Nash notes the increasing pervasiveness of 'the West' in popular travel accounts of Ireland throughout the boom years of the professional tourist industry during the 1880s and 1890s. The late Victorians' 'growing taste for the primitive' fuelled interest in the region and the late nineteenth- and early twentieth-century travel accounts of Connemara that Nash details are further seen to take part in a process of romanticisation whereby the west became an almost barbaric, but tantalisingly exotic, 'other' both within and without Ireland.[19] This overt primordial gloss, however, becomes problematic when viewed within a framework of British imperialist values. In his preface to an anthology of travel narratives on Ireland from 1800 to 2000, Glenn Hooper notes that: 'an ever increasing number of travel accounts reflected the discourse of British imperialism of the early and mid-nineteenth century, a discourse which was to flower supremely in the 1880s and 1890s.[20] 'The nineteenth century was stamped by the rhetoric of empire,' continues Hooper, and 'many of its travellers mirrored, and in some cases passionately articulated, empire politics'.[21] The idealised purity of Ireland's western corner was posited by ensuing travellers as a unique representation of untainted Irish authenticity which was simultaneously celebrated by the Irish-Ireland movement, as well as patronisingly denigrated by British empire politics. The west exuded Irish authenticity for the educated traveller and avid tourist alike, largely bypassing the ever-increasing cultural split that James Buzard identifies between the 'sensitive traveller' and the 'vulgar tourist'. As a result, the common iconic fodder of the west employed in both political and cultural circles gradually encouraged the establishment of an authentic discourse on the west of Ireland.[22] This textual dialogue was inscribed in the travel writing of the period and Melissa Fegan suggests that travel writers 'appeared to see themselves as successive editors of the text Ireland' and that the assumed stability of this text 'produced diachronic generalisations more often than synchronic truths'.[23] Fegan concludes that the travel book became a 'palimpsest' which was 'over-written by succeeding travellers' who preserved and added to its 'anachronistic interpretations'.[24] Subsequent to this layered narrative process, Martin Ryle argues that by the early twentieth century, the west of Ireland was decisively recognised both as 'a unique place within Ireland, and as quintessentially Irish'.[25] Its cultural status had become so time-honoured and anchored in its physical geography that any exposition on the subject was deemed almost redundant.

It was into this maelstrom of cultural certainty that Somerville and Ross launched their definitive account of Connemara in 1893 and arguably attempted a reversal of the trajectory Fegan describes above. *Through Connemara in a Governess Cart* becomes an endeavour to not only re-write, but also to re-fashion, ubiquitous images of the west of Ireland extolled in popular and commercial travel writing. It was Ross' abhorrence of an 'intolerably vulgar [railway] guide to Connemara' published in Dublin in the early 1880s, and detailed in a letter to Somerville in 1889, that provided the stimulation she and her writing partner needed to embark on their own travel narrative of Ross' native Irish district.[26] *Through Connemara*, however, is a very specific convolution of the traveller text, which is exposed by the fact that Somerville and Ross do not venture abroad to explore and report on foreign lands, but return home to Ireland. This manoeuvre forces the two writers to adopt the jarring position of both tourist and native, which in many ways mirrors their already anomalous and hyphenated Anglo-Irish identity and forces the issue of their dual identity to the surface of the narrative. Like their tour through the Aran Islands in 1895, *Through Connemara* begins elsewhere, in Galway and London, before inexorably moving westwards. Both texts are based on actual tours that Somerville and Ross embarked on in the 1890s and the factual details of both tours can be read in their diaries. To a certain extent, and despite the authors' proclamation that 'this is the record of a genuine expedition', the account given in *Through Connemara* is, in places, semi-fictionalised, as well as derived from textual sources and personal experiences in Ireland that occurred outside the actual trip.[27] In addition, many of Somerville's illustrations are not genuine depictions of Connemara or the people they met there, though she did make several sketches during the tour and these illustrations were utilised in the final publication. These working processes are not uncommon and most of the tours that Somerville and Ross wrote up for publication during the 1890s were a mixture of fact, fiction and other textual and visual sources.

The published Connemara tour begins in London and, by ship, moves to the Cork quayside. From there, the cousins travel by train through Limerick to Galway where they hire the governess cart of the book's title and a small jennet. The rest of the tour takes them on a somewhat well-worn loop around the Connemara district, travelling through Oughterard, Recess, Ballinahinch, Letterfrack, Renvyle, Leenane, Eshriff, Delphi, and finally back to Galway. The two travellers stay in a series of hotels and family homes and relate their encounters with the natives of Connemara, as well as their impressions of the landscape. *Through Connemara* was commissioned by, and originally serialised in, the *Lady's Pictorial*. Ross had originally envisaged writing a factual and functional guide 'à la Baedeker', a series of travel handbooks published by the German publisher, Karl Baedeker, which were geared towards independent travellers keen to throw off servants and tour guides.[28] Ross' friend Helps suggested approaching Thomas Cook, who produced a similar type of travel text, and Ross wrote to Somerville: 'Helps was very keen that I should write a guide book to the West of Ireland, for Cook; like some that have been brought out by him; you chuck in your interesting writing, & at the end of each chapter place the facts of hotels, distances and so forth, à la Baedeker.'[29] Somerville and Ross attempted to implement their 'Connemara and Cookian' idea in 1890 and visited Cook's offices in London with their proposal.[30] Unfortunately, they had little success there. It was on this same trip, however, that they also visited the offices of the *Lady's Pictorial* and though there is no mention of the guide proposal in Somerville's diary, it seems to be here that the two authors secured a commission for the series of travel articles that would eventually become *Through Connemara*. Shortly after their London visit they embark on the tour, and Somerville begins making sketches for their articles before the tour even begins.

The opening pages of *Through Connemara* are set in London and provide a scathing condemnation and reversal of the familiar rhetoric that emanated from various English quarters, from the typically wet Irish weather lamented by nearly every English traveller, to the degrading images of the Irish as Britain's dim-witted swine in the cartoons of *Punch* magazine:

> My second cousin and I came to London for ten days in the middle of last June, and we stayed there for three weeks waiting for a fine day.
>
> We were Irish, and all the English with whom we had hitherto come in contact had impressed upon us that we should never know what fine weather was till we came to England.
>
> ...

As the fifth party of moist ladies came in and propped their dripping umbrellas against the wall behind us, and remarked that they had never *seen* such rain, our resolution first began to take shape.

'Hansom!' said my second cousin.

'Home!' said I.

By home, of course we meant the lodgings –

...

'England is no fit place for a lady to be in,' said my second cousin, as we drove away in our hansom with the glass down.

'I'd be ashamed to show such weather to a Connemara pig,' I replied.

Now Connemara is a sore subject with my second cousin, who lives within sight of its mountains, and, as is usually the case, has never explored the glories of her native country, which is why I mentioned Connemara. She generally changes the conversation on these occasions; but this time she looked me steadily in the face and said,

'Well, let's go to Connemara!' (1–3)

This evident snubbing of England, using the very terms usually associated with Ireland, sets up a coded binary opposition which Somerville and Ross go on to navigate with both caution and a certain amount of relish. In London, the two travellers are able to assert with confidence that they are Irish, but their self-possession and their national identity is pointedly in the face of England's Englishness and they seem much less assured once back on native soil. In Connemara, their twofold national rivalry becomes a three-way affair as notions of Englishness and Irishness become entwined with the fact of political union and also with issues of class status. Somerville and Ross' boldly affirmed national identity, then, becomes a much more problematic topic during their tour of the west of Ireland and this complexity is foreshadowed early on in the text in the opening passage quoted above. The exuberant and finalised "Home!" is strangely and swiftly unnerving as we realise that they merely mean their lodgings in Bayswater. Connemara is introduced not as 'home' but as 'my second cousin's native country', which is notably a 'sore subject' and a place that is, as yet, unexplored by the two 'natives' (1–3).

While neither ratifying a strictly imperialist English viewpoint nor glorifying a wholly de-anglicised Ireland, *Through Connemara* thus sits, as Somerville once suggested of her and Ross' stance towards the Irish Revivalists, on the 'outer skin' of these cultural and political movements.[31] From this vantage point, Somerville and Ross create English-Irish 'unions' of their own which can be variously seen as attempts to assimilate their own familial and class histories to the dominant mode and they rather contentiously, but nonetheless trenchantly, stage these unions within *the* geographical arena of prototypical Irishness, the west. This battle of collaborative identities also challenges the dominant mode with which they are trying to integrate by displacing some of its core constituents, such as national homogeneity and conventional standards of femininity. Somerville and Ross interrogate the latter through the behaviour of their narrator and her cousin, and continually negotiate social expectations and socially constructed ideas about femininity. Significantly, and as this chapter will go on to argue, this negotiation relies on the unremitting play between the text and its collaborative authors and their self-awareness of the dual narrative voice. In *Through Connemara*, Somerville and Ross' dual authorial voice is used to create a singular narrative female voice, one that relates her travels with her 'second cousin'. This creates an authorial distance between the authors and their central narrator and, unusually for a travel text that relies for its success on its authenticity of events, blurs the boundaries between fact and fiction.

Despite adopting the collaborative mantle of Somerville and Ross' actual authorial lives, however, the imagined 'unions' within the text suffer from internal instabilities. The history of the landscape Somerville and Ross are so feverishly attempting to re-write acts as a destabilising force throughout the narrative, much as Romantic notions of singular authorship continually hinder and threaten to rupture the literary alliance of Somerville and Ross. However, as in *The Silver Fox*, the two authors take recourse in women's collaborative potential to overcome national and class divisions and, even if only temporarily, offer alternative and idealised possibilities for thinking about successful political union in Ireland.

The Irish sisterhood of Connemara: Caroline Blake, Mary Martin and Grace O'Malley

Dismissing the usual tirade of epithets to describe the idyllic wonders of Britain's Emerald Isle in much of the tourist literature written about Ireland, the landscape of the west takes a noted second place in Somerville and Ross' more populated account of Connemara. Somerville and Ross' *Through Connemara* continually pushes against the grain of the nineteenth-century's kitsch and colonial image of Ireland as preserved in the many popular commercial accounts of the region. Interactions with local people in these largely factual and functional guides, such as Charles and Adam Black's and Thomas Cook's, are few and far between. The landscape is instead engaged and appropriated within the commercialised language of the tour book, which foregrounds Connemara as a wild yet picturesque and untouched outdoor sporting playground. In contradistinction, the fishermen in *Through Connemara* are conspicuous failures at their sport and usually greeted with some disdain by the two lady travellers. The landscape is conversely transformed into an acquiescingly spectacular but deliberate backdrop upon which various exchanges between tourist and native take centre stage.

Encouraged by their editors to keep things at all times pleasant, the narrative is punctuated by human incident and, among this pint-sized and largely humorously depicted native population, Somerville and Ross accord special significance to three Irish women, both actual and legendary. In so doing, the text attempts to single out and forge a symbolic union between this triumvirate of women, namely Caroline Blake, Mary Martin and Grace O'Malley, who come to metaphorically adorn and redefine the political landscape of the west. All three are united as inimitable representatives of female empowerment while simultaneously serving as icons of an emblematic decline and fall trajectory, from the financial ruin of the once wealthy and landed Protestant gentry, to the faded glory and colonial disestablishment of Gaelic feudal society. In *Through Connemara*, their family homes still stand, but only as ruins (Curradh), hotels (Renvyle) and empty 'show places' for the eager tourist (Ballinahinch), and Somerville and Ross can only reconcile themselves 'to the loss of an ideal' as they travel this increasingly haunted wilderness (62 and 140).

This harmonious trinity, however, potentially suffer discordance at the very hands which bind them so tightly together, for hovering over the text is the question of how Caroline Blake's and Mary Martin's aristocratic endurance of Irish unrest can cordially amalgamate with Grace O'Malley's bloody and long-standing Gaelic resistance to English domination. The harmony of this alliance is further ruptured by the dispossession of Grace O'Malley's grandson from the Barony of Ballinahinch by Cromwellian forces in the mid-seventeenth century, which led directly to the estate's ownership by the ascendant Martin family from whom the Martins of Ross were directly descended. The Blakes at Renvyle also acquired their land in similar fashion, purchasing their estate from the privileged elite to whom Cromwell dispersed England's conquered lands. Both the Martins and the Blakes, leading Catholic merchant families of Galway, subsequently converted to Protestantism. Somerville and Ross knew their family histories intimately and with some amount of zeal and these facts won't have escaped their notice. Ireland's and their own familial history is forever catching up with them on this supposedly humorous tour and both continually disrupt the united English-Irish identities Somerville and Ross attempt to carve out.

Somerville and Ross nonetheless persevere in their bid to suture together these three women. Like their own partnership, and like the coming together of Lady Susan, Maria Quinn and Slaney Morris, there is a belief in the 'fundamental sympathy' that lies between these women in their independence and fortitude and Somerville and Ross attempt to bring this belief to the surface. This common ground in the text is one that attempts to overcome the 'practical difficulties' and 'inevitable divergences of opinion' that colour the political, racial and class divisions in late nineteenth-century Ireland, particularly in terms of Ireland's relationship with England. The potential feminist feeling that Somerville and Ross utilise to create a successful union between Caroline Blake, Mary Martin and Grace O'Malley is, firstly, placed against more traditional imperial master–slave dynamics, the latter of which are seen to be a repeated failure in the text. These dynamics are comically represented by the two female cousins' attempts to civilise and unite themselves with the half-breed jennet that leads their cart through Connemara and the cultivated and technologically progressive surroundings of Kylemore Abbey, Renvyle House Hotel, and the Ballinahinch estate. The human animation credited to 'Johnny Flaherty's … nice jinnet' goes beyond mere comic strategy as the colloquial and native 'Sibbie' graduates to the classical and Greek 'Sybylla' and the reformation of her moral character begins in earnest (27). The two cousins and their jennet symbolically parallel the uneasy relations between colonial master and colonised native and the antics of the jennet persistently disrupt the main narrative of the tour:

> It was painful to find that Oughterard credited the jennet with the sole conduct of the expedition, and regarded us as helpless dependents on her will and pleasure … With the subtlety of her race, she cloaked her design in a fulsome submissiveness, as the deadly spirit is sheathed in the syrup of the liqueur, and turning in full career, without so much as an indication from her long expressive ears, she made for the gate of which we had been warned … The seeds of distrust were from that moment sown in our hearts, and we proceeded with a want of confidence that we had never afterwards reason to regret. (34–6)

The enlightenment strategies of the two cousins upon their unfortunate mule centre predominantly around the oases of civilisation to which they direct her in the otherwise baleful and treacherous countryside around them.

Each sojourn in a hotel or country house brings Sibbie closer to attaining a higher level of social refinement and the influence of her aristocratic masters steadily begins to show in her supposedly educated behaviour:

No one could have supposed that in her short intimacy with 'the quality' she could have already developed a fine-ladyish affectation of horror at the sight of an estimable poor relation; yet so it was. Casting one wild look at the appalling spectacle, she sprang sideways across the road, whirled the trap round ... and fled at full speed in the direction from which she had just come. (84)

The scene is redolent of the two cousins' own horror at being accosted in public by 'my cousin's own little Judy from Menlo', a Galway beggarwoman persistent in her distant and embarrassing kinship to Miss Martin. This 'seventy-year-old nightmare of two foot nothing' is hastily dispatched with the 'necessary blackmail' money and the quick-thinking aristocrats make a swift exit with their horse and cart (17). It is notably Sibbie's 'pride' at having also run away from an intolerable familial confrontation that spurs her to toil gallantly onwards across the increasingly steep and stony shortcut to Letterfrack, encouraged 'in a way no mere whip could have done' (91). Furthermore, Sibbie's vulgarity is repeatedly overlooked because of the 'quality' company she keeps and is continually accorded 'brevet rank' wherever she goes, stabled in the finest accommodation each hotel has to offer, but this eventually seems to have little overall effect on her ethical principles and physical character (95):

> I am sure that Sibbie felt small gratitude to the sulphate of zinc that brought about the complete healing of her sore shoulder, which took place during her visit at Renvyle. Probably never before since her entrance into society had she spent three whole days in a stable on terms of delightful equality with real horses, and with at least two feeds a day of real oats. 'Beggars can't bear heat,' is a tried and trusted saying in Ireland, and it soon became apparent that the moral and physical temperature in which Sibbie had been living had been too high for her. (162)

Nonetheless, by the end of the journey, Miss Martin remains tentatively convinced that 'we have converted Sibbie' and her optimism at their successful master–servant union is only quenched when they reach Sibbie's hometown of Oughterard and their pampered jennet enthusiastically returns to Mr Flanigan's stable in like manner to the way in which she rather ostentatiously left it:

> 'I have noticed several little things about her lately that make me sure she regards us with a stern affection. I daresay,' she went on, 'that she will detest going back to her old life and surroundings.'

> ... Nothing was further from her expectations or from mine than the eel-like dive which, just as the sympathetic reflection was uttered, Sibbie made into the archway leading to Mr. Johnny Flanigan's stable; and we have ever since regretted that, owing to our both having fallen on to the floor of the governess-cart, Mr. Flanigan could not have credited the brilliant curve with which we entered his yard to our coachmanship. (199)

This admittance of failure brings Sibbie's fragmented story, as well as the tour itself, to an end, but it arguably leaves the main humorous narrative at odds with itself.

Heavy-handedness, as well as exposure to civilised surroundings and 'quality' company, have little effect on Sibbie, the text's untamed native. Neither violence nor paternalistic philanthropy, then, seems able to overcome the cultural and political divide in Ireland and this message is repeated with another anthropomorphic encounter. Early in the trip, the narrator and her cousin find themselves face to face with the sudden and threatening appearance of a large bulldog and a herd of villainous-looking cattle. During this scene, Miss Martin pulls out her contraband gun (Connemara was, as the cousins admit, a 'proclaimed' district (47)) and fires a shot into the air which sends the cows fleeing across the mountainside with the bulldog in hot pursuit of the largest cow in the herd. The bulldog finally latches himself onto the cow's nose with his teeth. The cousins quickly lament their hasty and despotic conduct and admit that 'this was a more appalling result than we could have possibly anticipated': '[n]ot only had we failed to intimidate, but we had positively instigated him to crime ... we had no time to argue away the illogical feeling that we were responsible for the bulldog's iniquities' (55–6). Miss Martin's felony and consequent misdemeanour become problematically intertwined with the bulldog's delinquency and this leaves Somerville and Ross' bold cousins in an insalubrious relationship with the now corrupted 'Stripes', a decidedly frosty union founded on blackmail tactics and dirty secrets. Upon unexpectedly meeting Stripes on the Ballinahinch avenue later on in the narrative, this time accompanied by his owners and restrained by a strong leash, Miss Martin and her second cousin remain cool in the assurance that: '"he won't tell. He knows if he gives us away about the revolver we will inform about the cow"' (70). The message behind this scene and its resonance with Sibbie's story seems doubly significant given that the events described occurred seven months before the Connemara tour took place. Somerville and Ross purposely embellish and re-write this incident from memory and their diary accounts for inclusion in the published version of the tour.

Similar frequent calamities along the road through Connemara bring untimely reminders of the Protestant Ascendancy's position within the political and social landscape of Ireland and are covertly signalled at the start of the text. Shortly after the party of three file through 'the entrance to Connemara', the weather changes for the worse and 'the first mishap to the expedition' occurs as the narrator's hat is blown off her head and plunges 'with the élan of a Marcus Curtius into a bed of waterlilies by the bank' (39–40). Unlike that legendary Roman's exploits, however, the hat fails in its suicide mission to gain the eternal prosperity of its people and is retrieved 'pale' and 'half-drowned' from the bank only to be swiftly replaced by a 'chilly knitted Tam O'Shanter' (40). The flamboyance of classical Roman courage and valour is here superseded by the comedy of modern parody, a Scottish mock-epic of the valiant hero returning home Odysseus-like over the River Doon, fuelled by superstition and embodying the transition from the natural to the supernatural, the earthly to the otherworldly. Again, the notion of 'home' is significantly disturbed as the exotic other they are about to enter is sufficiently foreign to destabilise the authors' homecoming from London, and their trip back to Ross House will first have to contend with this foreboding tour of the resident wilds of 'my second cousin's native country', a landscape that has previously only ever been within sight, actual but unexplored. These reminders of Ireland's current and historical political situation, as well as failed relationship with England, act as both a destabilising and contrasting force in the narrative as Somerville and Ross begin to explore a tentative alternative political landscape.

Malcolm Kelsall's recent study of Irish country house fiction under the union uses Somerville and Ross' *Through Connemara* to demonstrate the complex symbiosis of the savage and the civilised, a binary opposition that foregrounds Ireland's cultural and political relations with both England and Europe. His reading of the two cousins' visit to the Martin estate at Ballinahinch identifies the house and its surrounding signs of modernisation, such as the telegraph poles and developed roads, as 'the ultimate sign of "civilisation"' and argues that Ballinahinch is the 'crucial locus' of the tour, metaphorically representing 'both historical continuity ... and familial connection' but also significantly 'deserted'.[32] The disturbance of the house's now 'secured comfort and prosperity', which occurs as 'history reasserts itself' in the grounds of the estate by Mary Martin's garden seat, is rightly identified by Kelsall as an unwelcome '*frisson*' in the air that mars the house's current opulence.[33] However, this physical tremor, or textual shudder, is arguably not an isolated incident. Rather than a 'crucial locus', it is the first in a line of such episodes that both link and rent asunder the ambitious union of Mrs Blake, Mary Martin and Grace O'Malley. The significance of the house at Ballinahinch is only fully revealed in relation to the other houses to which the journey through Connemara takes the cousins, namely Kylemore Abbey, the Widow Joyce's cabin, Renvyle House, and the briefly glimpsed Curradh Castle.

The Ballinahinch estate provides the initial major stop of the tour and the first to yield a significant historical and local narrative from the two cousins, who describe in some detail the fate of the house's former inhabitants and of its famous last resident, the 'Princess of Connemara', Mary Martin:

> we had read up a certain amount of Lever's 'Martins of Cro' Martin', of which she was the heroine, and knew from other sources something of her gigantic estate, of the ruin of it during the famine, of the way in which she and her father completed that ruin by borrowing money to help their starving tenants, and of her tragic death, when she had lost everything, and had left Ireland forever. (64)

Before reaching the castle, the travellers pass a little Roman Catholic chapel; its broken windows are boarded up and its graveyard lies 'huddled under a few wind-worn trees', unnamed graves shelter in this 'forlorn hollow' with 'crooked wooden crosses' and 'single upright stake[s]' as the only 'landmarks of the dead' (62–3). This scene is both spellbinding and sinister and even the redoubtable Sibbie chafes and sighs to move on as her masters remain rooted to the spot. The pauper-like graves portend the cousins' necessary re-telling of the Martins' ruin and the famine history within which it is embroiled and which all the cultivation and modernisation of the Ballinahinch estate cannot erase. In fact, technological advancement is seen here as somewhat disappointing:

> We were prepared for anything, for an acre of gables and thatch to a twelfth century tower with a dozen rooms one on top of the other, and a kerne or a gallowglass looking out of every window, but this admirable mansion with plate-glass windows, and doubtless hot water to the very garrets, shook down our sentimentalities like apples in autumn. We drove on in silence. (64)

By the time of Mary Martin's flight to America, and subsequent death in 1850, her troubled and debt-ridden inheritance had passed through the Encumbered Estates Court and fallen into the hands of the London Law Life Assurance. There it remained while its indebted tenants were slowly evicted and its battlements erected until in 1872 a substantive amount of the property was bought by a wealthy London brewer, Richard Berridge. It was Berridge's son, also Richard, who had modernised the house and disappointed his two lady visitors, and yet his 'civilising hand' (67), which had also cultivated the estate and planted numerous varieties of trees, acts as a welcome break after the barren, windy and exposed roads the cousins have been forced to travel to get there. As they turn in at the estate's avenue and enter its large plantation, 'a great and sudden calm fell about us ... Here at all events the civilising hand had done its work, and we slackened pace in the greenness and shelter (67–8).

This affluent and woody oasis of tranquillity contrasts starkly with the roughly hewn stakes of the Catholic churchyard on the outer edges of the demesne and while this image is not allowed to directly interrupt the cousins' luncheon on the estate, their 'nightmare of yesterday', the 'insalubrious Stripes' rears his ugly head instead as an unsavoury reminder of the uneasy union between the estate and its natural surroundings (70). Furthermore, the travellers depart the estate without visiting 'the wonderful stables that cost Colonel Martin £15,000 to build, and are paved with blocks of the green and white Connemara marble', though Somerville and Ross did, in fact, make the half-mile journey out to the 'old marble stables' (81). The text is somewhat ambivalent at this point about the paternalistic generosity of the Martin family in helping their 'starving tenants'. The gross extravagance of the estate about which, the narrator recalls, Mary Martin boasts to a house guest, echoing her father's infamous brag to George IV over the length of the estate's approach, sits uneasily with both the reminders of the famine dead on the outskirts of the Ballinahinch demesne, and the impoverished Irish Catholic peasantry that remain (78). The beggar woman the two travellers encounter sitting in Mary Martin's neglected stone seat in the grounds of the estate reminds of the continuing destitution of the Irish Catholic peasants in the area, and the two travellers end their trip to Ballinahinch by hoping that 'our intended admiration was conveyed in some form to that costly [marble] flooring, in spite of an unpleasant saying about good intentions and a certain pavement that is their destination' (81).

The home of the Blakes, like the Martins', provides another troubled but sophisticated haven of aristocratic refinement and tranquillity that again yields a problematic family history. Their delight with Renvyle House and its 'old-fashioned, even mediaeval, dark, and comfortable' interior is at once contrasted with the modernity and ahistorical environment of Ballinahinch, the home of the Blakes retaining its 'cultured and artistic' status despite the '"Innkeeper's Regulation" Act hanging framed on the wall' (139–40). Even the Blakes' pet dog manages to exude its 'suave good breeding and friendliness' and the two travellers cannot help but contrast the 'refined behaviour of the Renvyle dog with the brutal cynicism of the Recess [Hotel] penwiper and the *blasé* effeteness of its fox-terrier' (142). The demoralising effect of hotel life and the boorish manners of its inhabitants has not yet penetrated Renvyle, which remains an anomalous icon of archetypal respectability and patrician fortitude amid the degrading ranks of the licensed home. Mrs Blake, like Mary Martin, is accorded her own historical narrative, which details the arduous and very public battle she fought with the Land Leaguers in her district:

> Anyone who knows Galway at all, knows the name of Blake; and anyone who read the reports of the Parnell Commission will remember that Mrs. Blake whose evidence there was thought by both sides to be of so remarkable a kind ... The bad times and the agitation hit Renvyle very hard; so hard that when the Land League was over, Mrs. Blake was not able to sit down and tranquilly enjoy her victory. She had, on the contrary, to rise up and give all her energies to repairing the ruin that such a victory meant. Her plan was a daring one for a boycotted woman to undertake ... We looked as hard at Mrs. Blake as politeness would permit, while the broad columns of the *Times* seemed to rise before our mind's eye, with the story sprinkled down it through examination and cross-examination of what she had gone through in the first years of the agitation. It required an effort to imagine her, with her refined, intellectual face and delicate physique, taking a stick in her hand and going out day after day to drive off her land the trespassing cattle, sheep, and horses that were as regularly driven onto it again as soon as her back was turned. (142–4)

Constant attempts to evade this disturbingly recent history – 'it is both easier and pleasanter to speak' of other things (137) – are futile as the cousins' narrative inexorably revisits Mrs Blake's unsettled past.

Their sojourn at Renvyle also brings them into close proximity with the ruins of Curradh Castle, one among many of the surviving but desolate relics of the O'Malley stronghold. It is here that we are also introduced to Connemara's pirate queen, Grace O'Malley, the infamous Granuaile: 'Grace O'Malley is a lady of too pronounced a type to be ignored, and even our very superficial acquaintance with her history compels us at least to express our regret that such a female suffragist as she would have made has been lost to our century' (151). Energetically discussing O'Malley's 'probable action in modern politics', however, merely leads the two cousins *further away* from their intended exploration of her nearby home and they instead settle into a heated stupor close to the shingled beach, playing an unproductive game of stone-throwing (152). After lunch, the tower 'seemed farther off than ever' and they opt for a more leisurely stroll on the beach only to be disturbed by the 'sinister suggestion of spying eyes', which turn out to belong to the rather reserved Englishman also staying at Renvyle House Hotel (153 and 155).

This sequence of events sets up a politicised geography marked on the one side by the 'untainted Atlantic' and the 'muffled ghosts of Innis Boffin and Achill Islands', the latter a mere 'cloudy possibility of the horizon', and on the other by the 'immense certainties of the north-eastern middle distance' and the dominating reassurance of Croagh Patrick and Mweelrea, which is also the way home to Ross House (144 and 154). Somerville and Ross choose to explore the middle ground that lies in between these two positions, their narrative creating an idyllic halfway point of childlike and paradisiacal proportions. The smooth and creamy sand embodies the 'romance of new-fallen snow' with 'none of its horrors', and the cousins are swept away by an 'insane and infantine ardour' (154). This unexpected zeal is, however, checked by the reality of colonial enterprise and the exploration of foreign lands and its flora and fauna: 'at our feet were laid lovely realities of long lace-like scarves of red seaweed, flattened out with such prim precision that we expected to find their Latin and English names written beneath them on the sand' (154). The cousins' perfectly constructed middle ground, a kind of romantic utopia positioned within the triangle of Anglo-Ireland, Gaelic Ireland and England, thus remains somewhat threatened by the misty piratical fortress of Grace O'Malley and the 'ghosts' of Ireland's western isles, as well as the menacing presence of the unnamed English scout.

The textually derived unions of west and east, Gael and Saxon, myth and reality, past and present are further soured by an internalised text of paternalistic Irish-English unionism, namely a Blake family-authored publication entitled *Letters from the Irish Highlands*, published in 1825. Evidence suggests that Somerville and Ross knew this book quite intimately, and it is possible that they came across and read the book while staying at Renvyle House. The fictionalised account of the cousins' stay in the Widow Joyce's cabin in *Through Connemara* is arguably an idea cribbed and expanded from the Blakes' *Letters*. Somerville and Ross' personal diaries pay testament to the fact that they never stayed in such a cabin and the incidents they describe therein are variously similar to a night spent in a hotel in Rossroe, which Henry Blake describes in one of the published family letters. The superficial acquaintance the cousins profess with the history of Grace O'Malley may also have derived from the personal details given of her in these same letters. Much of the information about the pirate queen in *Through Connemara* is identical to that related in the letters and both the Blakes and Somerville and Ross incorrectly cite Curradh Castle as one of Grace O'Malley's private abodes (it was, in fact, only her son who lived there).

This linkage between Somerville and Ross' travel narrative and the Blake letters lends some credence to an otherwise tenuous connection. With the writers' knowledge and use of the Blake text in mind, the almost tangible Latin and English names the cousins perceive written in the willing surface of the sand become significantly reminiscent of particular letters in the Blake book, namely those that habitually detail the Latin and English horticultural names of Connemara's wild fruits and flowers. This oblique reference to *Letters from the Irish Highlands* at a moment of, potentially, idealised union seems far from coincidental when the main thrust of the letters themselves is an attempt to portray what becomes an overly optimistic recipe for compatible relations between Ireland and England. This union is largely based on a kindly but superior paternalism and modernising impetus which chimes with Somerville and Ross' attempts to rewrite Ireland for an English audience:

> As the improvement of Ireland necessarily depends upon England, the first step towards that improvement must be, to make our English brethren acquainted with the true state of this portion of the empire ... It is therefore with an earnest desire to lend some assistance, however trifling, towards removing the veil which reveals the real state of Ireland, that the following work is offered to the British public.[34]

The Edgeworth family took some considerable interest in the book and Maria Edgeworth would later comment that despite Mr Henry Blake's ingenious philanthropy, he was altogether 'too Pierce Marvelish' and it had brought him much financial ruin.[35] His patronage, however benevolent, also did nothing to save Renvyle from the land agitation of the 1870s, as the story of his son's widow, Mrs Blake, painfully testifies in Somerville and Ross' *Through Connemara*. The Innkeeper's Regulation Act which welcomes the two cousins to Renvyle is a 'relief' to their weary travellers' feet looking for bed and board, but a 'shock' to their aristocratic sensibilities. It is also here at Renvyle that they markedly reconcile themselves to the 'loss of an ideal' (140).

Nonetheless, and however briefly asserted, the idyllic political and geographical middle ground that Somerville and Ross symbolically construct via the shared female fortitude of Mrs Blake, Mary Martin and Grace O'Malley pays testament to both their questioning of existing union relations between

Ireland and England, and the power of female collaborative thinking to potentially overcome the polarised, and often violent, actions and debates they see as governing political thinking in and about Ireland. Somerville and Ross' trio of Connemara women also sit in between competing versions of the west. The colonial construction of the Celtic as passive and female vies for authority with a home-grown refashioning of the west as Gaelic and masculine. *Through Connemara* rejects both these positions. In the text, the west is female-dominated, but not by the docile goddess figures that adorned the front cover of Thomas Cook's *Programme of Tours and Excursions in the Emerald Isle* (1899). Instead, Somerville and Ross' women are marked by the masculine strength and fortitude of the Gael and reinserted into national politics, their former actions exposed as having a bearing on the formulation of the Irish nation. Femininity, as well as Ireland, is being refashioned here and this recurs throughout the text.

Irish women and the exotic 'other'

Ubiquitous images of the west and its women, as extolled in popular and commercial British travel writing, repeatedly come under fire in *Through Connemara*. On meeting the Widow Joyce, an Irish peasant woman, for example, Somerville and Ross' female travellers muster the authority of their class position in Ireland and, lost and far from any hotel, seek bed and board for the night in the Joyce home: '[w]e did not ask the Widow Joyce if she could take us in. We simply walked into her house and stayed there' (94). This brashness of class might and right, however, does not seem to be a straightforward reflection of the authors' position, or of their own behaviour. Somerville and Ross happily spend several nights in the cabin of the Bordelais peasantry during their French tour in 1891. The overnight visit that takes place in the home of the French peasant woman, Suzanne, for example, is faithfully related from actual events and the travellers significantly ask Suzanne if they can lodge in her house for the night; they rather 'diffidently' suggest the idea to her and she delightfully accepts.[36] As noted earlier, Somerville and Ross' diaries prove that the encounter with the Widow Joyce is wholly fictionalised and that the two women never stayed in such a place. The scenes with the Widow Joyce appear to have been introduced for the purpose of both mocking the extremes of the master–slave dynamic inherent in British imperialism, and overturning colonial images of the Irish, particularly images of Connemara's women: 'We had heard a good deal of the Spanish type of beauty that is said to abound in Connemara, but the Widow Joyce was the first specimen of it that we had seen' (94). The subsequent account that the two cousins give of the Widow Joyce sits in opposition to the artful, exotic and bewitching characteristics often attributed to such women in other travel texts, not least an 'intolerably vulgar' Dublin railway guide, *The Midland Great Western Railway of Ireland Tourists' Handbook: Through Connemara and the West of Ireland* (1884). Ross took great umbrage with this particular travel text for its misinformation about the Martins of Galway, as well as its deplorable gender stereotypes. The railway guide describes the female peasant women of Claddagh as 'dark-eyed and dark-locked beauties, who peeped slyly out of the doorways of their miserable cabins'.[37] In this text, the women of Claddagh are accorded a foreign and near-destitute primitive status, and the British male colonial gaze of the narrator is both admiring and wary, ruminating on whether the women are descendants of continental European gypsy races. The Claddagh peasant women are thus posited as a temptation and a threat to the male traveller and the ruling colonial power that he represents.

In contradistinction, *Through Connemara* offers a wholly different portrayal of the same type of woman. The Widow Joyce's physical appearance and overall bearing is one of modesty, hospitality and friendliness, and her former courteous accommodation of an English major travelling through Connemara on a fishing expedition removes her as a threat to the English male tourist and his embodiment of colonial power. We are told that the Widow Joyce is 'a small, pale, refined woman, with large brown eyes, and dark hair tucked shiningly away under a snowy white frilled cap' (94). Her 'miserable cabin', as some would have it, reflects the Widow's poverty, but it is 'clean' and 'simple' and 'hot water was unexpectedly abundant' (99 and 109). While the two cousins claim much of the 'decorum' and 'civilisation' of the household for the English major and his influence during his stay with the Widow, it is also clear that they hold the Widow herself in some esteem. They receive an 'admirable meal' for dinner, and an 'excellent breakfast on departure', and they take their leave of the Widow Joyce with 'a mutually affectionate farewell' (96, 111 and 112). Indeed, the Widow Joyce is deserving of a place alongside Mrs Blake, Mary Martin and Grace O'Malley. Like Maria Quinn in *The Silver Fox*, the Widow is separated by her class status from the other women in *Through Connemara*, but she is united with them in the author's clear appraisal of her female fortitude. Despite her poverty and the loss of her husband, she is characterised by dignity and kindliness, and is both a sympathetic and admirable character. Her son, Pat James, 'the eldest hope of the house of Joyce' (111), seems to give recognition to, and be the successful fruit of, her venerable daily endeavours: 'he was an idyllically picturesque creature of seventeen or eighteen, with large, gentle grey eyes, set in a golden-brown face ... and the most charming voice and manner imaginable' (112). He sees the two cousins safely back to the main road at the request of his mother, and as they leave him behind to continue their journey, they agree that it '"was just as well we missed our way, for if we hadn't we should have missed Pat James"' (114).

While Somerville and Ross recognise the class and race divisions that exist between the Anglo-Irish and the native Irish, and briefly attempt to find a common ground upon which each can stand, they are also at pains to distinguish their female travellers from their English counterparts. By their own admission, the travellers are both native and tourist in Connemara, but in the face of England, they are indubitably Irish. Their opening thrust against the English in *Through Connemara* repeats itself further on in the text and combines with the two authors' gender concerns. On returning to Ireland from London, the two cousins relate their journey to Cork in an outside car and, in so doing, deliver another blow to the way in which women are often portrayed in travel texts, as well as exploit the experience to assert their full-blooded Irish heritage. Of their journey in the outside car, the narrator explains that 'no doubt, we should enter on a description of its perils which would convulse and alarm English readers in the old, old way' (11). Instead, the reader is informed that 'we know all about outside-cars; we believe we went to be christened on an outside-car, and we did not hold on even then – we have certainly not done so since' (11). A little later in the narrative, it is also pointed out to the text's 'English readers' that the 'word "peat" is not used in Ireland in reference to fuel by anyone except possibly the Saxon tourist. Let it therefore be accepted that when we say "turf" we mean peat, and when, if ever, we say Pete, we mean the diminutive of Peter, no matter what the spelling' (12–13).

Their defiance against being portrayed as 'English' also crops up in some of their other tours of the 1890s and is used to create a cultural passage through which Somerville and Ross can pass into mutually understood territory with the foreign land they are trying to translate for their readers. While travelling abroad in France, for example, the two travelling cousins are frequently introduced as 'les Anglaises', but the narrator quickly asserts that: '[w]e always found it advisable in France to announce our true nationality as soon as convenient. We found ourselves at once on a different and more friendly footing, and talk had a pleasant tendency to drift into confidential calumny of our mutual neighbour, perfidious Albion, and all things ran more smoother and more gaily.'[38] In *Through Connemara*, this issue of national identity coalesces with the book's gender concerns, as in the scene on the outside car. Ross, in particular, disliked the hackneyed gender stereotypes of the railway guide, and took much offence at the book's 'interesting facts about the disappearance of the Martins from the face of the earth'.[39] The guide, she tells Somerville, is 'written in description of a tour made by a party of people': 'Jack – very manly – the young ladies – very ladylike, a kind & humorous mother etc. Jack was much the most revolting.'[40] The journey in the outside car, like the description of the Widow Joyce, attempts to directly overturn a scene in the railway guide. On arriving in Ireland, the 'female portion' of the party in the guide, we are told, are full of 'feelings of nervousness ... inspired by the national vehicle'.[41] 'Dublin that evening was almost a blank' for the travelling women, a 'nightmare of jolts and bumps'.[42] Like many women travellers in the late nineteenth century, they are chaperoned by a guide while the 'ardent sportsman', Jack, goes in search of the best salmon fishing in Connemara's lakes.[43]

As unchaperoned female travellers and authors, Somerville and Ross already embody an explicit challenge to norms of femininity, and other female travel writers like them were seen as an increasing threat to serious travel literature. An anonymous review of Harriet Martineau's *Eastern Life. Past and Present* (1848) published in *Blackwood's Magazine* in 1848 railed against the modern tourist phenomenon and placed women writers at the heart of a perceived desecration of the 'rational travel ... and intelligent curiosity' undertaken by the 'manly investigator'.[44] '[O]ur *horror*' [emphasis in original], bemoans the author, is the 'professional tourist; the woman who runs abroad to forage for publication' and returns home with a 'periodical gathering of nonsense; and with a freight of folly'.[45] The article ends with a lengthy diatribe on the 'desperate evil' that is modern tourism and a longing for 'the return of that happy period when the chief occupations of the fair sex were cookery and samplers'.[46] James Buzard notes how these attitudes continued and hardened into the late nineteenth century where an ever-clearer distinction was made between the 'professional tourist' and the more serious traveller.[47] Buzard argues that the 'woman abroad was a natural "tourist" to the men who observed her: she was another avatar of that plural person destroying real travel'.[48] Somerville and Ross were also placed in a difficult position with regard to their publisher.

Writing for the *Lady's Pictorial* restrains Somerville and Ross in various ways. They are told from the outset that the editor 'wants Humour' and Somerville writes to Cameron that 'the Lady's Pictorial has commissioned us to go through Connemara (or anywhere else we like) and write a facetious account of our journey ... It will be rather expensive but the L. Pic. will pay well if we give them what they want.'[49] Looking back on their dealings with the periodical in *Irish Memories*, Somerville reiterates that, editorially, 'we were given ... to understand that the events ... were ever to be treated from the humorous point of view. "Pleasant" is the word employed, which means pleasant for the pampered reader, but not necessarily for someone else.'[50] Somerville and Ross' treatment of the west of Ireland thus had to straddle the demands of their editor, as well as their own ambitions to challenge colonial interpretations of their home country. Given the readership of the periodical, the two authors also had to abide by certain social conventions, particularly with regard to their depiction of women, and they achieved a somewhat mixed success with this. As Sara Mills demonstrates in her study of female colonial explorers, the conventions of travel writing 'present a framework of largely masculine narratorial positions and descriptive patterns with which women writers negotiate when they construct their travel accounts ... women could only write as gendered individuals with clearly delineated roles'.[51] While their text remained largely unchanged by the *Lady's Pictorial*, Somerville and Ross knew that they were treading a thin line. Ross' 'delicate' mother 'weakened frightfully' at some of the scenes Ross read to her in manuscript form, and all of Somerville's illustrations were modified by an in-house artist.[52] Violet Powell remarks of the redrawn pictures that they had been so 'softened and refined that the travellers appeared to have spent their time in a lady-like neatness ... Seated on window seats or grassy banks they yearned, most uncharacteristically, at the landscape.'[53] The vivacity and, often, uncompromising positions and state of dress of the female travellers that Somerville originally drew were nowhere to be found and Somerville complained (to no avail) that the finalised illustrations were 'simply intolerable'.[54]

Somerville and Ross were, therefore, only variously triumphant in containing their account of the west of Ireland within both the dictates of their editors, who demanded humour, and the more general prescriptions of Victorian femininity. The feminist unions Somerville and Ross create in *Through Connemara* are also, perhaps, never as stable as their authors would like them to be and yet they still manage to achieve several important effects. Firmly planting themselves on the 'outer skin' of English and Irish modes of archetypal Irishness enables Somerville and Ross to shift the goalposts that traditionally demarcate the permitted authenticities of Irish nationality, and by temporarily adopting the generic boundaries and rhetoric of the travel writer, they are further able to exploit the geographical and social spaces that this narrative occupies. The kind of national and gender contestation that the two authors re-enact within these spaces thus takes place in a shifting moment of transition between tourist and native.

Several critics of the travel-writing genre have suggested that the travel writer works in a space of cultural limbo, or transculturation, where each of two distinct cultures comes into contact and contests to appropriate the other within its own cultural and linguistic codes. Derek Gregory and James Duncan call this space of transculturation a 'tense space in-between', which is generated by the act of translating one culture into another, and Mary Louise Pratt defines it as the 'contact zone', a social space where 'disparate cultures meet, clash, and grapple with each other, often in highly asymmetrical relations of domination and subordination'.[55] The contact zone more than facilitates Somerville and Ross' tussle with competing versions of Irishness and femininity, yet they don't quite play within the rules of the game. As tourists in their own country, they get to revel in the grey areas that the middle ground affords them, blurring the divide between tourist and native. According to Lawless, this 'native tourist' is the exemplary traveller, someone not 'shackled by the shackles of the resident' or lacking in native knowledge but, most importantly, someone 'who has a prejudice ... in favour of forming his own views unbiased by the views of his predecessors'.[56] In Connemara, Somerville and Ross are Lawless' favoured and 'discriminating traveller[s]' and the middle ground in which they choose to play enables them to construct a series of national and gender unions which attempt to not only appropriate the other to which they are bound, but to significantly alter that other.[57] The Ireland to which Somerville and Ross purport to be natives has first to be revised or rescued from the successive English travel texts and Irish-Ireland cultural movements which have colonised its representation. The cultural passages through that this new Ireland is mediated in the travel text are English-Irish unions of differing sorts and varying strengths, but unions nonetheless.

During their travel-writing years, Somerville and Ross' political loyalties were seemingly clear-cut – they both campaigned for the Unionist Alliance in 1895 – and yet their travel narratives account for a much more complex and fluid notion of 'unionism' than their political activism perhaps suggests. Berating her brother for writing to her and telling her that he increasingly feels more English than Irish, Edith replies with the following:

> Nonsense about being 'English'! I don't mind if you say 'British' if you like, but the only pallid trickle of *English* blood comes from *one* marriage, when Hester Coghill married Colonel Tobias Cramer, *a pure blooded hun* – if not Jew! You might just as well say you were German! ... My family has eaten Irish food and shared Irish life for nearly three hundred years, and if that doesn't make me Irish I might as well say I was Scotch, or Norman, or Pre-Diluvian [emphasis in original]![58]

A British title allows Somerville and Ross to remain fully Irish in a colonised Ireland without relinquishing the English ties so essential to the sustenance of their class and without having to blur the cultural line between Irish and English. *Through Connemara* is largely a complex extrapolation of this position. While favouring the Unionist Alliance Somerville and Ross campaigned for in Ireland, it also foregrounds a 'feminocentric perspective' as integral and internal identities, which serve to complicate the broader political union it subtly advocates.[59] Pratt recognises this 'perspective' as a broader trend in the texts of female travel writers who, like Somerville and Ross, 'repeatedly point up instances of female strength and heroism' in their writing. In the case of Somerville and Ross, this is not isolated to *Through Connemara*, but reoccurs in their writing about other countries. In Denmark, for example, the two cousins visit Copenhagen's government art school for women and meet its founder, Fröken Krebs, as illustrated by Somerville on the cover of this book. The duo note that Krebs 'alone knows what long and hardy efforts were necessary before the government school for women was achieved; what interminable sessions of Parliament; what innumerable letters and audiences; what labyrinths of red tape.'[60]

Somerville and Ross' narrative of Ireland thus finally identifies and admits to the weaknesses within both the old unions that haunt the cousins' travels and the new unions they attempt to forge. The dual voice, and the complexities of that voice that are introduced into the text, also crucially influence the imagined alternative spaces that Somerville and Ross construct to challenge Ireland's intertwined gender and national politics. As the final chapter will go on to explore, the power of that dual voice during Somerville's and Ross' lifetimes continued to haunt and influence Somerville's post-Ross publications and extend the normative possibilities of literary collaboration.

CHAPTER FIVE

On opposite sides of the border

I t was in December 1915, six months after the death of Ross, that 'suddenly, and quite unexpectedly', Somerville began to successfully communicate once again with her friend and literary collaborator.[1] From these early 'few and faltering sentences', gained with the assistance of her friend and established local medium, J. E. M. Barlow, Somerville went on to publish a further fourteen books under the by then reputable dual signature of E.Œ. Somerville and Martin Ross.[2] Somerville's spirit communication with Ross was far from unusual in the early twentieth century. An international occult movement had been growing in popularity ever since the late 1840s and other literary figures both in Ireland and abroad also showed an interest to varying degrees in the Other World, including Yeats, Dickens, Conan Doyle, Bulwer Lytton and Elizabeth Barrett Browning. The history of Somerville's spiritualist practice spans two quite distinct periods of this much larger occult movement, which has combined roots in late eighteenth-century immigrant Swedenborgianism, as well as the much more popular séance culture that first spawned in 1848 in Hydesville, New York, in the form of the Fox sisters' renowned (but eventually discredited) spirit-guided table rappings.[3] After this first flourishing of à la mode dining-room spiritualism, which initiated a more serious and scientific investigative advance on paranormal activity, a second wave of intensive interest in mediumship swept through Britain and Europe as the unparalleled terrors of the Great War and its incalculable human losses slowly dawned.

Somerville's early forays into the spirit medium's circle came in the late 1870s in the shape of table-turning and automatic writing, the latter of which she was coerced to practise by her Uncle, Colonel Kendal Coghill, a keen and resolute spiritualist who was convinced of Somerville's and her brother Cameron's mediumistic powers.[4] This youthful and somewhat frivolous dabbling in the occult realm was largely carried out with a sense of adventure and a penchant for the latest new vogue, at least by Somerville, and it was only in the early decades of the twentieth century that Somerville had cause to take her spiritualist experiments more seriously. This marked volte-face came significantly in the midst of the First World War and on the death of Ross at the end of 1915. Somerville's spiritualism was thus born of the late nineteenth century's somewhat faddish mode of occult experimentalism, but its serious practice and cultivation was nurtured by a much later twentieth-century personal and international crisis of human loss and deep-seated bereavement. Her lifelong interest in the occult, however, is not simply a disjointed and somewhat alternative adjunct to the other social and cultural mediums in which she and Ross operated during their live working careers. Diana Basham argues that the nineteenth century's spiritualist movement was 'an integral part of that wider social change' that witnessed the rise of women in public writing and political roles.[5] Somerville and Ross' involvement and ardent practical support for female emancipation, plus their joint role as professional authors, are arguably all brought together in Somerville's spiritualist activities and form part of this wider emphasis on cultural, political and religious upheaval.

The historical contingency of Somerville's spirit communication with Ross, however, has rarely been taken into full account and many critics have simply viewed the occult narratives that Somerville produced in the later decades of her life as outlandish and nostalgic texts which, with the exception of *The Big House of Inver* (1925), engendered very little of literary note. Marginalised to a private sphere of emotion, the automatic writing transcripts that Somerville produced over many years of communicating with her deceased collaborator have either been ignored or read with a puerile interest in determining the sexual context of the lived relationship. However, as already witnessed through the affects and practices of the living bonds between Somerville and Ross, collaborative work and friendship lie at the core of the duo's partnership and this dynamic arguably continues to distinguish the occult relationship cultivated by Somerville after Ross' death. Recognition of this patterning across both the lived and spiritual relationship hence has a significant bearing on the ways in which Somerville and Ross' collaborative authorship is more broadly understood.

Somerville's first spirit communication with Ross certainly affirmed the dualistic nature of the two women's relationship. The intimacies of personal longing and grief manifested a psychic declaration that the work so crucial to their living partnership would go on, and Somerville's breakthrough message from the disembodied Ross was a clear call to literary arms: '[y]ou and I have not finished our work. Dear, we shall. Be comforted. V. M.'[6] That these words are delivered not through Somerville, but her friend and medium Barlow, perhaps pay testament to Barlow's first-hand understanding of the relationship between Somerville and Ross, as well as the entwined nature of their work–friendship bond. Writing for *Country Life* magazine on the death of Ross in 1916, Barlow recounts her first meeting with Somerville's writing partner and comes closer than most to comprehending the near existential relations that tied Somerville and Ross together:

> I early realised it was impossible to form a clear conception of Miss Martin's character without also having made the acquaintance of that friend of whom she spoke with infinite pride and affection, and Fate never did me a kinder turn than when one gave me the opportunity of observing what a truly splendid thing friendship between women may be.[7]

Barlow captures the ongoing relational sense of self that gives such vibrancy to the personal and professional dynamics of Somerville and Ross' friendship and collaboration, explicitly revealing the processes of mutual becoming that mark their lived communications. As Chapter 2 has already demonstrated, the two women's experience was one of incessant exchange, dialogue and passionately shared creativity, all of which was shaped by the movements between a well-established common ground and the necessary quakes of lively discordance. This dance of dissension within a harmonious framework forced continual moments of self-reflection that led to renewed gains in self-knowledge for both partners. In this sense, Somerville and Ross were, in part, Aristotelian mirror images for each other and this fortified their sense of professional worth against social and familial condemnation, but their images were as stones in water opposed to gilt-framed glass. The rippling and ever-changing sense of self that is reproduced via the personal and professional collaborative tie fails to settle into a cast-iron form, and is instead continually renewed and contested over time through the two women's ongoing personal and creative dialogue with each other, and is thus forever dependent on the relational other that constitutes its being.

It is this concept of identity dynamics that Barlow understands, and it is this same concept that is drastically altered for Somerville on the death of Ross and subsequently reanimated by her in diluted form via her occult activities. When Somerville lamented that 'no one can know what we were to each other', it was partially with the knowledge that Ross' death had forced her to know for herself the full extent of what this other woman had meant to her and, indeed, how this woman had altered and become part of her cognitive make-up. In his argument with Heidegger's views on death in *Being and Time* (1927), Emmanuel Levinas maintained that our relationships with others are constitutive of our selves and that the death of the other (far from severing this dialogue or remaining resistant to its loss) continued to play a role in our self-identity formations by configuring the self as a survivor and, therefore, enabling the continuation of a dialogue with the dead other.[8] Though Levinas denies the dead subject an actual speaking voice, Colin Davis argues that his stance does not preclude a signifying relationship with the dead and the possibilities of an alternative dialogue. 'The dead may not speak in any literal sense,' argues Davis, but they do signify to the survivor and death's non-response becomes 'another source of meaning': 'the self is no more the entire source of its own identity and its meanings than it was when the other was alive'.[9] As the surviving partner in the Somerville and Ross enterprise, Somerville's occult narratives can be usefully read as attempts to create 'another source of meaning' for her self, and re-enact the identity-forming dialogue which was the sustenance for that self. Contrary to Heidegger, then, Somerville's actions refute the imperviousness of the self to death and demonstrate the loss of being to the self which results in the death of the other. Ross's death is, therefore, a final extinguishing of her being, but it is also a literal cutting away of part of Somerville's own self. Yeats put it most succinctly when, through the hand of his Renaissance spirit correspondent, Leo Africanus, he wrote that the 'dead remain a portion of the living'.[10]

The dialogue through trance narrative that Somerville reanimates in order to resume this lost sense of self, however, is a far cry from the confidentialities, oppositions, self-reflections and creative finesse that distinguished her living relationship with Ross. Somerville makes live Levinas' intimation that a relationship with the dead is possible but, in fact, the conversations that Somerville produced with Ross in her automatic writing transcripts are, in reality, only an internal dialogue with the self. The dead, indeed, cannot speak. In this lies Somerville's greatest difficulty, and the nostalgia, idealisation and distortions of fact that are often attributed to Somerville's post-Ross writings, including parts of *Irish Memories*, arguably reside in this complex new dynamic Somerville creates in order to displace the psychological and practical consequences of Ross' death. Peter Goodrich has argued that the 'ideal of friendship belongs to the afterlife', and this is certainly true of Somerville's transformed friendship with Ross after her death.[11] Lewis and others have demonstrated that Somerville occasionally altered the historical narrative of her and Ross's life together after Ross' death, often to celebrate Ross as the greater partner in the collaboration and subsequently humble her own role in their writing. The same critics have also shown the ways in which Somerville occasionally revised her memories of their writing practice to paint it in a more idyllic light; as, for example, in *Irish Memories*, where the conception of the Irish R.M. tales is happily set amid the sunny dunes at Étaples and not, as was the case, in the two women's hotel room to escape the rain. Such narrative strategies, however, do not simply share in the processes of nostalgic reminiscence, but form part of Somerville's broader attempt to continue in dialogue with her dead partner and advance the friendship which lay at the core of that partnership. Goodrich argues that classical forms of friendship posit the relationship as a transcendent ideal where the friend exists as a 'specular double', and the 'proof' of such friendships lies in their ability to survive absence and, most notably, the 'absolute absence that takes the form of death'.[12] Goodrich here suggests that in the passing of one or other friend the possibilities of difference and discord (which constantly threaten the bonds of living friendship) are finally abolished, and the ideal of friendship can be witnessed. As a result, the subsequent relationship is conserved (or even trapped) in an 'autoerotic state'.[13] The idealisation of the dead thus returns the living friendship to an unattainable ideal, which is preserved and lived out through continuing dialogue (or what is believed to be a continuing dialogue) with the dead. Unable to relocate Ross as a living friend, the latter becomes confined in an idealised and internal dialogue that Somerville carries out with her own self and, in this sense, texts like *Irish Memories* become meditations on friendship itself. This also challenges the critical viewpoint that texts like 'Two of a Trade' and *Irish Memories* are merely a distortion of fact, or a nostalgic reminiscence. Rather, I would argue, they are, in part, conscious attempts to construct a social and philosophical narrative of female friendship, in both its lived and ideal forms.

The English composer and militant suffragette, Ethel Smyth, who became Somerville's friend and ardent correspondent after Ross' death, clearly recognised this dimension of *Irish Memories* when she read it in 1918, and it further prompted her to introduce herself to the author. Written in the form of a congratulatory review of Somerville's book, Smyth's first letter to Somerville praised her not so much for her portrait of Ross in *Irish Memories*, as for her depiction of female friendship: '[p]erhaps it is partly because of what friendship has been to me all my life that this book goes home to me so poignantly: I wish I could thank you adequately.'[14] She continued to return with enthusiasm and joy to the subject of the book in subsequent letters and went on to invoke the celebrated writings of Montaigne on his close friend and noted political philosopher, Étienne de la Boétie, in her desire that Somerville continue to write about Ross.[15] She further circulated the book among her extended circle of female friends, all of whom she maintained had 'the same feeling – to a hair – about it' as she did.[16] Smyth's later intimate advances towards Somerville, which Somerville rebuked, also suggest that Smyth recognised in *Irish Memories* the erotic dimensions of female friendship written into that text. Smyth here unconsciously moves the critical debate on *Irish Memories* from one of Somerville's personalised and oft-times idealised account of her life with Ross, to one which understands the political, intimate, and sometimes erotic and sexualised, discourse on female friendship on which Somerville's book is founded. Smyth's reaction to the book also unconsciously recognises the ways in which that book carves a place for itself amid what is otherwise a male-dominated tradition of narrative meditations on departed friends.

Despite, then, the realities of Somerville's somewhat calcified relationship with the deceased Ross, and the inevitable moments of romanticised looking back on a friend now gone, the emotive and critical response of other women to *Irish Memories* reveals both Somerville's ability to further understand and explicate 'what we were to each other', and her struggle with recapturing the dynamics of that friendship and its lived experience through spirit communications. The broad aims of this chapter, therefore, are to recontextualise Somerville's occult practices within the wider social contexts of the nineteenth and early twentieth century's mass interest in the occult, and understand her particular brand of trance narrative as not just the ravings of agonised personal loss, but the desire to consciously and actively sustain and enhance beyond the grave a personal and intellectual working relationship. In so doing, the chapter offers a more wide-ranging and comprehensive narrative of Somerville's occult activities, both before and after Ross' death, than has previously been the case. This largely personal and lifelong discourse on spiritualism allows for a conscious remapping of Somerville's trance communications with Ross onto the social and cultural frameworks of which Somerville's spiritual beliefs were always a part. Davis notes that even where the ability to literally speak to the dead is disavowed, it is the 'unanticipated meanings' of that communication that bestow significance to such activity.[17] In the light of such arguments, this chapter is thus finally about reconnecting Somerville's occult communication to the live collaboration from which it was cultivated, as well as verbalising the heretofore 'unanticipated meanings' it offers more widely on our understanding and theorising of collaborative female authorship.

Witches, wizards, roaring radicals and female Jacobins

Despite the fairly heady and lighthearted days of the early spiritualist movement in the second half of the nineteenth century, the reasons posited by recent research into its development cite far-reaching and more intellectually urgent contexts ensuring its popularity and successful evolution across America, Britain and continental Europe. Janet Oppenheim's study of the 'Other World' between 1850 and 1914 situates Victorian enthusiasm for all things spiritual in the perceived instability of the Victorians' religious institutions, arguing that the Victorians were 'fully aware that the place of religion in the cultural fabric of their times was scarcely secure'.[18] The ambiguity of the Church's answers to contemporary unease with the cultural, intellectual and emotional developments of the epoch led to thousands of British men and women turning to spiritualism and psychical research for a better understanding of their changing world.

Revolutions in teletechnologies also played their part in the growing acceptance of spiritualism. Scientific and rational developments in technological transmission in the late nineteenth and early twentieth centuries changed the way in which people began to view the physical world around them. Pamela Thurschwell's study of technology and magical thinking in this period suggests that 'the scientific study of the occult which emerged as a discipline in the late nineteenth century' was centrally related to a fascination with the means of cultural transmission and communication.[19] Thurschwell argues that teletechnologies such as the telegraph and the telephone 'suggested that science could help annihilate distances that separate bodies and minds from each other', and thus encourage and verify what could become spiritually viable in the popular imagination of those living at the *fin de siècle*.[20] Despite, then, the growing charm and titillation factor of psychics and séances for those seeking little more than popular entertainment, spiritualism was also providing more serious and consequential answers to a disillusioned population. Committed spiritualists and other faithful advocates also became determined to ascribe some scientific credence to their work and occult experiences, thereby acknowledging spiritualism's revolutionary potential. Institutions such as the London Dialectical Society, the National Secular Society, and the more popular Society for Psychical Research (SPR) all involved themselves in both collecting evidence for and attempting to justify through controlled experimentation all manner of psychic phenomena.

This oft-cited background of concurrent popular appeal, technological revolution, and socio-religious insurgency allows for the unusual participation in spiritualism of both the downtrodden and the elite. Furthermore, it situates the occult movement within what Peter Washington, in his book on theosophy and the emergence of the Western guru, has called an 'alternative synthesis': '[h]aving taken root in America, spiritualism rapidly colonised Europe. In the wake of failing political revolutions in 1848 – the very year of the Hydesville phenomena – it rapidly became part of an "alternative" synthesis which included vegetarianism, feminism, dress reform, homeopathy and every variety of social and religious dissent.'[21] Other historians have corroborated this theory, and research by Basham and Alex Owen, in particular, has gone on to explore in more detail the parallel relationship between the flourishing of the nineteenth century's feminist and spiritualist movements.[22] Owen, like Washington, concludes that 'spiritualism had the potential ... for subversion', and she goes on to argue that it was no accident that spiritualism attracted so many female believers.[23] Spiritualism privileged women 'during a period of gender disjunction and disparity between aspiration and reality', and spiritualist culture thus held 'possibilities for attention, opportunity, and status denied elsewhere'.[24]

Owen and Basham both agree that mediumship became, in certain circumstances, the key to opening up new professional career opportunities for women in that it allowed them to 'transgress taboos about female public articulacy without shouldering the burden of individual responsibility for their performances'.[25] It also allowed them, however, to alter the course of their personal lives by acting upon higher spiritual laws that were divined only to them. This enabled many women to act in ways that would normally have been unthinkable, but for which they escaped blame by pleading forced obeisance to otherworldly powers beyond their control. Owen gives the example of Louisa Lowe, an amateur medium living in the late 1870s, who left her unfaithful clergyman husband on the grounds that she had been spiritually encouraged to do so by her occult 'controls'.[26] Lowe firmly believed that her spirit guardians had bestowed upon her the frequently denied and greatest gift of all, that of 'freedom of thought and belief'.[27] Yeats' wife, George Hyde-Lees, also managed to coerce her husband into satisfying her sexual and other welfare needs by putting her personal demands into the mouths of her spirit mentors. If George wasn't content in body and soul, warned the mentors, then it would be impossible for the creative spirit muses in which Yeats was so absorbed to continue sending their messages through her. Jeff Holdridge notes that in *A Vision*, Yeats erects a 'complicated geometrical system meant to show how lyric moments illuminate the sexual-religious basis of psychological or historical change', and that it is 'not surprising that the automatic writing from which [*A Vision*] was conceived was also intimately connected to improving Yeats's sexual life' with his wife.[28]

In certain cases, spiritualism also allowed women to adopt leading and influential public roles within the occult movement. One of the most famous and significant figures in the nineteenth century's Western esoteric tradition was a woman: Russian-born Helena Blavatsky. Blavatsky commanded a strong and long-lasting political hold on the Theosophical Society via her spirit masters, Morya and Koot Hoomi. The society was founded in 1875 by Blavatsky and fellow spiritual enthusiast, Colonel Henry Olcott, and its organisation and ambitions quickly became dependent on the phantom communications only Blavatsky could conduct with the unearthly 'Great White Brotherhood of Masters'.[29] These spirit messages constantly reaffirmed her psychic authority, particularly in times of crisis and doubt, and for many years fended off her main rival and original disciple, co-founder and president, Olcott. Her position within the society wielded social power and influence, and also gave her theories on the link between spiritual knowledge and science an international audience.

Women, it seems, also found temporary imaginative relief from their usual subservient lives by adopting a variety of remarkably ultra-male and usually impermissible social roles while in a trance state. In his study of spiritualism and parapsychology in American culture, Laurence R. Moore notes that women turned into 'swearing sailors, strong Indian braves, or oversexed male suitors' while under the influence of their spirit controls.[30] Henry James' *The Bostonians* is perhaps one of the clearest literary examples of the ways in which feminism and spiritualism were inextricably linked in the nineteenth century, as well as the ways in which the prevalent reputations of these differing socio-cultural movements merely combined to create a double public censure against them. The opening pages of James' novel unsympathetically amalgamate both the female emancipation movement and occultism by citing a meeting of feminist sympathisers as a 'rendezvous of witches on the Brocken': 'all witches and wizards, mediums, and spirit-rappers and roaring radicals ... female Jacobin[s] ... nihilist[s]'.[31] With her stirring and hypnotic trance speeches of female oppression and the need for liberation, the transcendental Bohemianism of the novel's protagonist, Verena Tarrant, is central to the successful progress and expansion of the book's feminist movement. But in its association with occultism, Verena's suffrage is derisively portrayed as another dissident social and political activity, one which has significantly contributed to the perceived overall feminisation of the age. The somewhat unsympathetic narrator notes that Verena had been raised under the wings of a litany of female professional influences: 'the girl had grown up among lady-doctors, lady-mediums, lady-editors, lady-preachers, lady-healers, women who, having rescued themselves from a passive existence, could illustrate only partially the misery of the sex at large' (83–4). Verena's ability to give a public voice to these women and their ambition, however, is excoriated as part of the nineteenth century's 'damnable feminization'. Basil Ransom, Verena's unnecessary saviour from the clutches of feminism and occultism, laments the loss of the 'masculine character' in all walks of professional life and views the spiritualist movement as an avoidance of life's brute realities:

> 'The whole generation is womanised; the masculine tone is passing out of the world; it's a feminine, a nervous, hysterical, chattering, canting age, an age of hollow phrases and false delicacy and exaggerated solicitudes and coddled sensibilities, which, if we don't soon look out, will usher in the reign of mediocrity, of the feeblest and flattest and the most pretentious that has ever been. The masculine character, the ability to dare and endure, to know and yet not fear reality, to look the world in the face and take it for what it is – a very queer and partly very base mixture – that is what I want to preserve, or rather, as I may say, to recover.' (289)

Such thinking is not isolated to the nineteenth century. Writing in the 1970s, Theodor Adorno's 'Theses Against Occultism' posited similar charges against spiritualist practitioners whose 'judicious reason' had crumbled in the face of man's exorbitant and fascist desire to control Nature, as well as his disillusion at the commodification of a 'world congealed into products'.[32] Adorno argues that the tendency to occultism 'is a symptom of regression in consciousness', a loss of power to 'think the unconditional and to endure the conditional': '[b]ecause objects have frozen in the cold light of reason, lost their illusory animation, the social quality that now animates them is given an independent existence both natural and supernatural, a thing among things.'[33]

Adorno's thesis pinpoints a popular sourcing of the sweeping move towards occultism in the loss of conventional rational thought, but this kind of reasoned thinking in the nineteenth century was almost exclusively considered a masculine affair. Indeed, male practitioners of the occult were equally vilified for their womanish irrationality and ostracised in the nineteenth-century press as 'addle-headed feminine men'.[34] Even the celebrated and internationally renowned spirit medium, Daniel Dunglas Home (1833–86), was slighted by his enemies with lurid suggestions of his assumed homosexuality.[35] Moore delineates the gendered qualities ascribed to spirit mediumship in the nineteenth century, demonstrating that mediums were considered weak 'in what were considered to be the masculine qualities of will and reason', and strong 'in what were considered to be the female qualities of intuition and nervousness'.[36] Mediums were further considered 'impressionable (i.e. responsive to outside influence) and extremely sensitive'.[37] Above all else, they were deemed wholly passive.

This assumed passivity was deeply problematic for women advocating feminist values, and such hostile and archetypal attitudes towards the occult frequently undercut the advantageous positions women had gained through spiritualist practice. Verena's oratorical command in *The Bostonians*, for example, is recognised by herself and those around her as something outside her own powers of thinking and speaking and this clearly places her as the recipient oracle of a much higher authority beyond her control:

> They had just heard her say 'It is not *me*, mother,' and he and Mrs Tarrant and the girl herself were equally aware it was not she. It was some power outside – it seemed to flow through her; he couldn't pretend to say why his daughter should be called, more than anyone else. But it seemed as if she *was* called. (59)

Verena is thus only privileged within the more conventional limits of a Victorian taxonomy of gender roles and this circumscription confines women's empowerment within the spiritualist movement more generally to a sphere of already accepted womanhood and a nineteenth-century understanding of femininity. Nonetheless, there remained a fear of female spiritual power spiralling out of male social and moral control, and this was often symbolised by interpreting the realm of the occult as a maternal and colonial space. Linking the metaphoric dimensions of the spiritualist movement with masculine projects of imperialism and empire revealed oblique overtones of female usurpation of male power structures. Basham argues that the 'Occult Mother' figure of the period's press is 'both a figure of Empire and of over-reach', dominating the psychic and geographical 'uncertain borderlands' which mark a country's jurisprudent limit.[38] She is finally 'a female embodiment of phallic domination and its collapse into farce and pathos'.[39] Maureen O'Connor and Roz Cowman recognise this dynamic in Somerville and Ross' Irish R.M. stories, citing the supernatural powers of their female characters, and often animals (e.g. foxes), as something that is seen to constantly rout the authority of the stories' 'representative of masculine colonial power, the R.M. himself'.[40] Helen Sword confirms this theorising and maintains that nineteenth-century spiritualism 'replicated problematic imperialist attitudes'.[41]

Sir Arthur Conan Doyle, a staunch public supporter of spiritualism in the early twentieth century, corroborates in practice the metaphoric correlation of imperial doctrines and Victorian spiritualism by offering a pacifying and religious explanation of paranormal activity in *Pheneas Speaks* (1927). The book is a trance narrative account of direct communications reported by

members of the Conan Doyle family, including transcripts with Conan Doyle's
son Kingsley, who died in combat in the First World War. In the introduction
to the book, Conan Doyle creates an analogy of the hierarchy of souls between
man on earth and Christ in Eternity, and the chain of command between the
lowly Indian peasant and the British occupying forces in India:

> Let us compare a man's position under the eternal with that of an Indian
> Villager under the British Raj. When he is in trouble, or claims redress,
> he does not make a personal appeal to the king. He turns to the king's
> representative, who may be no more than the local police inspector. If the
> matter is more than can be dealt with, it goes back to the local magistrate,
> to the district commissioner, to the provincial governor, to the viceroy,
> finally to the high authorities in London.[42]

Progressively concerned with the corporeal stability of the spiritual law-giver
in occult communications, the Victorians thus found themselves increasingly
more determined to establish either the fraudulence of the female mediums
involved, or the authenticity of their claims of obeisance to a legitimate higher
power.

This persistent question spiralled around the validity of the spirits
themselves, questioning whether or not the spirits were 'genuine entities' or
merely, and perhaps more threateningly, a 'metaphor for some other agency
whose agency was as yet undetermined'.[43] It was the indeterminacy of this
agency that proved so troubling to the Victorian mind. The unspecified cultural
and political outfit governing the spirit world was one that could be neither
controlled nor usurped while it remained unidentified and, moreover, its
literal ascendancy was being divined and circulated by women and supposedly
effeminate men who were gaining the vestige of an imperial authority in
the process. This occult sanction was bestowed and remained outside of the
traditional political system, acting as a destabilising force against the norms
of patriarchal governance and allowing women to be perceived, once again, as
a threat to standard political and social relations. The fear remained that the
mediums themselves were in fact the authors of the texts they produced and
the speeches they gave and, hence, such figures were able to gain an unofficial
autonomy that threatened conventional standards of behaviour, particularly in
the case of female mediums. If these women did indeed enjoy the powers, both
literal and spiritual, that they were often slanderously accused of possessing,
then the fearful question remained of 'how far did this power stretch, and
what could it accomplish?'[44] Furthermore, how could these female influences

be curbed and guided into benefiting a more traditional path of female social responsibility and domestic obligation?

It was only with the dramatic political events of the first half of the twentieth century that such questions began to be overshadowed. The world wars of that period instigated a mass turn towards all things spiritual, and went some way in deflecting from the impropriety of the spiritual act. In the introduction to Somerville's unpublished essay (*c.*1940) on her and Ross' spiritual communication, she gestures towards these global conflicts as being responsible for swathes of the population turning to the occult and attempting communication with the spirits: '[f]or a reason that is dark to one, the subject which has been comprehensively labelled Spiritualism is, in general society, a somewhat risky one. Less so, perhaps, since a Second Great War has more or less regularised it, and a guarded reference to a Future Life is less improper than it used to be.'[45] Both the First and the Second World War have frequently been cited as the turning point for many people who took up the spiritualist cause in the hope of getting in touch with their grieved loved ones. The innumerable social and cultural frameworks previously discussed as the subtle driving forces of the occult movement in Europe arguably take a back seat in the theorising of the occult movement's popularity in this later period, as the prevailing emotional force of intense national grief begins to take centre stage. Oppenheim argues that the Great War substantially 'enhanced the appeal of psychics and séances,' not because the context had changed, but because the new converts were responding to the unprecedented horrors of the world wars, rather than the intellectual and emotional crises of the mid- and late Victorian decades.[46]

Both wars took their toll on the emotional psyche of the populations involved and, as Somerville's writing on the subject repeatedly emphasises, spiritualism helped these populations through the mourning process. The shifting rationale for spiritualism's continued popularity and importance was also duly noted by Conan Doyle, whose interest in and attitude towards the occult bears a noteworthy congruence to that of Somerville. Conan Doyle's interest in spiritualism, like Somerville's, was slowly nurtured over almost twenty years of his life, throughout spiritualism's halcyon days in the 1880s and 1890s. After obtaining his degree in medicine in 1882, spiritualism gradually came to his notice but, while curious, he frequently dismissed it as the workings of the 'weak side' of men's brains.[47] The serious undertakings to understand the occult by the period's prominent scientists such as Crookes, Wallace and Flammarion, however, impressed Doyle enough to rethink the spiritualist phenomena of the late nineteenth century. The oaths of these 'men of honour and repute', which testified to the validity of their occult experiences, plus the staid reports of the Dialectical Society, moved Conan Doyle to finally join the SPR in 1896 and begin a more concerted effort to investigate for himself the paranormal activity in which he was increasingly interested.[48] He read a wide range of spiritualist literature, including *Human Personality and its Survival of Bodily Death* (1903), whose author, F. W. H. Myers, was one of the founding members in 1882 of the SPR, as well as a lecturer in Classics at Trinity College Dublin. Conan Doyle also read Sir Oliver Lodge's *Raymond, or Life and Death* (1916), an account of Lodge's trance communications with his son, who was killed in the First World War. Finally, in 1916, Conan Doyle publicly announced his committed allegiance to the spiritualist movement in *Light* magazine and began publishing his own spiritualist texts.

Looking back on this major transition, which considerably and quite negatively affected his public reputation, Conan Doyle explains and defends his motives in his two-volume *History of Spiritualism*, published in 1926:

> The sight of the world which was distraught with sorrow and which was eagerly asking for help and knowledge, did certainly affect my mind and cause me to understand that these psychic studies, which I had so long pursued, were of immense practical importance and could no longer be regarded as a mere intellectual hobby or fascinating pursuit of a novel research. It was this realization which, from early in 1916, caused me and my wife to devote ourselves largely to this subject, to lecture upon it in many countries, and to travel to Australia, New Zealand, America and Canada upon missions of instruction.[49]

Again, the emotional impact of the Great War is cited as a leading factor in Conan Doyle's serious and very public turn to the occult and critics have gone on to argue that the death of his son, Kingsley, in 1918 further cemented his dedication to the dissemination and scientific investigation of occult practices.[50] In the early 1920s his wife developed the 'great gift of inspired writing' and her trance texts form the core of the spirit narratives published in Conan Doyle's *Pheneas Speaks*.[51] The introduction to this slim volume sets out, again like Somerville, to determine a positive relationship between spiritualism and religion, allowing for a hierarchy of dead souls to exist between man and God, 'Higher Spiritual beings who may exist between ourselves and the level of Christ':

> it seems to me a very human and reasonable scheme that our immediate spirit guides have others behind them, and yet others, extending in an infinite hierarchy through such a great spirit as the Christ up to the

unthinkable centre of life and love, and that the lowest vibration may, if needful, be transmitted to the highest.[52]

Conan Doyle's dedication to and staunch belief in spiritualism is perhaps one of the clearest and most public examples of the way in which the Great War changed early twentieth-century attitudes towards the movement and reveals the extent of its cultural influence on a grieving population.

Despite this decidedly less complex incentive for the second wave of popular spiritualism in Britain, therefore, it is nonetheless a significant motive in the history of spiritualism's social and cultural impact, and equally as potent as the other factors previously evaluated in this chapter. Moreover, Somerville's later personal involvement with the occult movement was, for the most part, a result of a combined individual and national grieving, and it was this emotional impact that led Somerville onto the more professional path of the established spirit medium. Mediumship arguably provided both a public and domestic way forward for Somerville, and radically altered the collaborative status of her future literary projects. It was also a practice which was nurtured over a considerable period of time, crossing the boundary between the late nineteenth century's somewhat illicit vogue for communicating with the dead, and the early twentieth century's more mainstream acceptance of spiritual transmissions.

The occult world of Castletownshend

In her diary of 1874, Somerville admitted that in Castletownshend there was at least one 'ruling mania' at all times which occupied the young and old alike.[53] Throughout the closing decades of the nineteenth century, spiritualism flirted on and off as the number one activity and acted as both popular entertainment and serious scientific pursuit. Somerville acknowledges in her brief autobiographical essay, 'Extra-Mundane Communications', that her mother had 'a special *flair* for the occult' [emphasis in original] and remembers and records the 'light-hearted' adult fascination with spiritualism in Castletownshend during her childhood.[54] Somerville's uncles, Kendal and Joscelyn Coghill, appear to be the main driving force behind this sustained preoccupation and they both kept up a lively interest in the occult that spanned a broad remit, from stirring the Castletownshend young with fantastical psychic exploits and tales of public séances in London, to the more serious founding of the local Cosheen Psychical Society. Both were members of the SPR and, in 1885, Joscelyn presided, as vice-president of the society, over the

Hodgson Report, which discredited the activities of the by now internationally renowned medium, Madame Blavatsky. Kendal Coghill also contributed articles to the proceedings of the SPR on the subjects of dream premonitions, charms and cures, and formally lectured on spiritualism across the British Isles throughout the later years of his life. The Somerville family were also friends with SPR presidents and cofounders, Arthur and Gerald Balfour, both variously chief secretaries for Ireland and (in the case of the former) British prime minister in the early years of the twentieth century. Somerville's brother, Aylmer, served with the Admiralty Intelligence Department during the First World War, which coincided with Arthur Balfour's tenure as First Sea Lord, and he also had a keen interest in spiritualism and was an active practitioner of psychometry – the study of paranormal extrasensory perception. Further to this, he was an expert on stone circles, ley lines (the alleged alignment of places of geographical interest), and astronomy.

This both international and oft-times esoterically conducted spiritual enthusiasm of the adults at Castletownshend influenced and fostered an inquisitive huddle of youngsters who weren't averse to conducting their own occult experiments, much to the disapproval of their elders, who felt they were too young to accord their practices with the respectful seriousness it deserved. An early entry in Somerville's diary in August 1873 records that she, along with her brother, Cameron, and the 'Aylmer Brothers', turned their hand to a little table-turning of their own:

> After tea the boys came up & after some planchetting we tried table turning & Percy, Eddy, Cam, & I actually made a small round table turn, & rap out some questions, when Mother put a stop to it, being a <u>questionable</u> amusement.[55]

Nonetheless, Somerville and Cameron certainly seem to have been heavily involved with and exposed to spiritualist beliefs and exercises as young children and this left them rather immune and open-minded to its otherwise outlandish doctrines. They were very much singled out by their Uncle Kendal for their collaborative ability to transmit 'replies from the Unknown', which they would conduct via automatic writing, and it was here that they first gained formal access to their mother's group of spirit inquirers, even if only reluctantly:

> I may admit that we were very unenthusiastic mediums. When one has but recently escaped from the trammels of the schoolroom, interest in problems touching the next world is negligible. My brother and I

accepted the role suddenly thrust upon us of mouthpiece, or rather private secretaries, of the Oracle, with more reluctance than we ventured to exhibit.[56]

According to Somerville, their séances were very fruitful and, in response to their uncle's questions, the automatic writing flowed 'in an abundant and fairly legible stream over sheet after sheet of foolscap paper'.[57]

In early 1878 there seems to have been a flurry of occult activity in the Drishane household, Somerville and Cameron claiming to have made contact with an ancient Dublin ancestress, Elizabeth Cockhill, as well as establishing a connection with a female spirit, Florence Bigg, professing to have known their Uncle Kendal.[58] Exciting occult reports were also flowing in from Uncle Joscelyn, who was in London attending a public séance: 'Mother heard from Uncle Jos. who was at a grand séance & was "levitated" chair & all till he could touch the ceiling.'[59] Lewis confirms that this séance was conducted by the celebrated Home and demonstrates the wider occult circles into which the Coghill brothers were moving and, in turn, the broader popular movement by which those in Castletownshend were increasingly influenced.[60] Later that same year, on 25 August, Somerville records her own miraculous physical spirit manifestation at Drishane: 'Aunt Flo's basket has suddenly (11.30 P.M.) become possessed of an evil spirit & has waved its lid about on its own accord. I am going to sleep with her in my character as "materializer and strengthener".'[61]

Not unlike her and Ross' early forays into authorship in the compilation of the family dictionary, Somerville's spiritualism thus began as a familial occupation within the safe haven of Castletownshend, one which was often extended to social visitors:

> Afterwards the yachts came up. I was talking to Captain Kerison about Madame Blavatsky (he is much interested in her) when it occurred to us to try and turn a table. Katy, Lucy, Mr Geddes and I put our hands on and very soon it began to skip in a most lively manner ... they all came up here that evening and we had some splendid willing.[62]

With the sprouting of local psychical societies following in the wake of the London-based SPR, Uncle Kendal announced in 1894 that he was starting up a 'Psychical Enquiry Society', and that year proved to be another prosperous time for the spirits in Castletownshend.[63] In a rare letter to Cameron, Ross refers to the new occult phenomenon sweeping its way through the Somerville-Coghill family via the arrival of one of the SPR's founding members, Stainton Moses.

Although lengthy, the letter is worth quoting for its insight into Ross' rather sceptical attitude towards spiritualism, as well as her interloping perspective:

> You may think and believe in your ignorance that your elders at Castletownshend are drowsing along in the lines of the Church of Ireland or in indifference to them, either way without excitement, but you are mistaken. A gentleman called Stainton-Moses has arisen, with a resident Djin for his prophet, called Imperator, and I solemnly assure you that on the creed of Imperator, Egerton, the Bart [Uncle Joscelyn], Uncle Kendal, and, in a kind of way, your mother are ordering their theories and lives ... Egerton takes it with a sort of very logical intelligent credulity, you know the kind of way the Coghills take new things, the Bart ditto, but without the desire to act on it, Uncle K. very darkly and mysteriously, your mother by bursts of the most delightful kind. Last winter she said to me that she believed the apostles when they spoke with tongues were 'people hypnotised by God' which the more I think of it the more awfully I laugh. Now she says it's all very well talking about Abraham being the friend of God, and that he was a good man – 'Imperator says that it was nothing of the sort, that Abraham was <u>anything</u> but what he ought to be'. This time next year all will be forgotten, except by Uncle Kendal, who has for a long time been going steadily on with his spirits and spirit writing.[64]

Somerville admits in her unpublished history of the Somerville family's spirit communications that Ross maintained a lifelong cynicism of the occult movement and its arcane practices: 'she had not cared to inquire into things psychic. In fact, she mocked at me, and told me I was an "Othernian" who wanted "nothing else but either to tell or to hear some new thing".'[65] Ross' attitude also seems to have discouraged Somerville's occult pursuits as their collaboration began to take precedence in their lives, and Somerville admits that she gradually became more 'immersed in strenuous and enjoyable wordly matters' with her new writing partner and, for a time, 'forgot my friends the Ghosts'.[66] Despite her continued interest in the occult, therefore, there is also the slightest hint of condescension and derision at Uncle Kendal's persistent 'gubbing'.[67] It wasn't until Somerville's friendship with Barlow in 1912 that her serious interest in spiritualist matters began to have some currency again.[68] It was Barlow who would eventually go on to aid Somerville in her spirit communications with Ross but, as Collis notes, it was their friendship prior to Ross' death that began to encourage Somerville's more serious attempts to understand the occult world:

> Spiritualism had now begun to fascinate her ... By the autumn [of 1912]
> she was holding séances with Uncle Kendal, in which they were soon
> joined by Egerton, whose keenness had been much enhanced by his
> experiences when in London ... Edith herself began reading books on the
> occult.[69]

Barlow's temporary move to Castletownshend in September 1912 seems to
have cemented her friendship with Somerville and there are many mentions in
the latter's diary of their spirit-writing experiments together. In the following
years, Barlow gradually became a significant authority in Somerville's eyes on
all spiritual matters. When Ross passed away at the end of 1915, Somerville's
spiritual development had thus already passed from being a youthful and
frivolous pastime into a more considered and concerted effort to communicate
with the dead.

Collis's biography already records in full detail the events that led up to
Somerville's eventual spirit communication with Ross in 1916, including
transcripts of the original séances that established contact, and these are not
worth repeating here. It seems sufficient to reiterate that it was through Barlow
that initial contact was made and it was many months before Somerville had
the ability and confidence to conduct her own spirit-writing sessions with Ross
without Barlow's help.[70] It also took some time before she was fully assured of
the validity of her spirit-writing with Ross, and on the day of their first occult
communication Somerville writes in her diary: '[r]eceived communications of
which I hardly know what to think.'[71] By January 1917, however, she was writing
to her friend, Alice Kinkead, to tell her that she 'writes' with Ross 'every day
at 7pm' and that it 'has made everything different, and I cannot now feel any
doubt, or fear, that I am deceiving myself'.[72] In 1924, Somerville even attempted
a spirit materialisation with the help of Hildegarde, Cameron and Barlow,
which she named 'The Experiment', but despite several attempts throughout
January and February of that year, Ross' spirit did not appear.[73]

Somerville's acceptance of spiritualism as a serious practice after Ross' death
was further facilitated by a much-needed reconciliation of the occult with
her religious beliefs and she appears to have found comfort in the sermons of
Basil Wilberforce (1841–1916), an Anglican priest and author who was also
appointed archdeacon of Westminster in 1900 and was a strong supporter
of spirituality within the Church. Wilberforce preached that the 'continued
existence of the individual after death was but simple Christianity,' and much
of his association with the occult was arguably prompted by his anguish over
the premature death of his wife, Emily Sargent.[74] At the end of her 1916 diary,

the year she began communicating with Ross, Somerville recorded a quotation from Wilberforce's book, *New Theology* (1908), which took the form of a prayer concerning Sargent:

> 'Suffer her to know, O gracious Lord, if it may be, how much I love her and miss her, & long to see her again; & if there are ways in which her influence may be felt by me, vouchsafe her to me as a guide & guard, & grant me a sense of her nearness in such degree as thy laws permit.
>
> If in anything I can minister to her peace, be pleased of thy love to let this be; & mercifully keep one from every act which may hinder me from union with her as soon as this earth-life is over, or mar the fullness of our joy when the end of the days has come.'[75]

Her essay 'Extra-Mundane Communications' also shows that she was familiar with the spirit works of Myers, and Somerville ends her essay with another affirmation of her religious beliefs and now fully fledged spiritualism with a quote from Myers:

> Not then, with tears and lamentations, should we think of the Blessed Dead. Rather should we rejoice with them in their enfranchisement, and know that they are still minded to keep us as sharers of their joy. Nay, it may be that our response, our devotion, is a needful element in their ascending joy.[76]

After 1916, both Somerville's spiritual communications with the dead Ross and her writings on the occult invoke this fused sense of the religious and the spiritual, and her narratives and spirit-writing are given practical value by their responsiveness to the nation's collective grief during and after the First World War.

Throughout the Great War years, Somerville's occult communications also took on a very practical import and she communicated with Ross to consult her on the whereabouts and welfare of her brothers and nephews fighting abroad. During the 1920s and the onset of the Irish Troubles, Somerville further believed that the spirits of her family and friends (led by Kendal Coghill, who died in 1919) set up watch over the living in Castletownshend as their 'guardians'.[77] Somerville's letters to her friend and fellow spiritualist, Smyth, during this period provide one of the most detailed accounts available of the troubles those in Castletownshend and Skibbereen suffered during these difficult years, as well as the extent of her spiritualist practices during this period. These letters also pay testimony to Somerville's determination to remain in Ireland in the face of a virtual state of chaos and complete isolation fuelled by republican raids and house burnings, as well as the atrocities of the Crown's 'Black and Tan' forces, the latter of which Somerville believed to be as bad as, if not worse than, the extreme republicans: 'there is no cohesion between soldiers and police, & the auxiliaries are as unspeakable as ever, in <u>most</u> places. Here & there one hears less shame-inspiring accounts of them.'[78]

There was some light relief in the spring of 1921 when Somerville travelled to England and spent time with several friends and SPR members, including Lady Troubridge, Radclyffe Hall and the Balfours, with whom she had 'much talk about spiritualism', as well as debate over the state of Ireland.[79] On 24 March of that year, she '[t]alked things psychic' with Troubridge and Hall, and on 2 April she attended a séance at Fishers Hill, the home of Gerald Balfour.[80] While this visit may have bolstered her spiritualist beliefs, the state of affairs back home in Ireland remained bleak, and she received news of another local house-burning by republicans, Colonel Spaight's Union Hall, on 1 April, which almost settled her into cutting her trip short and returning to her Drishane home. Somerville and her neighbouring relations repeatedly suffered throughout the early 1920s at the hands of republican looters. Somerville fended off raiders in Drishane several times, often with the help of the off-shore British naval destroyer posted in the bay, and also had horses and tackle stolen. Her sister, Hildegarde, had her house raided several times by republicans looking for arms, and Cameron, as a long-serving and yet retired colonel in the British Army, received a death threat from the republicans and only returned from England to Castletownshend in July 1922. He was smuggled back to Ireland across the sea by his brother, Hugh, who served in the navy and was, during the troubles, positioned off-shore near Skibbereen with the British destroyer.

The family also experienced grave financial losses as Somerville's horse-coping business began to fail with sinking farming prices, and the enthusiasm of Somerville's publishers in London began to wane considerably with the lack of literary appetite from English audiences for all things Irish: '[w]e are broke, Irish farmers and Irish writers alike.'[81] Her political position also placed her in danger from both sides as she made no secret of the fact that she was emotionally and ideologically torn between her traditional Irish roots and her allegiance to the British establishment, calling herself a 'Mr. Facing-both-ways'[82] in letters that were regularly intercepted and opened by republicans.[83] She also further endangered herself by becoming politically active in the civil war that erupted after the 1921 truce between Britain and Ireland, this time taking a much more definitive stance by acting, with Cameron, as intermediary between the Free

State guards who now held Skibbereen, and the captains of the British naval fleet that flanked the Castletownshend shore.[84] Previous to this, Somerville and Cameron had made a trip to Skibbereen that coincided with the arrival of Michael Collins, then commander of the Irish Free State forces, and Somerville sent Cameron forth to impress upon him Castletownshend's plighted situation against defiant republican rebels: 'I made C[ameron]. go & talk to him, as we want a guard here, badly, & C[ameron]. liked him, & thought he seemed straightforward & sincere.'[85] Collins admitted that there were no guards to spare and later that day he was killed in an ambush on the Bantry–Cork road, plunging Castletownshend into ever blacker despair at anti-treaty republican outrages.[86]

During this depressing period, Somerville's regular séances with Ross became the only unhampered and dependable source of communication left to her, providing much-needed consolation, security, good-spirits, and predictions of peace to come, as well as quashing the enormous sense of isolation that prevailed in Castletownshend. As the Free State troops inexorably began to restore order amid continuing republican resistance, Somerville was able to report to Smyth that Castletownshend had 'escaped as by a miracle':

> Firstly by the splendid effort, ... & secondly, by the sudden descent of the F[ree]. S[tate]. troops. Also, as I entirely believe, by the dint of special help and effort from the Other Side. Martin says there has been an unwearied cordon of spiritual protection around us, provided by my father, Egerton [Hildegarde's husband], Uncle Kendal & many others. They can't ensure protection, but by their devotion & concentration they can, & do, influence affairs here. Absolutely there is no other reason why we have escaped so easily. In comparison with other places, *nothing* has happened to us, altho' we have had some horrible people here ... I think I will ask Martin if she can go to see you and tell me how you are.[87]

Somerville even believed that the spirit of her Uncle Kendal had physically intervened against raiders looting vacant Coghill-Somerville residences, rapping out ghostly footsteps in empty rooms which supposedly frightened them away mid-raid, as well as interfering with the movements of the living to 'lay traps' for unsuspecting republicans.[88] Despite the outlandishness and speciousness of most of her claims, the occult guardians paradoxically helped to conserve a large part of her sanity against the chaos and helplessness that surrounded her and which had driven most of the rest of the gentry away from Castletownshend, including Hildegarde in late 1922. Cameron and

Somerville were the only two Somerville family members left in Drishane during the civil war and, given the information available in the Smyth–Somerville correspondence, the strength to remain there seems to have largely derived from both physical and spiritual sources. The occult communications Somerville managed to receive from the familial guardians that watched over her and her home arguably provided both mental and quite tangible assurances which were reinforced by the significant and active physical presence of the British destroyer off the south-western Irish coast.

Somerville's fluency in communicating with Ross also had another practical application in that it enabled her to continue with the publishing career that had been temporarily cut short by Ross' death. During the troubled years in Castletownshend, Somerville was writing *An Enthusiast* (1921), a politically charged novel expressing through its doomed protagonist the national double-bind in which Somerville found herself during this strained period, and which was also composed with the help of Ross.[89] Painting and writing were the only distractions to be found against the ongoing atrocities and they provided a life-saving sense of normalcy amid the everyday disorder and, once again, were enabled by Ross and Somerville's spirit communications: 'I know Martin is working with me.'[90]

She continued with her spirit-writing practices right up until the end of her life and made many friends in spiritualist circles, including the renowned London-based medium, Geraldine Cummins, who went on to write the first biography of Somerville after her death.[91] Somerville also conducted spiritualist sittings with some of the best-known mediums and Anglo-Irish automists of the day, including Hester Dowden and Eileen Garrett. By the 1930s, her interest in the occult had broadened beyond Castletownshend and she had opened up her opinions to public debate, as well as read all the books she could get hold of on the subject, and attended spiritualist meetings in London with her other interested friends.[92] Further to this, her biography of her great-grandfather, Charles Bushe, was facilitated by séances conducted through Cummins in November and December 1930 and September 1931. Manuscripts reveal that Cummins and Somerville called up the spirit of the dead Bushe and asked him questions about his life in order to fill the gaps Somerville had stumbled across in her bibliographic research. In November 1930, while researching the biography in the British Museum in London, Somerville records in her diary: 'Geraldine and I ... had most interesting writing, more than an hour, M.[artin] passing on the Chief's [Bushe's] views &c. 'Astor', Geraldine's control, brought M.[artin], saying "the woman with the white soul is here"'.[93] By the end of that year Somerville was in direct communication with the spirit of her great-grandfather, who gave a 'long & very interesting account of himself and "Nan" [Nancy Crampton]' on 5 December.[94] Although the final published volume makes no explicit reference to these séances and the information obtained through them, the book does rely quite closely on séance transcripts in chapters eight and twenty-four in particular. The book was duly published in 1932 under Somerville and Ross' dual signature.

In 1933 Somerville attended an Irish Academy dinner after receiving her honorary doctorate from Trinity College Dublin, and had 'a great talk about spiritualism' with a 'rather splendid-looking' Mr Yeats.[95] The following year, on 27 October, she attended the inaugural meeting of 'The International Institute for Psychical Research' in London, which was attended by the acclaimed Hungarian-born champion of the spiritualist movement, Nandor Fodor (1895– 1964), who gave a 'very long address' to the meeting's participants.[96] Her book, *Notions in Garrison* (1941), is further evidence of her lifelong commitment to the occult and is a selection of largely autobiographical stories detailing an array of 'miscellaneous marvels', which range from serious séances to ghost stories and the local activities of Irish fairies.[97] The book also pays testament to the dual nature of Somerville's interest in the occult, combining as it does the influence of the English spiritualist circles in which she moved, and the myths, superstitions and folklores of the native Irish among whom she lived. She also published several reviews and letters in the pages of *Light* magazine, an American journal dedicated to the investigative research of psychical phenomena, as well as co-authored (via spirit-writing) the Somerville family records with her deceased brother, Boyle.[98] When Somerville died in 1945, therefore, it was with the firm belief that the relatives and friends who had passed away before her were in Ross' safekeeping on the Other Side and that she would go on to join them all there.

This personal history of spiritualist practice clearly parallels and is influenced by the nineteenth century's larger occult movement, moving as it does through the early decades of spiritualism's popular rebirth in the 1880s and 1890s onto the more serious spirit communications that followed the Great War. Despite its initial insularity and parochial genesis, the Coghill brothers imbued local occult experiments with a flavour of the larger developments in spiritualism taking place in London and Europe, and Somerville certainly seems to have kept up with these external advances. The mood of revolution that spiritualism encapsulated in the late nineteenth century was thus felt even as far as the quiet corners of south-western Cork, and the social and intellectual frameworks of the movement became essential to understanding the deeper ramifications of Somerville's occult involvement and her post-Ross collaborative writings.

'This is her enterprise, not mine'

In his essay on Yeats and 'Protestant Magic', Roy Foster argues that the occult preoccupations of the marginalised Irish Protestant classes of the late nineteenth and early twentieth centuries mirrored 'a sense of displacement, a loss of social and psychological integration, and an escapism motivated by the threat of a takeover by the Catholic middle classes'.[99] Selina Guinness and Julie Anne Stevens further locate this particular appeal of the occult for the Anglo-Irish in the latter's Anglican backgrounds and the context of religious revival.[100] Stevens notes that '[r]eligious revival as well as political developments such as the increasing distance of the Anglo-Irish from the workings of government and the disruption and loss caused by war may have intensified interest in the rites of spiritualism'.[101] Rightly so, Foster's essay several times cites Somerville and Ross as the most significant literary documenters of Ascendancy reality and, in particular, the socio-economic upheavals of the late nineteenth century which finally usurped Protestant economic, political and spiritual agency in Ireland. He further situates Irish Protestant gothic fiction, including that of Maturin, Le Fanu and Stoker, as part of the cultural and intellectual historical narrative of Ireland's embattled Protestant figure, and the predilections to the occult that such figures exhibited.

Surprisingly, however, the intense and long-standing spiritual occupations of Somerville play no role in the essay, despite their congruence with Foster's theorising. Whether in a serious or comic vein, and from their earliest publication, *An Irish Cousin*, right through to Somerville's post-Ross publication, *The Big House of Inver*, and beyond, Somerville and Ross' works are consistently alive to the external menace of Protestant usurpation, as well as the internalised machinations and miscegenation of their own class that was further placing Protestant economic and political control at risk. Chapter 4 has already demonstrated the territorial disarticulation of the Anglo-Irish felt by Somerville and Ross, and their attempts to forge a geographical and cultural safe haven for their Protestant Ascendancy roots in their travel writing. The latter texts defaced the purity of the Western Irish Gael, and resituated Anglo-Irish relations as a hybrid and modern zone of potentially amicable national bonding. Following Foster's lead, these concerns can be traced to Somerville's spiritualist tastes.

The occult activities of the Somervilles and Coghills throughout the late nineteenth and early twentieth centuries creates an alternative and somewhat subterranean passage to England in the spiritualist adventuring of the Coghill brothers, and reconnects their otherwise marginalised Protestant enclave of Castletownshend with their increasingly distanced political motherland. Moreover, the 'loss of social and psychological integration' is nowhere more keenly felt than in Drishane during the civil war, and most notably by Somerville as she is slowly deserted by family and friends who leave Castletownshend to seek safety in England. It is at this point that Somerville's spiritualism takes a heightened turn and her over-wrought mind conjures the intercession of her familial spirit communicators in the realms of the living. Somerville's spirit circle of Protestant guardians are made to move against the ever-more savage attacks of the Irish republican militias and arguably represent an otherworldly army of deceased Somerville-Coghill family members, stretching right back to the venerable chief justice of Ireland, Charles Bushe. This ghostly force attempts to both preserve the geographic territories and properties belonging to the Protestant elite in southwestern Cork, and serve as hopeful reminders to the increasingly encumbered Somerville that Protestant influence and rule has yet to be snuffed out. The actual and psychological uncertainties of Protestant domination as played out in her and Ross' fiction finally reach an apocalyptic and factual level as the big houses around Somerville begin to burn and the architectural symbols of Protestant governance in Ireland are reduced to ashes. Somerville's recourse to the occult at this time thus acutely mirrors, as Foster more broadly suggests, the social and psychological ramifications of a marginalised and increasingly threatened Protestant minority.

The political and emotional support that Somerville clearly derives from her occult activities also recurs in other trance narratives, notably those she carries out with Bushe in 1932. On the eve of the Irish general election, which would see the first change in government since the establishment of the Irish Free State, the spirit of Bushe reassured Somerville that 'we here are making efforts': 'I think light is breaking. I feel that the coming elections will make the world know the full soul of the country. We are doing all we can. I feel that there is hope ... I have so much to say, but above all I long to encourage and inspire you with hope for Ireland.'[102] Despite the drastically altered state of Irish politics in the 1930s compared with the comparatively untroubled days of Protestant rule that Bushe presided over as chief justice, his spirit nonetheless confidently encourages Somerville in the knowledge that the Somerville-Coghill guardians still retain political influence over modern Ireland and are making the necessary 'efforts' for the best outcome in the election.

These confluences between the anxieties over the socio-political state of Protestant Ireland and the occult are further prevalent long before Ross' death and most conspicuously in Somerville and Ross' fiction. The gothic strains, for example, of *An Irish Cousin* and *The Silver Fox* consciously frame the changing and diminishing conditions of Protestant authority in Ireland within the supernatural world of ghosts, haunted houses and native Irish superstitions. Nowhere, however, are the relations between Anglo-Irish occult activity and the disquiet over Protestant political weight more zealously felt than in Somerville and Ross' first Irish R.M. tale, 'Great-Uncle McCarthy', published in 1888 for the London-based *Badminton Magazine*. In that story, the racial and class fragmentation of the ruling Protestant tribes of Ireland is already self-evident in Flurry Knox's crossbreed position as 'a stable boy among gentlemen, and a gentleman among stable boys'.[103] His 'shifting position about midway in the tribe' of the Knox family is emblematised by the variations on his name, segueing with ease from Mr Florence McCarthy Knox to Flurry Knox, depending on the local situation: '[h]e belonged to a clan that cropped up in every grade of society in the county, from Sir Valentine Knox of Castle Knox down to the auctioneer Knox, who bore the attractive title of Larry the Liar' (7). He was as likely to be met 'at dinner at Sir Valentine's' as he was to be heard of 'at an illicit auction, held by Larry the Liar, of brandy stolen from a wreck' (7). On taking up his residency as Knox's tenant at Shreelane, Major Yeates (the R.M. of the series' title) admits that he is 'a believer in ghosts' and even takes in 'a paper that deals with their culture' (10). He looks forward to the 'prospect of writing a monograph on Great-Uncle McCarthy for a Spiritualistic Journal', believing early on in the story that the whisperings and rappings he hears late at night in Shreelane are the ghostly perambulations of the deceased and senile old McCarthy (25–6). By the end of the tale, however, the nocturnal rumblings that Yeates has been forced to listen to turn out to be none other than those of Knox's 'disreputable relations' (25), the McCarthy Gannons. The largely disowned family members have been illicitly roosting in unrestrained squalor in the attic rooms of Shreelane, living off jackdaws, rabbits and Yeates' whiskey, while profiteering from the sale of Shreelane's foxes in Yeates' name and destroying the local hunt in the process. As the colourful (and complicit) housekeeper, Mrs Cadogan, neatly puts it of the Gannons' living conditions: '[a] Turk couldn't stand it' (26).

Once again, the familial Protestant 'ghosts' of Shreelane remind the living of their increasingly threatened and marginalised position but, unlike the Somerville-Coghill guardians who represent a united and privileged Protestant force against external threats to their homes and traditions, the McCarthy Gannons of Shreelane's attics are a repellent and frightening *aide-memoire* of how far the elite can, and indeed have, fallen by their own hand. Yeates notes that Mrs McCarthy Gannon had an 'unspeakably vulgar voice, yet it was not the voice of a countrywoman, and there were frowzy remnants of respectability about her general aspect' (24). The McCarthy Gannons also turn out to be a concrete reality, opposed to mere familial hauntings, which the now 'uncomfortable' Knox cannot escape (24). Somerville and Ross are perhaps, then, even more deserving of a place in Foster's essay than he seems to realise. Their particular brand of 'Protestant magic', however, goes even beyond the theorising of the essay as the dislocations and sense of displacement that Somerville suffers after Ross' death prove to be of an explicit twofold nature. While the political instability of Anglo-Ireland certainly haunts and contributes to Somerville's lost sense of social and psychological assimilation, so also does the loss of Ross on a much more personal and professional level. The lost sense of self that Somerville suffers after Ross' death parallels the socio-political fragmentation of Protestant Ireland, and her occult activities thus have a twin purpose. Somerville's heightened awareness of a shared sense of self and consciousness with Ross after her partner's death is something that Stevens argues is a preoccupation of the writing couple even before Ross' death. Her study of Somerville and Ross' short fiction and the modern ghost story in Ireland clearly demonstrates that the duo's interest in spiritualism is reflected in their writing and 'directs itself as much at the workings of consciousness and altered states of awareness as it does at revealing the supernatural'.[104]

The mutual affirmation of self that characterises Somerville and Ross' living friendship, as well as sustains an adaptive and developing intellectual and personal identity, is one which is nurtured both physically and textually. The geographical distances that frequently separated the two collaborators during their joint working lives forced significant reliance on textual communication as a space within which to nurture the two women's authorial and intimate ambitions. The spiritual and psychic distance which Ross' death created in 1915, however, is not entirely unlike the living separation and such modes of intimate interaction exist as both experiential and linguistic relations for both the living and spiritual friendship of Somerville and Ross. Gerhardt Richter argues that in times of separation 'we interact not with the empirical friend, but with his image, posing questions to his image and reconfiguring it on the basis of our imagined response'.[105] The resulting disparity between the actual friend and his image thus causes the referentiality of the image to become unstable and, concludes Richter, the friend haunts us in the moment that opens up between the friend and his image: 'we interact with him as though with a spectre, a ghost that returns to us the unfinished relation with the other'.[106] Somerville's spirit relationship with Ross takes to a literal extreme the hauntings of lived friendship whereby the temporary reconfiguring of the friend's image in their absence takes on permanent proportions. Just as Somerville's occult guardians exist to preserve her sense of political selfhood with regard to her threatened Anglo-Irish heritage, her ongoing spirit communications with Ross serve to heal the severed sense of self that Somerville endures with Ross' death by protracting the women's friendship (and the politicised intellectual activities which are part of that friendship) beyond Ross' lifetime.

The intellectual tenor of this spirit friendship is early set out when Somerville questions Ross on the viability of cross-border collaboration with the dead through the medium of automatic writing. In a trance séance with Ross in 1937, Somerville exclaims that, 'I shouldn't know which were my own thoughts and which yours,' to which the spirit of Ross replies, '[t]hat would not matter.'[107] Ross' prophetic foreshadowing of Foucault's conclusion to 'What is an Author?' ('What matter who's speaking') establishes the ideological parameters of her and Somerville's esoteric authorship as akin to those that governed their living collaboration. In death, as in life, the duo's joint authorship will defy the norms of the singular author figure, demonstrating a dispersal of authority rendering Somerville and Ross as the function of their own texts, opposed to a central signified origin. Stevens suggests that Somerville and Ross' preoccupation with the 'shifting nature of identity' derives from their modernist comic sensibilities, but it is also clear here that their collaborative practice has a strong bearing on how they question and understand 'the workings of consciousness'.[108] The hallmarks of authorial dissidence that have already been shown to individuate Somerville and Ross' collaboration from the conventions of nineteenth-century models of authorship and literary ownership thus continue to imprint themselves on the mystic working processes of the two women's continued collaboration beyond the grave. Moreover, the ideologies of their pluralised authorship in life go some way towards normalising the technicalities of their joint authorship in the light of Ross' death, and this is played out in practice by Somerville's attempts (post-Ross) to keep intact the collaborative methodologies of their corporeal authorship.

Somerville's favoured style of spirit communication with Ross largely took the form of automatic writing, an occult technique developed by Somerville in a way that appreciably mimics and adopts strategies similar to their actual literary collaboration, as well as providing a space in which the friendship can advance and continue. The letters Somerville and Ross wrote to each other during their live careers, as well as the manuscript texts on which they jointly worked and the conversations in which they partook, formed the crux of the textual and oral narrative of their real-life collaboration. It is this living narrative that arguably makes possible Somerville's psychical manifestation of her later spiritual conversations with Ross, her occult technique modelling itself on an already successful method of living communication and thus establishing an out of the ordinary parallel process. In her unpublished essay on her and Ross' spirit communication, written *c*.1940, Somerville writes that: 'Martin Ross and I had learnt the art of corresponding with one another by "automatic writing", almost as easily as in the old way.'[109] She further frames her spiritual correspondence with Ross within an explicit epistolary context, equating their daily occult interactions with letters received from abroad: '[t]hey almost began to feel as normal and natural as the "foreign letters" from far countries that we might hope for, once a week perhaps, from distant kinsfolk. But my letters from Martin Ross came every night.'[110]

In the same essay, this naturalisation of an otherwise implausible feat of communication is additionally authenticated by analogous recourse to the advances in telecommunications to which Somerville bore witness in her more earthly twentieth-century world. Somerville recounts Ross' spirit complaint that '"getting through" to us here was as exasperating as trying to deliver a message through a refractory telephone' and, in so doing, conflates the radical dismantling of traditional authorship that the living collaboration enacted, with the esoteric methodologies of her spirit communications with Ross.[111] It is worth reiterating Stevens' point here that interest in spiritualism and 'second sight' within Anglo-Irish communities coincided with other 'visually centred activities', many of them involving new technologies, such as photography and stereoscopic viewing.[112] It was Somerville's uncle, Joscelyn, notes Stevens, who 'introduced photography into County Cork in the 1850s'.[113]

Inventions such as the telephone and telegraph had already extended the boundaries of what was humanly possible in the late nineteenth century, and such technologies had a profound effect on the ways in which the limits of human communication were understood. The debates of prominent psychical researchers in the late nineteenth century, argues Thurschwell, contributed to wider reconceptualisations of the 'borders of individual consciousness', and the technological advances and economic changes of the period further interlinked with occult developments to exacerbate the anxieties surrounding the measurable limits of individual human knowledge.[114] Daniel Pick additionally argues that mesmerism, hypnotism, thought transference, somnambulism and telepathy were all 'examples of a wider set of challenges to the notion of the commanding, single, fully-conscious self' in this period, and incredulity at scientific advances in telecommunications were on a par with the astonishment and curiosity felt at psychical interaction.[115] Through the lens of such historical contexts, then, Somerville's essay can be read as a conscious framing of her occult activities within an increased awareness of technology's known ability to compress time and distance, which lends some scientific credence to her spirit collaboration. It can also be simultaneously understood through her and Ross' celebrated breakdown of the 'commanding' singular author, which her living authorship with Ross had already ratified and was now arguably part of a wider discourse on the recognised social and plural constitution of the self, or what Roger MacFarlane has called a new-found sense of the 'interanimation of minds'.[116]

In her study of ghost writing and modernism, Sword has argued that 'mediumship has always been closely allied with authorship' and, like the pseudonymous (or ghost-)writer, the spirit medium erodes the barriers of individual consciousness by purporting to speak with the mind of another.[117] One of the most common features of spirit mediumship is the medium's repeated disclaimer of responsibility for the end product, whether this is an oral trance message or a text written via automatic writing. Moore writes that the success of spirit communication depends on the medium's ability to 'give up their own identity to become the instruments of others'.[118] Somerville certainly seems to initially adhere to this characterisation of the spirit medium's practice in her deference to Ross' role in their occult communications: 'this was her enterprise, not mine'.[119] Somerville further explains that she is merely 'yielding to the determination of my Collaborator', and that the early frustrating days of attempting to communicate via automatic writing left her to be 'the helpless accessory of a brilliant intellect handicapped by the mysterious limitations of this correspondence'.[120] Unlike other disempowered female mediums, however, whose temporary gains over patriarchal strictures are devalued by their submissive obeisance to higher oratorical powers, Somerville's spirit communication with Ross is not a giving up of individual identity, but the formation of a joint literary alliance. By straddling the divide between passive medium and creative author, Somerville was, in several respects, reliving the oscillating parts of reflexive recipient and proactive writer in her living correspondence with Ross. Within this carefully constructed and symbolic authentication of her continuing dual authorship, Somerville reproduced endless pages of automatically written scripts, often alone and yet frequently with the aid of other mediums, notably Barlow and Cummins. In so doing, Somerville generated the kinds of epistolary and rhetorical texts that could and did replace the now suspended physical letters and conversations since Ross' death. The dual signature, which always accompanied the publications that derived from this spirit collaboration, is further suggestive of the levels of responsibility Somerville duly felt towards her and Ross' joint artistic work.

The peculiarities of Somerville's continuing collaboration with the dead Ross, as revealed in the séance transcripts, are thus less outlandish than at first appears. In these transcripts, the spirit voice of Ross is often tutoring Somerville in the ways of psychic interanimation:

> Let the idea of it germinate in your mind, don't hurry over it, you might say aloud to yourself "<u>I am writing a series of stories – or a story with Martin, that will be like those we wrote together long ago</u>". If you say this aloud quite passively <u>before</u> you fall asleep, the message goes to your deeper mind & it begins to carry out the order, & it will open the door to me, & we will fabricate the stories together.[121]

The other female mediums in Somerville's midst also often corroborated Somerville's belief in the authenticity of her ongoing spiritual collaboration. In 1931, Cummins claimed that her spirit control, Astor, spoke to her of Somerville and Ross' occult collaboration and the intermingling of the two women's minds:

> The woman with the white soul is here. I open the door to her. It is strange to me to watch her inner mind making one with the living woman's mind. Their thoughts are like coloured mist, & they achieve the impossible – They blend and make one. I have never seen this before.[122]

The social and technological realities of Somerville's life without Ross are thus ever present in their ongoing collaboration, regularly surfacing in Somerville's subconscious fabrication of an ongoing dialogue with her dead writing partner.

Often stationed apart during their live collaboration, Somerville further drew on her past lifetime of lived plural authorship with Ross to endorse and enable her occult narratives. The two authors were well used to conducting their joint literary projects via personal letters and the postal exchange of draft manuscripts, and this allowed for a somewhat smooth transition from actual letters to spirit communications. Transcripts of Somerville's automatic writing during séances with the dead Ross are seen to provide ideas, plots and characters for new novels in much the same way as did the letters and conversations during Ross' lifetime. Somerville's novel, *Sarah's Youth* (1938), for example, was probably inspired by a séance carried out by Somerville and Cummins in September 1933 in the Drishane studio, when the spirit of Ross suggests to Somerville a 'book in three periods' which concerns the 'life of a woman who lived as you have lived'.[123] As the novel takes shape, séance transcripts in 1937 reveal Ross' continuing input to the manuscript:

I feel your instinct is the right one – Keep the treatment light and don't let any tragedy, such as an unfortunate marriage, for Sarah, come into it. I feel however that you might make a little more of Sarah's father and Richard. Remember that Sarah will have a reaction when she realises that Tim does not care.[124]

Somerville also continued to use archived personal material produced while Ross was alive to continue with their writing, a technique that Chapter 3 has already demonstrated they both used during the actual collaboration, mining their personal letters and literary notebooks for retold stories, tales, superstitions and speech patterns, which they had collected from the local populaces of Cork and Galway. It was, for example, a letter written from the living Ross to Somerville in 1912 concerning the inhabitants of Tyrone House that prompted and produced Somerville's most noteworthy novel after Ross' death, *The Big House of Inver*, in 1925.[125] Robinson's detailed analysis of this novel, alongside an earlier one, *Mount Music* (1919), discloses the extent to which Somerville continued to crib speech and incorporate tales from the notebooks and letters into her post-Ross fiction.[126] Somerville also believed Ross to be carrying on with this literary practice on the Other Side, executing a parallel occult process by 'digging in old memories' for literary inspiration, of which the latter would then 'plant the seed' in Somerville's mind.[127] Finally, the séances also yielded practical advice on what publishers to approach for the novels on which they were collaborating, in much the same way as they had debated such corporeal issues during Ross' lifetime through their letters.[128]

Despite these attempts at maintaining the methodologies of the living collaboration, however, many of Somerville's occult narratives clearly lack the spontaneous creative moments of the living correspondence and their aesthetically minded narratives, as well as the intense levels of preparation of ideas that, for example, went into Ross' letters about the drowning at Pouleen-a-Fearla discussed in Chapter 3. Nonetheless, there are some attempts to make up for the limits of the occult communication and Lewis argues that, in lieu of the kind of detailed textual literary debate witnessed in the living correspondence, Somerville repeatedly 'rehearsed' her literary themes in letters to Hildegarde during the composition of *The Big House of Inver*.[129] Indeed, letter-writing retained its significance to Somerville even after Ross' death and her epistolary output to her remaining female companions was as prolific as ever, substituting perhaps at least a small part of the creative space she had found with Ross in their close correspondence. Somerville's letters to her friend Smyth during the early 1920s, for example, could also constitute a rehearsal of ideas for *An Enthusiast* (1921). Despite the censoriousness of their tone, many of these letters rage and debate the local and national positions of her fellow countrymen and -women, foreshadowing the political heat of her novel. During this period, Somerville also sustained the utility of the literary notebooks compiled during Ross' lifetime by adding to these same working notebooks the local grievances of those in Castletownshend, and the tales told to her of the troubling events in the environs beyond Drishane.

Equally at a discount to the live collaboration are the spirited arguments that formed such a crucial element of Somerville and Ross' creative process and overall intellectual and emotional bond. In 1939, Somerville's subconscious hankering after this vital dynamic is expressed in the spirit words of Ross, which acknowledge the inability to partake in argument via Somerville's mediumship, and lament 'I want to argue with you.'[130] Without this fundamental aspect of the two women's partnership, both the working and personal facets of the collaboration suffer a certain calcification and this, in part, is recognised in the texts that Somerville produces after Ross' death. Very few of Somerville's post-Ross writings reach the same levels of aesthetic merit as the ones produced through their living collaboration and, yet, this is not to dismiss Somerville as the inferior surviving partner, but to further substantiate what both women understood during their respective life spans – that it was the combination of their talents which made for the creative brilliance of their work. Even during Ross' lifetime, Somerville expressed this knowledge to Cameron when she wrote in 1895 that writing was something she knew she could not 'excel' at as a lone artist.[131] This need continued to be felt, and reciprocated, after Ross' death, and the words '[i]t is a necessity for me to write with you' came through to Somerville in 1933 via a trance séance conducted by Cummins.[132] The message was purported to be, of course, from the deceased Ross.

Such 'necessity' redraws the critical lines of inquiry which have thus far governed Somerville's occult activities with Ross by situating such procedures outside the claims of personal grief and nostalgic longing. This chapter has attempted to demonstrate that Somerville's ongoing collaboration with Ross is believed by Somerville to be a personal but also crucially professional necessity for both women, and the mechanisms of that collaboration remain largely unchanged (if admittedly esoterically adapted) even after Ross' death. Somerville's youthful interest in the occult thus prepared her for an unprecedented task on the premature death of her writing partner as she attempted to reproduce and give life to their literary partnership in Ross' physical absence, and the technicalities of the lived partnership also contributed to her professional ambitions. Even long after Ross' death, the séances Somerville continued to conduct with her literary partner encourage their work together, increasingly with the promise of an everlasting artistic and familial bond and a life of 'immortality together'.[133] To dismiss Somerville and Ross' epistolary and automatic writing from their creative equation is to dismiss the intertextual layers of both their collaborative methodology and their texts. This chapter has delineated a fully contextualised narrative of Somerville's occult collaboration with Ross in order to extend our critical understanding of literary collaboration more generally, and complete the historical account of Somerville and Ross' joint authorship with which this book began.

Afterword

In 2003, Catriona Crowe retrospectively described the publication of *The Field Day Anthology of Irish Writing* as 'one of the most intensely anticipated literary events in Ireland in many years'.[1] The (original) three-volume anthology was launched in October 1991 in Newman House, the site of Ireland's first Catholic University, by Seamus Deane, Seamus Heaney, Brian Friel, and the then taoiseach, Charles Haughey. During the launch, Haughey hailed *The Field Day Anthology* as 'one of the most important events of our era', and journalist Fintan O'Toole later commented that the four men 'seemed for a moment like a cultural cabinet, like people who run a country in their imagination'.[2] The anthology was also heavily promoted in the US as 'a landmark event in twentieth-century literature' and 'the most comprehensive exhibition of the wealth and diversity of Irish literature ever published'.[3] Canon-making in Ireland is a big deal. Moreover, as Julia McElhatton Williams notes, the Field Day volumes exposed the 'ideological nature of the literary canon', and represented 'the meta-narrative of anthology-making'.[4]

Like the contemporary Irish poet, Eavan Boland, who was included in these first three Field Day volumes, Somerville and Ross may well have felt 'sorry to be included in an anthology that excludes women'.[5] Despite its high-flying beginnings, the original anthology is perhaps now more widely remembered for the furore that erupted shortly after its publication. The objections to those earlier volumes were vociferous and manifold, but they also distinctly coalesced around two interlaced key issues: the perceived Northern and unreconstructed nationalist bias of the anthology, and the paucity of women writers and women's texts contained therein. The latter feminist critique proved hard to deny or to challenge, and so began the long process of what literary critic, Edna Longley, dismissed early on as a 'damage-limitation exercise'.[6] Arguably, once published, the final two volumes (four and five), which appeared in 2002, 'Irish Women's Writing and Traditions', transpired to represent far more than a workout in either compensating the injured parties or controlling the angry fallout. As its all-female editorial team argued in the preface to the two concluding volumes, far from an addendum or an extension of an existing canon, these volumes sought to both supplement and 'interrogate' the 1991 Field Day publication, as well as empower Irish women to 'know about their history, culture and traditions' by offering a 'sample of texts which are historically interesting, aesthetically accomplished, and politically indispensable'.[7]

Somerville and Ross were included in both sets of volumes, though in radically different guises, and, as with their relationship with Victorian authorship, the duo sit uncomfortably with the foundational values of national canon-formation in Ireland. This book has demonstrated the ways in which Somerville and Ross' dual authorship was legally and aesthetically devalued in a cultural climate that valorised a particular type of author (male, singular and originary), but it has also significantly shown how this devaluation was compounded by the authors' gender and the popular and comic genres of writing in which they engaged. In so doing, it also makes an important point about the way in which Somerville and Ross are currently positioned in the Irish canon. Julie Anne Stevens argues that the privileging of the writers' social and sexual significance within literary studies has closed off potentially diverse critical avenues and confines the duo's output to two somewhat limited 'central discourses': 'first, a feminist/sexual argument, and second, the Anglo-Irish tradition of country-house writing'.[8] It is these privileged discourses that this book has sought to widen and it is clear that it is these same discourses that frame Somerville and Ross' canonicity.

More than just sharing Boland's dismay at her inclusion in a sorely gender-biased anthology, Somerville and Ross would probably also have strongly lamented the inclusion of extracts from *The Real Charlotte* in volume two of the Field Day anthology, where the novel is represented as an over-simplified and prosaic illustration of Anglo-Irish Big House class and character, as well as an unimaginative demonstration of Protestant Ascendancy superciliousness. This over-familiar critical rhetoric sidelines the novel's modernity and largely ignores altogether its composite gender concerns, reducing it to an example of an already too-easily dismissed tradition of women's 'Big House' writing. Augustine Martin writes in the anthology that: '[i]t is strange that the novel's modernity and strong moral realism should admit such a contemptuous tone towards the "natives" ... *The Real Charlotte* is perhaps most significant in being the last unselfconscious novel of this "Big House" tradition.'[9] Since their Field Day debut, Somerville and Ross have been utilised by other somewhat grandiose (and male) canon-making publications, such as Declan Kiberd's *Inventing Ireland: the literature of the modern nation* (1995). Despite its nationalist and post-colonial outlook, Kiberd recruits the female duo and *The*

Real Charlotte on rather dissimilar grounds to Field Day, and reclaims both for the modern Irish nation by artfully (and with some partiality) foregrounding the two women's nationalist sympathies and, in particular, their antipathy towards the English.[10] A similar tactical manoeuvre is arguably used to include Somerville and Ross' *The Silver Fox* (1897) in Kiberd's follow-up to *Inventing Ireland* in 2000, *Irish Classics*.[11]

Within these contexts and critical scenarios, and whether being berated for their condescension to the Irish Catholic peasantry or welcomed back into the Irish fold for their antagonism towards all things Anglo-Saxon, Somerville and Ross are (in these various volumes) only of interest for what they can tell us about Ireland's difficult colonial relations with England in the nineteenth century. They become objects in a larger cultural political game, and are denied a more complex authorial subjectivity. In his review of the first set of Field Day volumes, and more general interrogation of Irish canon-formation, Roy Foster makes a connection between the anthology's politics, particularly its definition of who is (and who is not) Irish, and its exclusion/inclusion of women writers. Foster points out the under-representation of, for example, Elizabeth Bowen, and argues that there is some 'indication of a deliberate decision to cut down on "Anglo-Irish" literature', especially Anglo-Irish literature which the editors seem to have 'firmly tagged as British' and which doesn't 'specifically deal with Irish themes'.[12] Foster goes on to note a similar problem with the absence of writers such as Molly Keane, and the very few pages devoted to Somerville and Ross. '[A] suspicion begins to arise,' argues Foster, that 'these particular figures [have] been banished, not so much for their wrong gender, as because they speak with the wrong accent'.[13]

Somerville and Ross' relegation to the social and historical framework of the Anglo-Irish Big House literary tradition is, thus, a politicised one and *The Real Charlotte* is reduced to a mere personalised historical document. Moreover, the two writers are pigeon-holed within nationalist canon-building in Ireland for their seeming capacity to illustrate and serve specific nationalist and/or post-colonial narratives and political agendas. This oversimplified presentation of Somerville and Ross and their works ignores the much more intricate and gender-influenced political outlook of the two authors and their writing. Such a perspective also unhelpfully conflates texts and characters with the assumed personal opinions of their creators. This, by itself, seems to do the authors a grave disservice, but given the complex dynamics of Somerville and Ross' collaborative modes of writing and composition that this book demonstrates, this critical attitude appears increasingly out of place and enormously reductive.

Volumes four and five of the Field Day anthology broaden this critical perception of Somerville and Ross and consciously attempt to respond to, and cross-examine, the two women's position in the earlier volumes. Gerardine Meaney points out in her introduction to women's writing between 1890 and 1960 in volume five that, alongside Elizabeth Bowen, Kate O'Brien and Mary Lavin, Somerville and Ross are indeed considered one of the key female 'canonical writers of this period'.[14] In terms of the prior inclusion of brief extracts from *The Real Charlotte* in the earlier volumes, Somerville and Ross are more fully included in Emma Donoghue's section in volume four on 'Lesbian Encounters' as part of Donoghue's attempt to showcase writing which is 'lesbian in content, not necessarily in authorship': 'I have prioritized women writers whose lives revolved around attachments to women ... as well as those women writing today who are "out" as lesbians or bi-sexual, because writers in both groups have an insider's perspective on love between women, and because their work has often gone unread or misread.'[15] Donoghue chooses to include an extract from Somerville's memoir, *Irish Memories*.[16]

This is a significant recontextualisation of the two authors in the light of their earlier appearance in volume two. As Siobhán Kilfeather points out in her review of the original volumes, sexuality is ignored as a 'vexatious political issue in Irish history' and 'sexual identities are occluded'.[17] In addition, Kilfeather argues, the major sex scandals involving Charles Parnell, Oscar Wilde and Roger Casement 'are all treated as if they took their meaning primarily in a context of British repression and misrepresentation'.[18] Foster makes a similar point by noting the 'missing link' in the volumes of an 'Irish feminist critique': 'there is no sexual politics (and practically no sex)'.[19] The sexual contexts of Somerville and Ross' partnership are thus rescued in volume four from the limiting colonial framework of the earlier volumes, but both sets of volumes still frame Somerville and Ross within the social and sexual discourses that Stevens points out have become so central and so limiting to studies of the writing couple.

This book has attempted to open up these discourses and demonstrate how central Somerville and Ross' collaboration is to any understanding of their writing, but it has also predominantly relied on texts and sources, most of which are difficult to categorise within canonical forms of literature. Somerville and Ross' authorship defies centralised and singular modes of literary authority, as well as concepts of literary greatness or genius, and this further disrupts how well they can be accommodated in canonical literary projects. As Chapter 1 of this book points out, even within the covers of Kiberd's *Inventing Ireland*, the accommodation of Somerville and Ross' partnership is uneasy. The writing duo are seen to pale in comparison to the steely individualism of a writer like Jane Austen. Interestingly, it is perhaps in the feminist methodology of Field Day's final volumes, rather than in its pages, that a more accommodating type of thinking can be found.

Seamus Deane, the single general editor of the first set of Field Day volumes, described (as a looker-on) the editorial structure and methodologies of the follow-on Field Day volumes as 'democratic', committee-based, and ultimately 'nightmarish', as well as in clear opposition to the 'more authoritarian' methods he had employed with the earlier volumes.[20] This 'freedom' given to section editors was a point of disgruntlement for some readers, and Eileen Battersby's review of the volumes for *The Irish Times* in 2002 lamented the loss of a 'central editor presence' and the necessary cohesiveness that Deane had given to the earlier volumes.[21] There was an 'immense sense of disappointment' that publicly surrounded the final volumes on publication, particularly in the mainstream Irish press, and much of this discontent seems to have been due to the (arguably) impossible expectations that had been placed on them, as well as an unfair comparison between the structure and historical emphasis of the earlier and later volumes.[22] As with all anthologies, there were also the inevitable accusations of partiality in terms of textual choices, as well as debate over what was *not* included. Many of these criticisms and ongoing reflections over the volumes' significance continue to coalesce around the structure and editorial methodologies employed on the project. Even while defending the volumes against much of this mainstream criticism, for example, Rebecca Pelan still cites as problematic the loss of a centralised 'general editor to oversee the project'.[23]

Meaney has since defended the volumes from this recurring charge and argues that the collaborative and multidisciplinary nature of the project resulted in a much more diverse and complex picture of women's history and creative output than might otherwise have been the case. Due to their structure, and the editorial attitudes and processes that made them possible, the final volumes have also, Meaney contends, been able to avoid any 'claim to totality or truth' and have, instead, opened up new 'conceptual spaces and dialogue'.[24] There was, claims Meaney, for her and the other general editors, always 'one constant' in the editorial process: '[t]he multiplicity of sources and voices and texts and editors can be understood ... as the mark of a narrative in process, the refusal to construct one story which will make sense – finally – of woman's relation to Irishness and the alternative proposal of a point of dialogue with the past for future use.'[25]

If there is a 'point of dialogue' between the final Field Day volumes and Somerville and Ross, as well as a staunch challenge to the canon-making processes of the earlier volumes, it is here in this 'multiplicity of sources and voices and texts'. Somerville and Ross' authorship was, in many ways, a 'narrative in process', defined by its ceaseless exchange of dialogue that took place both in conversation and through writing. It challenged authoritarian ways of thinking about authorship, literary property and literary genius, and opened up new avenues for the writers in debating the social, gender and national politics of their home country. As the closing words of this book have attempted to demonstrate, Somerville and Ross's authorship finally continues to have an impact through its challenge to how we currently value literature and the aesthetic and political hierarchies that govern national canon-formation in Ireland.

Notes

Introduction

1. T. S. Eliot, 'Phillip Massinger', in *Elizabethan Essays* (New York: Haskell House, 1964), p. 154.
2. Roland Barthes, 'The Death of the Author', in Stephen Heath (ed. and trans.), *Image, Music, Text* (London: Fontana, 1977), p. 115.
3. Somerville and Ross have increasingly been acknowledged in recent contemporary criticism as key figures in the study of women's literary partnerships in the nineteenth century. See, in particular, Lorraine York, *Rethinking Women's Collaborative Writing* (Toronto: University of Toronto Press, 2002).
4. Edith Somerville, *Irish Memories* (London: Longmans, 1917), p. 129.
5. Martin Ross, letter to Edith Somerville, 18 May 1889, in Gifford Lewis (ed.), *The Selected Letters of Somerville and Ross* (London: Faber & Faber, 1989), p. 135.
6. 'Though the Earth, and all inferior Creatures be common to all Men, yet every Man has a *Property* in his own *Person*. This no Body has any Right to but himself. The *Labour* of his Body, and the *Work* of his Hands, we may say, are properly his. Whatsoever then he removes out of the State that Nature hath provided, and left it in, he hath mixed his *Labour* with, and joyned to it something that is his own, and thereby makes it his *Property* [emphasis in original].' John Locke, 'The Second Treatise of Government: an essay concerning the true original, extent, and end of civil government', in Peter Laslett (ed.), *Two Treatises on Government* (Cambridge: Cambridge University Press, 1988), pp. 287–8.
7. Walter Besant, *The Pen and the Book* (London: Thomas Burleigh, 1899), p. 59.
8. Besant, 'On Literary Collaboration', *The New Review*, vol. 6, no. 33, 1892, pp. 203–4. The American author and literary critic Brander Matthews also offers a similar opinion in 'The Art and Mystery of Collaboration', *Longman's Magazine*, vol. 15, 1890, pp. 157–70.
9. Martha Woodmansee, 'The Genius and the Copyright: Economic and Legal Conditions of the Emergence of the "Author"', *Eighteenth-Century Studies*, vol. 17, no. 4, 1984, p. 427. Also see William Duff, *An Essay on Original Genius* (London: E. & C. Dilly, 1767); and Edward Young, *Conjectures on Original Composition: in a letter to the author of Sir Charles Grandison* (London: R. & J. Dodsley, 1759).
10. Woodmansee, p. 427. Also see Mark Rose, 'The Author as Proprietor: *Donaldson v. Becket* and the Genealogy of Modern Authorship', *Representations*, no. 23, 1988, pp. 51–85; and Peter Jaszi, 'On the Author Effect: contemporary copyright and collective creativity', in Martha Woodmansee and Peter Jaszi (eds), *The Construction of Authorship: textual appropriation in law and literature* (London: Duke University Press, 1994), pp. 29–56.
11. The revised Copyright Act of 1842 was largely driven by English judge, author and MP, Sir Thomas Noon Talfourd, and was publicly supported by a wealth of high-profile poets and novelists. Despite the overt pecuniary gloss to the revised act, it has been recognised that Talfourd's vision of copyright 'as a recognition of cultural worth' was coded into the new parliamentary bill by demanding that the term of copyright extend to the life of the

author plus a sixty-year period after the author's death. Talfourd and his proponents eventually had to concede to a term of forty-two years, or the life of the author plus seven years, but Catherine Seville argues that it was, in particular, the fact of the post-mortem term that held the most significance for Talfourd: 'Talfourd regarded the term as primarily something of symbolic importance, and not as a parameter to be determined by economic argument … Talfourd had seen the life plus sixty year term as a fundamental clause which expressed the concentrated weight of all the moral arguments for protecting authors' works.' *Literary Copyright Reform in Early Victorian England: the framing of the 1842 Copyright Act* (Cambridge: Cambridge University Press, 1999), pp. 5–6, 19. The convention that first met in Berne, Switzerland, in 1883 was an attempt to extend this (and other countries') domestic copyright across international boundaries by founding a global union for the protection of literary and artistic work. It was conceived of and organised by the International Literary and Artistic Association, which the French novelist Victor Hugo helped to establish. As B. Zorina Kahn notes: 'perhaps the most significant aspect of the convention was not its specific provisions, but the underlying property rights philosophy which was decidedly from [the] natural rights school. Berne abolished compliance with formalities as a prerequisite for copyright protection since the "creative act" itself was regarded as the source of the property right.' *The Democratization of Invention: patents and copyrights in American economic development, 1790–1920* (Cambridge: Cambridge University Press, 2005), p. 302. Both domestic and international copyright laws in the nineteenth century thus quite explicitly seal the moral rights of authors, the latter of which rely on a Romantic and singular definition of the author figure.

12. Terry Eagleton, *The Ideology of the Aesthetic* (Oxford: Basil Blackwell, 1990), pp. 64–5. It is also worth noting that Dickens' earlier attempts to found a society of authors with Thackeray and Carlyle in 1843, as well as his sponsorship and direction of Forster and Bulwer Lytton's Guild of Literature and Art in 1850, were less triumphant but nonetheless ideologically similar enterprises to the Society of Authors. The guild, for example, promoted 'a plan of collective patronage to disassociate writers from the market place', as well as secure their financial positions. See Margaret Shaw, 'Constructing the "Literate Woman": nineteenth-century reviews and emerging literacies', in Michael Timko, Fred Kaplan and Edward Guiliano (eds), *Dickens Studies Annual: essays on Victorian fiction*, vol. 21 (New York: AMS Press, 1992), p. 197. The Society of Authors thus represented the first successful institution of its type, but was nonetheless founded on a much-longer-suffering grievance of which its failed predecessors are indicative.

13. The Society of Authors became the main facilitator for the formal professionalisation of authorship in the late nineteenth century and assisted the growing acknowledgement of writing practice as a vocation which required the same kind of legal and business support as other professional occupations. By the beginning of the twentieth century it operated as a fully recognised and representative voice for authors, battling and negotiating with publishers on behalf of its members on issues largely concerned with copyright, royalty agreements and contract-making. The society thus publicly sealed the notion of literary property, and its key founder has since been credited with the instigation and maintenance of the significant ideological breakthrough that emerged between author and publisher as a consequence of this conception of literary property: '[Besant's] main achievement was probably establishing for all time the principle that the author has control over his or her product, as a partner, or shareholder, with the publisher, not a hireling.' Robert Colby, 'Authorship and the Book Trade', in J. Don Vann and Rosemary T. VanArsdel (eds), *Victorian Periodicals and Victorian Society* (Aldershot: Scholar Press, 1994), p. 147. Other institutions and publications were quickly founded to rally around the Society of Authors. Periodicals such as the *Literary Yearbook* published directories of publishers and

magazines, and provided practical information for all different types of writer. This rising professionalism in the literary establishment also influenced the commercial outlets they utilised, and the naissance of the Publishers Association and Booksellers Association were arguably in reaction to the new pressures placed upon them by the Society of Authors and the state's improved copyright regulations for authors.

14. See Linda H. Peterson, *Becoming a Woman of Letters: myths of authorship and facts of the Victorian market place* (Princeton: Princeton University Press, 2009), p. 208.

15. Myriam Boucharenc, 'Plural Authorship in Automatic Writing', in Paul Gifford and Johnnie Gratton (eds), *Subject Matters: subject and self in French literature from Descartes to the present* (Amsterdam: Rodopi, 2000), p. 100.

16. Woodmansee and Jaszi, 'Introduction', in Woodmansee and Jaszi (eds), p. 11. Copyright law does encompass joint authorship of literary and artistic commodities, but as Margaret Chon points out, the definitions of joint authorship are 'influenced by the cult of the Romantic author' and do not recognise the 'morphability, flexibility and fluidity' of a true collective enterprise. 'New Wine Bursting from Old Bottles: collaborative internet art, joint works, and entrepreneurship', *Oregon Law Review*, vol. 75, 1996, pp. 257, 264. Peter Jaszi adds that copyright 'refuses to acknowledge the existence of joint authorship, or does so grudgingly'. 'Towards a Theory of Copyright: the metamorphoses of "authorship"', *Duke Law Journal*, vol. 455, 1991, p. 51.

17. Bette London, *Writing Double: women's literary partnerships* (Ithaca: Cornell University Press, 1999), p. 9.

18. See in particular Maurice Collis, *Somerville and Ross: a biography* (London: Faber, 1968), and Gifford Lewis, *Somerville and Ross and the World of the Irish R.M.* (New York: Viking, 1985). Even more recent analyses, such as Jill R. Ehnenn's *Women's Literary Collaboration, Queerness, and Late-Victorian Culture* (Aldershot: Ashgate, 2008), which attempt to explore the sexual dynamics of literary collaboration within much more diverse and material-based contexts, still seem to privilege (indeed construct) the sexual over the textual manifestations of Somerville and Ross' partnership.

19. Janice Raymond, *A Passion for Friends: towards a philosophy of female affection* (Boston: Beacon Press, 1986), p. 15.

20. Marilyn Friedman, *What Are Friends For? Feminist perspectives on personal relationships and moral theory* (New York: Cornell University Press, 1993), p. 248.

21. Peterson, p. 5; see also Catherine Gallagher, *Nobody's Story: the vanishing acts of women writers in the marketplace, 1670–1820* (Princeton: Princeton University Press, 1994); Betty A. Schellenburg, *The Professionalization of Women Writers in Eighteenth-Century Britain* (Cambridge: Cambridge University Press, 2005); and Gaye Tuchman with Nina E. Fortin, *Edging Women Out: Victorian novelists, publishers, and social change* (New Haven: Yale University Press, 1989).

22. See, for example, Ehnenn, York and London.

23. See, for example, Collis and Lewis.

24. York, p. 32.

1. The legality and aesthetics of Victorian authorship

1. Gilles Deleuze and Claire Parnet, *Dialogues II* (London: Continuum, 2002), p. 17.

2. Ibid.

3. Michel Foucault, 'What is an Author?', in J. V. Harari (ed.), *Textual Strategies: perspectives in poststructuralist criticism* (Ithaca: Cornell University Press, 1979), p. 141.

4. The terms of argument here are Jeffrey Masten's, who makes this same point in his study of collaboration and authorship in Renaissance drama, arguing that individual authorial

control is minimised or diffused in plural authorship, resulting in a 'dispersal of author/ ity, rather than a simple doubling of it'. *Textual Intercourse: collaboration, authorship, and sexualities in Renaissance drama* (Cambridge: Cambridge University Press, 1997), p. 19.

5. Gary Genosko, 'Introduction', in Gary Genosko (ed.), *Deleuze and Guattari: critical assessments of leading philosophers* (New York: Routledge, 2001), p. 4.

6. In discussion with Charles Stivale in 1985, Guattari admitted that his intellectual collaboration with Deleuze had often been figured as an 'unfortunate episode' in Deleuze's life and, consequently, that certain critics had simply denied his existence: 'Sometimes, one even sees references to *L'Anti-Oedipe* or *Mille plateaux* in which my name is quite simply omitted, in which I no longer exist at all.' Charles Stivale, 'Pragmatic Machinic: discussion with Félix Guattari', 1985, www.dc.peachnet.edu/~mnunes/guatarri.html, accessed 25 August 2012, n. pag.

7. Martin Ross, letter to Edith Somerville, 16 January 1895, in Gifford Lewis (ed.), *The Selected Letters of Somerville and Ross* (London: Faber & Faber, 1989), p. 209.

8. Quoted in E.Œ. Somerville and Martin Ross, *Irish Memories* (London: Longman, 1917), p. 134.

9. Quoted in Gifford Lewis, *Somerville and Ross: the world of the Irish R.M.* (Harmondsworth: Penguin, 1987), p. 110.

10. Edith Somerville, letter to Cameron Somerville, 6 January 1916, ms. L.A.938.a–c, Edith Œnone Somerville Archive, Drishane House, Co. Cork.

11. Edith Somerville, letter to Martin Ross, c. 1904, quoted in Somerville and Ross, *Irish Memories*, p. 132.

12. Edith Somerville, letter to Martin Ross, 25 April 1897, in Lewis (ed.), *The Selected Letters*, p. 243.

13. Edith Somerville, letter to Martin Ross, 25 April 1897, in Lewis (ed.), *The Selected Letters*, p. 243; and, Edith Somerville, letter to Cameron Somerville, 6 January 1916, ms. L.A.938.a–c, Edith Œnone Somerville Archive, Drishane House, County Cork.

14. Lewis, *Somerville and Ross*, p. 127; also see Maurice Collis, *Somerville and Ross: a biography* (London: Faber, 1989); and Violet Powell, *The Irish Cousins: the books and background of Somerville and Ross* (London: Heinemann, 1970).

15. Terence Brown, *The Life of W. B. Yeats: a critical biography* (Oxford: Blackwell, 1999), p. 147; and Julie Anne Stevens, 'The Irish Landscape in Somerville and Ross's Fiction and Illustrations, 1890–1915', PhD diss., Trinity College Dublin, 2000, p. 24.

16. Declan Kiberd, *Inventing Ireland: the literature of the modern nation* (London: Vintage, 1996), pp. 75–6.

17. Bette London, *Writing Double: women's literary partnerships* (New York: Cornell University Press, 1992), p. 5. Also see more generally, Holly Laird, *Women Coauthors* (Chicago: University of Illinois Press, 2000); Lorraine York, *Rethinking Women's Collaborative Writing: power, difference, property* (Toronto: Toronto University Press, 2002); and Jill Ehnenn, *Women's Literary Collaboration, Queerness, and Victorian Culture* (Aldershot: Ashgate, 2008).

18. Lorraine York, 'Crowding the Garrett: women's collaborative writing and the problematics of space', in Marjorie Stone and Judith Thompson (eds), *Literary Couplings: writing couples, collaborators, and the construction of authorship* (Madison: University of Wisconsin Press, 2006), p. 300.

19. Richard Badenhausen, *T. S. Eliot and the Art of Collaboration* (Cambridge: Cambridge University Press, 2005), p. 74.

20. Ibid.

21. Hélène Cixous, 'The Laugh of the Medusa', in Elaine Marks and Isabelle de Courtivron (eds), *New French Feminism* (Hemel Hempstead: Harvester, 1981), p. 46.

22. Paul K. Saint-Amour, *The Copywrights: intellectual property and the literary imagination* (London: Cornell University Press, 2003), p. 3; also see Catherine Seville, *The Internationalisation of Copyright Law: books, buccaneers and the black flag in the nineteenth century* (Cambridge: Cambridge University Press, 2006), p. 216.

23. See Howard B. Abrams, 'Originality and Creativity in Copyright', *Law and Contemporary Problems*, vol. 55, 1992, pp. 53–94; and Christopher May, 'Cosmopolitan Legalism Meets "Thin Community": problems in the global governance of intellectual property', *Governance and Opposition*, vol. 39, no. 3, 2004, pp. 393–422.

24. Brad Sherman and Lionel Bently, *The Making of Modern Intellectual Property Law: the British experience, 1760–1911* (Cambridge: Cambridge University Press, 1999), pp. 11–14.

25. For a more detailed history of these developments see the following: Ronan Deazley, *On the Origin of the Right to Copy: charting the movement of copyright law in eighteenth-century Britain, 1695–1775* (Portland: Hart, 1994); Mark Rose, *Authors and Owners: the invention of copyright* (Cambridge, MA: Harvard University Press, 1993); Lyman Ray Patterson, *Copyright in Historical Perspective* (Nashville: Vanderbilt University Press, 1968); David Saunders, *Authorship and Copyright* (London: Routledge, 1992); and Sherman and Bently.

26. Roger Chartier, 'Figures of the Author', in Brad Sherman and Alain Strowel (eds), *Of Authors and Origins: essays on copyright law* (Oxford: Clarendon Press, 1994), p. 12.

27. William Enfield, *Observations on Literary Property* (London: Joseph Johnson, 1774), p. 21.

28. See William Warburton's, William Blackstone's and Francis Hargrave's summarised argumentation in Rose, 'The Author as Proprietor: *Donaldson v. Beckett* and the genealogy of modern authorship', *Representations*, vol. 23, 1988, pp. 62, 63–5, 71–5. Also see William Warburton, *A Letter from an Author, to a Member of Parliament, Concerning Literary Property* (London: John & Paul Knapton, 1747); William Blackstone, *Commentaries on the Laws of England*, 4 vols, 1765–9 (London: Cavendish, 2001), vol. 2, p. 57; Francis Hargrave, *Argument in Defence of Literary Property* (London: W. Otridge, 1774), reprinted in Stephen Parks (ed.), *Four Tracts on Freedom of the Press, 1790–1821* (New York: Garland, 1974), p. 79; and Duncan Kennedy, 'The Structure of Blackstone's *Commentaries*', *Buffalo Law Review*, vol. 28, 1978, pp. 205–382.

29. Hegel argues that 'property is the first embodiment of [rational] freedom and so is in itself a substantive end'. Georg Hegel, *Philosophy of Right*, trans. S. W. Dyde (New York: Cosimo, 2008), p. 10. This freedom is essentially a freedom from dependence on the will of others and marks the beginning of man's personal, political and social development.

30. Blackstone, p. 58.

31. Hargrave, p. 74.

32. Hegel, p. 45.

33. Edward Young, *Conjectures on Original Composition: in a letter to the author of Sir Charles Grandison* (London: R. & J. Dodsley, 1759), p. 59.

34. Rose, 'The Author as Proprietor', pp. 68–9.

35. Ibid., p. 68.

36. This also goes some way in supporting Robert MacFarlane's recent contention that the myth of Romantic authorship, originality and genius did not arise with the Romantics *per se*, but that it 'crystallized afterwards ... when Romantic doctrine on the subject of originality was simplified and mythified [and] brought into line with the ideal of *creation* promulgated in the late 1700s'. *Original Copy: plagiarism and originality in nineteenth-century literature* (Oxford: Oxford University Press, 2007), p. 33. My argument does suggest, however, that Wordsworth (despite his often conflicting pronouncements) was not entirely immune from this selective editing and the simplification of these doctrines for his own purposes.

37. Mark Shoenfield, *The Professional Wordsworth: law, labor, and the poet's contract* (Athens, GA: University of Georgia Press, 1996).

38. Ibid., p. 110.

39. Jack Stillinger, *Multiple Authorship and the Myth of Solitary Genius* (Oxford: Oxford University Press, 1991), p. 69. Also see Wayne Koestenbaum's useful discussion of Wordsworth's authorial relationship with Coleridge during the composition and publication of *Lyrical Ballads* in *Double Talk: the erotics of male literary collaboration* (New York: Routledge, 1989).

40. Alison Hickey, 'Double Bonds: Charles Lamb's Romantic collaborations', *English Language History*, vol. 63, 1996, p. 735. Also see Hickey, 'Coleridge, Southey, "and Co.": collaboration and authority', *Studies in Romanticism*, vol. 37, 1998, pp. 305–49.

41. William Wordsworth, 'Essay, Supplementary to the Preface (1815)', in W. J. B. Owen and Jane Worthington Smyser (eds), *The Prose Works of William Wordsworth*, vol. 3 (Oxford: Clarendon Press, 1974), p. 80.

42. Wordsworth, 'Essay, Supplementary to the Preface (1815)', pp. 82, 83–4.

43. Talfourd quoted in Thomas Edward Scrutton, *The Laws of Literary Property: an examination of the principles which should regulate literary and artistic property in England and other countries* (London: John Murray, 1883), p. 107.

44. Seville, p. 164.

45. Extract from Lord Camden's speech in parliament during the 1774 court case, *Donaldson v. Becket*, quoted in Scrutton, p. 103. Camden went on to argue that: 'When the bookseller offered Milton five pounds for his "Paradise Lost", he did not reject it and commit his poem to the flames, nor did he accept the miserable pittance as the reward for his labour; he knew that the real price of his work was immortality, and that posterity would pay it.' Scrutton, p. 103.

46. Wordsworth alludes to Camden's opposition to an author's natural rights in a letter to Talfourd in 1838, stating that: 'This right I hold to be more deeply inherent in that species of [literary] property than in any other.' William Wordsworth, letter to Thomas Noon Talfourd, 1838, in Owen and Smyser (eds), *The Prose Works of William Wordsworth*, vol. 3, p. 13.

47. William Wordsworth, letter to the *Kendal Mercury*, 12 April 1838, in Owen and Smyser (eds), *The Prose Works of William Wordsworth*, vol. 3, p. 312.

48. Wordsworth further maintained to Talfourd that: 'Authors as a Class could not but be in some degree put upon exertions that would raise them in public estimation – and say what you will, the possession of Property tends to make any body of men more respectable, however high may be their claims to respect upon other considerations.' Letter from Wordsworth to Talfourd, 25 October 1838, in Alan G. Hill (eds), *The Letters of William and Dorothy Wordsworth*, vol. 5 (Oxford: Oxford University Press, 1969–88), p. 636.

49. James Holston, *Insurgent Citizenship: disjunctions of democracy and modernity in Brazil* (Princeton: Princeton University Press, 2008), p. 115.

50. Archibald Alison, 'The Copyright Question', *Blackwood's Magazine*, vol. 51, 1842, p. 108.

51. Matthew Arnold, 'Copyright', *Fortnightly Review*, vol. 27, no. 159, 1880, pp. 321, 333.

52. See Immanuel Kant, *Anthropology from a Pragmatic Point of View*, ed. Robert B. Loudon (Cambridge: Cambridge University Press, 2006), §20; and, Kant, *Critique of the Power of Judgement*, ed. Paul Guyer (Cambridge: Cambridge University Press, 2000), §49. Saint-Amour also offers a similarly useful definition of this type of 'fanatical' originality as one that is marked off from other lesser forms of originality: 'To be designated radically original, a work must break detectably with its antecedents, and in order to make such a claim, the claimant purports to know not just the *best* that has been known and thought but *all* that has been known and thought ... Once it is denominated original, however, the work puts on the near invulnerable glamour of the self-generating, self-legislating Romantic artefact. Dissevered from not only the collective sources and modes of its own production but from the hypothetical nature of its originality, it attains the theological rank of a "classic",

a "masterpiece", a work of "genius". What ought to have been a rhizomatic process of evaluation has become an indwelling monolithic value.' Saint-Amour, p. 8.

53. W. B. Yeats, 'A General Introduction for My Work', in *Essays and Introductions* (London: Macmillan, 1961), p. 522.

54. S. T. Coleridge, letter to Joseph Cottle, 28 May 1798, in Earl Leslie Griggs (ed.), *The Collected Letters of Samuel Taylor Coleridge, 1785–1800*, vol. 1 (Oxford: Clarendon Press, 1956), p. 412.

55. Stillinger, p. 70.

56. Prickett argues that 'both poets saw the *Lyrical Ballads* as a particular kind of artistic unity that would be lost on many readers if it were known that the poems were by two different authors'. *Wordsworth and Coleridge: 'The Lyrical Ballads'* (London: Edward Arnold, 1975), p. 17.

57. Hickey, 'Coleridge, Southey, "and Co."', p. 317.

58. S. T. Coleridge, letter to Joseph Cottle, 28 May 1798, in Griggs (ed.), vol. 1, p. 412.

59. S. T. Coleridge, *Biographia Literaria; or Biographical Sketches of My Literary Life and Opinions*, ed. J. Shawcross, vol. 2 (Oxford: Oxford University Press, 1973), pp. 5–6.

60. John Beer, 'The Unity of *Lyrical Ballads*', in Nicola Trott and Seamus Perry (eds), *1800: The New 'Lyrical Ballads'* (Basingstoke: Palgrave, 2001), p. 11.

61. Quoted in Mary Moorman, *William Wordsworth: a biography*, vol. 1 (Oxford: Clarendon Press, 1957), p. 348.

62. William Wordsworth, Preface to *Lyrical Ballads* (1800), rpt. in William Wordsworth and S. T. Coleridge, *Lyrical Ballads*, ed. W. J. B. Owen (Oxford: Oxford University Press, 1995), p 153.

63. Wordsworth, Preface, pp. 153–4.

64. Prickett, p. 21; and, Beer, p. 21. Prickett maintains this argument in more detail in an earlier work: 'In stressing how similar Wordsworth's and Coleridge's ideas were about their own poetic growth, it may seem that we have, up till now, been ignoring their very obvious differences. The reason for this is that I believe, as I have tried to show, that if we look at them together as a unity they offer a coherent whole greater than either of its parts. Each poet tends to illuminate the other. Reading Wordsworth tells us more about Coleridge, and vice versa. But I think, too, there is more to it than that. If, as I have argued, there is no such thing as 'Romanticism', but only a number of casually connected 'romanticisms', then the theory of Imagination held by Wordsworth and Coleridge together would constitute the centre, or core, of one such "romanticism". In suggesting this, I am suggesting that their differences are as important a part of this unity as their points of agreement.' Prickett, *Coleridge and Wordsworth: the poetry of growth* (Cambridge: Cambridge University Press, 1970), p. 147.

65. Coleridge, letter to an unknown correspondent, c.15–21 December 1811, in Griggs (ed.), vol. 1, pp. 355, 361.

66. S. T. Coleridge, explanatory note to 'Kubla Khan: or, A Vision in a Dream. A Fragment', in Ernest Hartley Coleridge (ed.), *The Complete Poetical Works of Samuel Taylor Coleridge Including Poems and Versions of Poems Now Published for the First Time*, vol. 1 (Oxford: Clarendon Press, 1912), p. 296.

67. T. S. Eliot, 'Tradition and the Individual Talent', in *Selected Essays* (London: Faber & Faber, 1975), p. 19.

68. Michael P. Farrell, *Collaborative Circles: friendship dynamics and creative work* (Chicago: Chicago University Press, 2001), p. 115.

69. Jerome J. McGann, *The Romantic Ideology: a critical investigation* (London: University of Chicago Press, 1983), pp. 98, 104–6.

70. Coleridge, *Biographia Literaria*, vol. 1, pp. 65–74; and McGann, p. 105.

71. Coleridge, *Biographia Literaria*, vol. 1, p. 72.

72. Ibid., p. 29.

73. Robert Southey, letter to Charles Wynn, 1813, in John Wood Warter (ed.), *Selections from the Letters of Robert Southey*, vol. 3 (London: Longmans, 1856), p. 323.

74. Coleridge, *Biographia Literaria*, vol. 1, p. 72.

75. Jerome Christenson, *Coleridge's Blessed Machine of Language* (Ithaca: Cornell University Press, 1981), p. 119.

76. Christenson, p. 120.

77. Saint-Amour, p. 130.

78. Robert MacFarlane, *Original Copy: plagiarism and originality in nineteenth-century literature* (Oxford: Oxford University Press, 2007), p. 32. Tilar J. Mazzeo's *Plagiarism and Literary Property in the Romantic Period* (Philadelphia: University of Pennsylvania Press, 2007) is also particularly good at highlighting and attempting to disentangle the startling contradictions inherent in several Romantic poets' stances on originality and authorship.

79. *Royal Commission on Copyright. 1876. Report and minutes of evidence. The Royal commissions and the report of the Commissioners. Minutes of evidence, together with an appendix, preceded by tables of the witnesses and of the contents of the appendix* (London: HMSO, 1878), quoted in Arnold, 'Copyright', p. 321.

80. Quoted in Max Saunders, 'Secret Agencies: Conrad, collaboration and conspiracy', in *Collaboration in the Arts from the Middle Ages to the Present*, eds Silvia Bigliazzi and Sharon Wood (Aldershot: Ashgate, 2006), p. 93.

81. Saunders, pp. 100, 101.

82. Ibid., p. 116.

83. Henry James, 'Collaboration', *The English Illustrated Magazine*, vol. 9, 1892, p. 912.

84. Ibid., p. 915.

85. Ibid., p. 916.

86. Ibid., p. 919.

87. Ibid., p. 921.

88. Duncan Aswell, 'James's Treatment of Artistic Collaboration', *Criticism*, vol. 8, no. 2, 1966, p. 181.

89. James, 'Collaboration', p. 920.

90. Quoted in Saunders, p. 120.

91. Edith Somerville, letter to Cameron Somerville, 31 January 1906, L.A.492.a, Edith Œnone Somerville Archive, Drishane House, Co. Cork.

92. Martin Ross, letter to Edith Somerville, 1901, in Lewis (ed.), *The Selected Letters of Somerville and Ross*, p. 256.

93. Anna Mary Howitt, 'The Sisters in Art', *The Illustrated Exhibitor and Magazine of Art*, vol. 2, 1852, p. 319.

94. See Linda Peterson, *Becoming a Woman of Letters: myths of authorship and facts of the Victorian market* (Princeton: Princeton University Press, 2009), pp. 96–130.

95. Ibid., p. 97.

96. James Cahalan, *Double Visions: women and men in modern and contemporary Irish fiction* (New York: Syracuse University Press, 1999), p. 67.

97. Koestenbaum, p. 95.

98. Martin Ross, letter to Edith Somerville, 16 January 1895, in Lewis (ed.), *The Selected Letters of Somerville and Ross*, p. 209.

99. Walter Besant, 'On Literary Collaboration', *New Review*, vol. 6, no. 33, 1892, pp. 204–5.

100. Brander Matthews, 'The Art and Mystery of Collaboration', in *With My Friends: tales told in partnership* (New York: Longmans, 1891), p. 15.

101. Ibid., p. 162.

102. Martin Ross, letter to Edith Somerville, 16 January 1895, in Lewis (ed.), *The Selected Letters of Somerville and Ross*, p. 209.
103. Somerville, *Irish Memories*, p. 98.
104. Ehnenn, p. 72.
105. Quoted in Mary Sturgeon, *Michael Field* (London: Harrap, 1922), p. 47.
106. Edith Somerville, 'Two of a Trade', in Geraldine Cummins, *Dr. E.Œ. Somerville: a biography* (London: Andrew Dakers, 1952), p. 182.
107. Michael Field, *Works and Days: from the journal of Michael Field*, ed. T. and D. C. Sturge Moore (London: John Murray, 1933), p. 6.
108. Marilyn Butler, *Maria Edgeworth: a literary biography* (Oxford: Clarendon Press, 1972), p. 49.
109. Maria Edgeworth, letter to Sophy Ruxton, October 1797, in *A Memoir of Maria Edgeworth*, ed. The Edgeworth Family, vol. 1 (London: Joseph Masters, 1867), p. 76.
110. Maria Edgeworth, letter to Charlotte Sneyd, 2 April 1799, in *A Memoir of Maria Edgeworth*, p. 95.
111. Maria Edgeworth, letter to Sophy Ruxton, 27 February 1796, in *A Memoir of Maria Edgeworth*, p. 76.
112. Martin Ross, letter to Edith Somerville, 21 August 1889, in Lewis (ed.), *The Selected Letters of Somerville and Ross*, p. 143.
113. Howitt, p. 318.
114. Somerville, *Irish Memories*, p. 112.
115. Edith Somerville, diary, 15 October 1880, MS. 17/875, Queen's University Belfast.
116. Edith Somerville, diary, 16 December 1880, MS. 17/875, Queen's University Belfast.
117. Jem Barlow, 'A Memory of Martin Ross', *Country Life*, vol. 39, no. 995, 1916, p. 136.
118. Somerville, *Irish Memories*, p. 114.
119. Peterson, p. 145.
120. London, p. 56.

2. The erotics and politics of female collaboration

1. E.Œ. Somerville and Martin Ross, *Irish Memories* (London: Longmans, 1919), p. 326.
2. Virginia Woolf, 'A Room of One's Own' in Morag Shiach (ed.), *Virginia Woolf: A Room of One's Own and Three Guineas* (Oxford: Oxford University Press, 2000), p. 107.
3. Sasha Roseneil, 'Foregrounding Friendship: feminist pasts, feminist futures', in Kathy Davis, Mary Evans and Judith Lorber (eds), *The SAGE Handbook of Gender and Women's Studies* (London: SAGE, 2006), pp. 323–4.
4. Elaine Showalter, *A Literature of their Own: from Charlotte Brontë to Doris Lessing* (London: Virago, 1999), pp. 29–30.
5. Carey Kaplan and Ellen Cronan Rose, 'Strange Bedfellows: feminist collaboration', *Signs*, vol. 18, no. 3, 1993, p. 547.
6. Janice Doan and Devon Hodges, 'Writing from the Trenches and Collaborative Writing', *Tulsa Studies in Women's Literature*, vol. 14, no. 1, 1995, pp. 53–4.
7. Edith Somerville, letter to Cameron Somerville, 6 September 1916, MS. L.A.938.a–c, Edith Œnone Somerville Archive, Drishane House, County Cork.
8. Maryanne Dever, '"No Mine and Thine But Ours": finding M. Barnard Eldershaw', *Tulsa Studies in Women's Literature*, vol. 14, no. 1, 1995, p. 71.
9. Bette London, *Writing Double: women's literary partnerships* (New York: Cornell University Press, 1999), p. 96.
10. Lorraine York, *Rethinking Women's Collaborative Writing: power, difference, property* (Toronto: University of Toronto Press, 2002), p. 6.

11. Ibid.
12. Ibid., p. 7.
13. Ibid., pp. 10–11.
14. Janet Surrey, 'Relationship and Empowerment', in Judith Jordan, Alexandra Kaplan, Jean Miller, Irene Stiver and Janet Surrey (eds), *Women's Growth in Connection: writings from the Stone Center* (New York: Guidford Press, 1991), p. 170.
15. Ibid., pp. 165–6.
16. Edith Somerville, 'Two of a Trade', in Geraldine Cummins, *Dr. E.Œ. Somerville: a biography* (London: Andrew Dakers, 1952), p. 182.
17. Edith Somerville, letter to Cameron Somerville, 6 January 1916, MS. L.A.938.a–c, Edith Œnone Somerville Archive, Drishane House, County Cork.
18. Holly A. Laird, *Women Coauthors* (Chicago: University of Illinois Press, 2000), p. 14.
19. Jill Ehnenn, *Women's Literary Collaboration, Queerness, and Victorian Culture* (Aldershot: Ashgate, 2008), pp. 13, 14.
20. Ibid., p. 45.
21. Cummins, p. 180.
22. Somerville, 'Two of a Trade', p. 182.
23. Cummins, p. 180.
24. Somerville, 'Two of a Trade', pp. 181–2.
25. Ibid., p. 185.
26. Somerville, *Irish Memories*, p. 133.
27. Somerville, 'Two of a Trade', p. 185.
28. Ibid., pp. 184–5.
29. Ibid., p. 181.
30. Ibid., p. 183.
31. Somerville, *Irish Memories*, p. 185.
32. Ibid., p. 186.
33. Ibid., p. 54.
34. Janice G. Raymond, *A Passion for Friends: towards a philosophy of female affection* (Boston: Beacon Press, 1986), p. 9.
35. Somerville, *Irish Memories*, p. 129.
36. Ibid., p. 138.
37. Ibid., p. 326.
38. Marilyn Friedman, *What Are Friends For? Feminist perspectives on personal relationships and moral theory* (New York: Cornell University Press, 1993), pp. 248–9.
39. Edith Somerville, letter to Cameron Somerville, 18 January 1895, MS. L.A.177.a, Edith Œnone Somerville Archive, Drishane House, County Cork.
40. E.Œ. Somerville and Martin Ross, *The Silver Fox* (London: Longmans, 1927), p. 79. Subsequent references to this text are cited parenthetically in the text.
41. E. Lynn Linton, 'The Girl of the Period', in Linton (ed.), *The Girl of the Period and other Social Essays*, vol. 1 (London: Richard Bentley & Son, 1883), pp. 2–3.
42. E. Lynn Linton, 'The Wild Women as Social Insurgents', *The Nineteenth Century*, vol. 30, October 1891, p. 596.
43. See, for example, Declan Kiberd, *Irish Classics* (London: Granta, 2001), p. 324.
44. Raymond, p. 199.
45. Ibid.
46. Mary Wollstonecraft, *A Vindication of the Rights of Men with A Vindication of the Rights of Woman* (Cambridge: Cambridge University Press, 2003), p. 99.
47. Ibid.

48. Maureen O'Connnor, *Female and the Species: the animal in Irish women's writing* (Bern: Peter Lang, 2010), p. 118.

49. Roz Cowman, 'The Smell and Taste of Castle T.', in Eibhear Walshe (ed.), *Sex, Nation, and Dissent in Irish Writing* (Cork: Cork University Press, 1997), p. 99.

50. Susan J. Leonardi and Rebecca A. Pope, 'Screaming Divas: collaboration as feminist practice', *Tulsa Studies in Women's Literature*, vol. 13, no. 2, 1994, pp. 268–9.

51. Edith Somerville, letter to Cameron Somerville, 5 December 1888, MS. L.A.108.a–c, Edith Œnone Somerville Archive, Drishane House, Co. Cork.

52. Thomas Gisborne, *An Inquiry into the Duties of the Female Sex* (London: T. Caldwell & W. Davies, 1797), p. 111.

53. Barbara Maria Zaczek, *Censored Sentiments* (London: Associated London Presses, 1997), p. 14.

54. Ibid., p. 55.

55. Stephanie Tingley, '"A Letter is a Joy of Earth": Emily Dickinson's letters and Victorian epistolary conventions', *The Emily Dickinson Journal*, vol. 5, no. 2, 1996, p. 202.

56. Mary Favret, *Romantic Correspondence: women, politics, and the fiction of letters* (Cambridge: Cambridge University Press, 1993), p. 19.

57. Ibid.

58. Brigitte Glaser, *The Creation of the Self in Autobiographical Forms of Writing in Seventeenth-Century England: subjectivity and self-fashioning in memoirs, diaries and letters* (Heidelberg: Universität Sverlag C. Winter, 2001), p. 30.

59. Nicola Watson, *Revolution and the Form of the British Novel, 1790–1825: intercepted letters, interrupted seductions* (Oxford: Oxford University Press, 1994), p. 57.

60. Elizabeth Cook, *Epistolary Bodies: gender and genre in the eighteenth-century Republic of Letters* (Redwood: Stanford University Press, 1996), p. 145.

61. Michel Foucault, *The History of Sexuality*, vol. 1 (London: Penguin, 1991).

62. Leonardi and Pope, p. 269.

63. Glaser, p. 55.

64. Martin Ross, letter to Edith Somerville, May 1886, in Gifford Lewis (ed.), *The Selected Letters of Somerville and Ross* (London: Faber, 1989), p. 6.

65. Ibid.

66. Lewis, *Somerville and Ross: the world of the Irish R.M.*, p. 98. Also see Sharon Marcus, *Between Women: friendship, desire, and marriage in Victorian England* (Princeton: Princeton University Press, 2007).

67. Martin Ross, letter to Edith Somerville, 1895, in Lewis (ed.), *Selected Letters*, p. 222.

68. Somerville, 'Two of a Trade', p. 185.

69. Sandra Butler and Barbara Rosenblum, *Cancer in Two Voices* (San Francisco: Spinsters, 1991), p. 141.

70. Raymond, p. 225.

71. Ibid.

72. Ibid.

73. See in particular Lewis' *Selected Letters,* which repeatedly highlights dialogue and plots Somerville and Ross borrowed from their own letters to each other to use in their fiction. As Lewis has already performed the arduous task of locating dialogue and stories in the letters in much of Somerville and Ross' fiction, many of her observations will simply be quoted and repeated in this chapter in an attempt to explain their further significance beyond being what Lewis calls the 'seeds of their stories'. Lewis (ed.), *Selected Letters*, p. xxvi.

74. Martin Ross, letter to Edith Somerville, 3 December 1887, in Lewis (ed.), *Selected Letters*, p. 62.

75. Martin Ross, letter to Edith Somerville, 21 August 1889, in Lewis (ed.), *Selected Letters*, p. 143.

76. Martin Ross, letter to Edith Somerville, 6 September 1889, in Lewis (ed.), *Selected Letters*, p. 153.

77. Martin Ross, letter to Edith Somerville, 4 September 1889, in Lewis (ed.), *Selected Letters*, p. 147.

78. Martin Ross, letter to Edith Somerville, 12 September 1889, in Lewis (ed.), *Selected Letters*, p. 158.

79. Kaplan and Cronan Rose, p. 555.

80. Jennifer Cognard-Black and Elizabeth MacLeod Walls, 'Introduction', in Cognard-Black and MacLeod Walls (eds), *Kindred Hands: letters on writing by British and American women authors, 1865–1935* (Iowa City: University of Iowa Press, 2006), p. 3.

81. Cognard-Black and MacLeod Walls, *Kindred Hands*, p. 3.

82. Martin Ross, letter to Edith Somerville, 9 July 1888, in Lewis (ed.), *Selected Letters*, p. 87.

83. Walter Ong, *Orality and Literacy: the technologizing of the word* (New York: Routledge, 2002), p. 131.

84. Robert MacFarlane, *Original Copy: plagiarism and originality in nineteenth-century literature* (Oxford: Oxford University Press), p. 142.

85. Ibid., pp. 136–41.

86. Martin Ross, letter to Edith Somerville, 9 July 1888, in Lewis (ed.), *Selected Letters*, p. 83.

87. Ibid.

88. Martin Ross, transcript in E.Œ. Somerville's hand of a séance with Martin Ross aided by Geraldine Cummins, notebook 43, 3 October 1937, MS. 17/904/2, Queen's University Belfast.

89. Edith Somerville, letter to Martin Ross [envelope marked 'Hunting'], 27 December 1893, mic. 147, Berg Collection, New York Public Library, New York; Edith Somerville, letter to Martin Ross [envelope marked 'Hunting' and 'Hunt Ball'], mic. 147, Berg Collection, New York Public Library, New York; Martin Ross, letter to Edith Somerville [incomplete], *c.*1895 [letter marked 'Dogs'], mic. 147, Berg Collection, New York Public Library, New York; Edith Somerville, letter to Martin Ross [envelope marked 'Agric. Show – Races'], mic. 147, Berg Collection, New York Public Library, New York.

90. Martin Ross, letter to Edith Somerville, incomplete, *c.*1893, mic. 147, Berg Collection, New York Public Library, New York.

91. Martin Ross, letter to Edith Somerville, 19 May 1886, in Lewis (ed.), *Selected Letters*, p. 8.

92. Martin Ross, letter to Edith Somerville, incomplete, *c.*1895, in Lewis (ed.), *Selected Letters*, pp. 221–2.

93. Martin Ross, letter to Edith Somerville, 9 July 1888, in Lewis (ed.), *Selected Letters*, p. 85.

94. Martin Ross, letter to Edith Somerville, 9 July 1888, in Lewis (ed.), *Selected Letters*, p. 242.

95. Lewis (ed.), *Selected Letters*, p. xxvi.

96. Ibid.

97. Edith Somerville, letter to Martin Ross, 19 August 1888, in Lewis (ed.), *Selected Letters*, p. 101. Somerville is responding to Ross' description of the welcome bonfire for her sister Geraldine and her husband, who returned to Ross House after sixteen years of living away from home. During that time Ross House was leased out for rent money and gradually deteriorated until the Martins returned to live there in the summer of 1888 and attempted to resurrect it from its sorely dilapidated state: 'In the strictest privacy I may say that I felt all of a heap to see the bonfire blazing there just as it used to in my father's time – when he and the boys used to come down and all of us, and it was all the most natural thing in the world. It was very different to see Geraldine walk in front us through the gates, with her

white face and shabby clothes. Thady Connor (who is the bailiff and was the steward) met her at the gate, and not in any vice regal circles could be surpassed the way he took off his hat and came silently forward to her, while everyone else kept back in dead silence too. I know Thady is not what he ought to be, or any of them for the matter of that, but I think they felt seeing her – of course they had all known her well. What with that glare of the bonfire that *we* have described [in *An Irish Cousin*], and the welcome killed with memories for her, I wonder how she stood it. It was the attempt of the old times that was painful and wretched – at least I thought so.' Martin Ross, letter to Edith Somerville, 17 August 1888, in Lewis (ed.), *Selected Letters*, p. 107.

98. Martin Ross, letter to Edith Somerville, 3 January 1894, in Lewis (ed.), *Selected Letters*, p. 198.

99. Martin Ross, letter to Edith Somerville, incomplete, *c.*December/January 1893/4, in Lewis (ed.), *Selected Letters*, p. 196.

100. 'It fills my mind with its dramatic aspect mostly and perhaps after a talk with you it might take shape.' Martin Ross, letter to Edith Somerville, 3 January 1894, in Lewis (ed.), *Selected Letters*, p. 198.

101. Commenting on Somerville's critique of her review of the Irish Exhibition at Olympia, Ross exclaims: 'These last two letters of yours have put a backbone into me.' Martin Ross, letter to Edith Somerville, 17 August 1888, in Lewis (ed.), *Selected Letters*, p. 103.

102. Edith Somerville, letter to Martin Ross, 15 August 1888, in Lewis (ed.), *Selected Letters*, p. 101.

103. Martin Ross, letter to Edith Somerville, 26 July 1888, in Lewis (ed.), *Selected Letters*, p. 88.

104. Edith Somerville, letter to Martin Ross, 21 January 1888, in Lewis (ed.), *Selected Letters*, p. 63.

105. Edith Somerville, 'Étaples: where the Irish R.M. began', p. 70.

106. York, p. 5.

107. Martin Ross, letter to Edith Somerville, 26 July 1888, in Lewis (ed.), *Selected Letters*, p. 88.

108. Martin Ross, diary, 4 January 1892, MS. 17/874, Queen's University Belfast.

109. Somerville and Ross, *Irish Memories*, p. 133.

110. See Neville Coghill's account of the partnership quoted in Lewis, *Somerville and Ross: the world of the Irish R.M.*, p. 76.

111. Martin Ross, letter to Edith Somerville, September 1889, in Somerville, *Irish Memories*, p. 134.

112. Edith Somerville, letter to Martin Ross, 5 December 1895, in Lewis (ed.), *Selected Letters*, p. 227.

113. Martin Ross, letter to Edith Somerville, 18 May 1889, in Lewis (ed.), *Selected Letters*, p. 135.

3. Women's popular literature in the commercial marketplace

1. Marjorie Barnard, 'The Gentle Art of Collaboration', in Hilarie Lindsay (ed.), *Ink No. 2*, 1977 (Sydney: Society of Women Writers), p. 126.

2. Quoted in Gifford Lewis, *Somerville and Ross: the world of the Irish R.M.* (Harmondsworth: Penguin, 1985), p. 74.

3. Quoted in Mary Sturgeon, *Michael Field* (London: George G. Harrap, 1922), p. 47.

4. Jill Ehnenn, *Women's Literary Collaboration, Queerness, and Victorian Culture* (Aldershot: Ashgate, 2008), p. 33.

5. Ibid., pp. 33–4.

6. Yopie Prins, *Victorian Sappho* (Princeton: Princeton University Press, 1999), p. 89.

7. Bette London, *Writing Double: women's literary partnerships* (New York: Cornell University Press, 1999), p. 110.

8.   Martin Ross, letter to Edith Somerville, 18 September 1890, in Gifford Lewis (ed.), *The Selected Letters of Somerville and Ross* (London: Faber, 1989), p. 64.

9.   Edith Somerville, *Happy Days* (London: Longmans, 1946), p. 69.

10. Edith Somerville, letter to Martin Ross, 25 April 1897, in Lewis (ed.), *The Selected Letters*, p. 243.

11. Martin Ross, letter to Edith Somerville, 29 January 1895, in Lewis (ed.), *The Selected Letters*, p. 220.

12. Mary Ann Gillies, *The Professional Literary Agent in Britain, 1880–1920* (Toronto: University of Toronto Press, 2007), p. 6.

13. James B. Pinker, interview, *The Bookman*, vol. 14, no. 79, April 1898, p. 9.

14. *The Literary Yearbook and Bookman's Directory*, 1901, p. 119.

15. See Gillies, pp. 90–3.

16. Ibid., p. 93.

17. Martin Ross, letter to Edith Somerville, 21 August 1889, in Lewis (ed.), *The Selected Letters*, p. 243.

18. Martin Ross, letter to Edith Somerville, 24 August 1889, in Lewis (ed.), *The Selected Letters*, p. 243.

19. Edith Somerville, letter to Cameron Somerville, 9 January 1889, MS. L.A.109.a–b, Edith Œnone Somerville Archive, Drishane House, County Cork, Ireland.

20. Edith Somerville, letter to Cameron Somerville, 26 November 1889, MS. L.A.121.a–b, Edith Œnone Somerville Archive, Drishane House, County Cork, Ireland.

21. Edith Somerville, letter to Cameron Somerville, 11 July 1890, MS. L.A.131.a–b, Edith Œnone Somerville Archive, Drishane House, County Cork, Ireland.

22. Edith Somerville, letter to Cameron Somerville, 17 September 1889, MS. L.A.114.a, Edith Œnone Somerville Archive, Drishane House, County Cork, Ireland.

23. Edith Somerville, letter to Cameron Somerville, 24 October 1894, MS. L.A.174.a–c, Edith Œnone Somerville Archive, Drishane House, County Cork, Ireland.

24. Editor of *The Book-lover*, letter to Edith Somerville and Martin Ross, 5 February 1904, MS. TCD 4276–7194, Trinity College Dublin.

25. Edith Somerville, letter to Cameron Somerville, 22 February 1891, MS. L.A.139.a–b, Edith Œnone Somerville Archive, Drishane House, County Cork, Ireland.

26. Edith Somerville, letter to Cameron Somerville, 26 January 1890, MS. L.A.121.a–b, Edith Œnone Somerville Archive, Drishane House, County Cork, Ireland.

27. Edith Somerville, letter to Cameron Somerville, 1 December 1893, MS. L.A.167.a–b, Edith Œnone Somerville Archive, Drishane House, County Cork, Ireland.

28. Edith Somerville, letter to Cameron Somerville, 2 November 1893, MS. L.A.166.a–c, Edith Œnone Somerville Archive, Drishane House, County Cork, Ireland.

29. Edith Somerville, letter to Cameron Somerville, 28 July 1889, MS. L.A.110.a, Edith Œnone Somerville Archive, Drishane House, County Cork, Ireland.

30. William Heinemann, 'The Middleman as Viewed by a Publisher', *Athenaeum*, 3446.

31. Edith Somerville, letter to Cameron Somerville, 11 July 1890, MS. L.A.131.a–b, Edith Œnone Somerville Archive, Drishane House, County Cork, Ireland.

32. Edith Somerville, letter to Cameron Somerville, May 1893, MS. L.A.165.a–b, Edith Œnone Somerville Archive, Drishane House, County Cork, Ireland.

33. Edith Somerville, letter to Cameron Somerville, 6 March 1897, MS. L.A.210.a–b, Edith Œnone Somerville Archive, Drishane House, County Cork, Ireland.

34. Somerville, *Irish Memories*, p. 128; and, Edith Somerville, letter to Cameron Somerville, 10 March 1898, MS. L.A.246.a–b, Edith Œnone Somerville Archive, Drishane House, County Cork, Ireland.

35. Edith Somerville, letter to Hildegarde Somerville, 6 August 1893, quoted in Gifford Lewis, *Somerville and Ross: the world of the Irish R.M.* (New York: Viking, 1989), p. 196.

36. Edith Somerville, letter to Hildegarde Somerville, 30 March 1886, quoted in Gifford Lewis, *Edith Somerville: a biography* (Dublin: Four Courts Press, 2005), p. 103.

37. Martin Ross, letter to Edith Somerville, 10 July 1906, in Lewis (ed.), *The Selected Letters*, p. 278.

38. William Gregory, letter to Mrs. Ross, 21 October 1889, MS. 17/920, Somerville and Ross Papers, Queen's University Belfast.

39. Augusta Gregory, letter to Martin Ross, c.1914, MS. 17/920, Somerville and Ross Papers, Queen's University Belfast.

40. Augusta Gregory, letter to Martin Ross, 20 February 1905, MS. 17/920, Somerville and Ross Papers, Queen's University Belfast.

41. Martin Ross, letter to Edith Somerville, 30 April 1905, in Lewis (ed.), *The Selected Letters*, pp. 273–4.

42. Martin Ross, letter to Edith Somerville, 30 April 1905, in Lewis (ed.), *The Selected Letters*, p. 274.

43. Ibid.

44. Martin Ross, letter to Edith Somerville, 10 July 1906, in Lewis (ed.), *The Selected Letters*, p. 278.

45. Augusta Gregory, letter to Martin Ross, 8 July 1915, MS. 17/920, Somerville and Ross Papers, Queen's University Belfast.

46. See Lewis (ed.), *The Selected Letters*, p. 257.

47. Martin Ross, letter to Edith Somerville, 8 August 1901, in Lewis (ed.), *The Selected Letters*, p. 252.

48. Edith Somerville, letter to J. B. Pinker, 9 January 1905, MS. TCD 3330–1/152, Somerville and Ross Papers, Trinity College Dublin.

49. Ibid.

50. Edith Somerville, letter to Cameron Somerville, 1 December 1904, MS. L.A.452.a–c, Edith Œnone Somerville Archive, Drishane House, County Cork, Ireland.

51. Edith Somerville, letter to Cameron Somerville, 14 December 1898, MS. L.A.267.a–c, Edith Œnone Somerville Archive, Drishane House, County Cork, Ireland.

52. Walter Besant, 'On Literary Collaboration', *The New Review*, vol. 6, no. 33, 1892, pp. 203–4.

53. Brander Matthews, 'The Art and Mystery of Collaboration', in *With My Friends: tales told in partnership* (New York: Longmans, 1891), p. 15.

54. William G. Wills, letter to Martin Ross, n.d., MS. 17/876, Somerville and Ross Papers, Queen's University Belfast.

55. Ibid.

56. Julie Anne Stevens, 'The Staging of Protestant Ireland in Somerville and Ross's *The Real Charlotte*', in *Critical Ireland: new essays in literature and culture*, eds Aaron Kelly and Alan Gillis (Dublin: Four Courts Press, 2001), p. 67.

57. Julie Anne Stevens, 'The Irish Landscape in Somerville and Ross's Fiction and Illustrations, 1890–1915', PhD diss., Trinity College Dublin, 2000, p. 192.

58. Wills, n. pag.

59. Besant, p. 209.

60. Ibid.

61. Edith Somerville, 'The Educational Aspect of Suffrage', 1912, MS. 17/898/d, Queen's University Belfast.

62. Ibid.

63. Ibid.

64. Ibid.

65. Edith Somerville, letter to Mrs. Anstey, 10 December 1932, quoted in Otto Rauchbauer, *The Edith Œnone Somerville Archive in Drishane: a catalogue and an evaluative essay* (Dublin: Irish Manuscript Commission, 1995), p. 234; and Edith Somerville, letter to Jack Somerville, 19 December 1932, quoted in Rauchbauer, p. 235.

66. Edith Somerville, letter to Cameron Somerville, 4 February 1914, MS. L.A.851.a–d, Edith Œnone Somerville Archive, Drishane House, County Cork.

67. Ibid.

68. Edith Somerville, letters to Cameron Somerville, 1 December 1904 and 27 May 1909, MSS. L.A.452.a–c and L.A.658.a–f, Edith Œnone Somerville Archive, Drishane House, County Cork.

69. Brander Matthews, 'The Ethics of Plagiarism', *Longman's Magazine*, vol. 8, October 1886, p. 622.

70. Andrew J. Strahan, 25 June 1913, copy of Strahan's report in the hand of E.Œ. Somerville, MS. 17/914, Somerville and Ross Papers, Queen's University Belfast.

71. Edith Somerville, letter to Cameron Somerville, 5 August 1913, MS. L.A.829.a–b, Edith Œnone Somerville Archive, Drishane House, County Cork.

72. J. B. Pinker, letter to Edith Somerville, 24 June 1913, MS. 17/917, Somerville and Ross Papers, Queen's University Belfast.

73. MacFarlane, p. 43.

74. Michael Wiley, 'Romantic Amplification: the way of plagiarism', *English Language History*, vol. 75, no. 1, 2008, p. 219.

75. Matthews, 'The Ethics of Plagiarism', p. 634.

76. Saint-Amour, p. 38.

77. MacFarlane, p. 43.

78. Matthews, 'The Ethics of Plagiarism', p. 623.

79. Andrew Lang, 'Literary Plagiarism', *The Contemporary Review*, 1887, p. 832.

80. Ibid.

81. W. H. Davenport-Adams, 'Imitators and Plagiarists', *The Gentleman's Magazine*, 1892, pp. 502, 613.

82. Edward Wright, 'The Art of Plagiarism', *The Contemporary Review*, 1904, p. 514.

83. Ibid.

84. Ibid., pp. 514–15.

85. Ibid., p. 515.

86. Davenport-Adams, p. 506; and Matthews, 'The Ethics of Plagiarism', p. 628.

87. Matthews, 'The Ethics of Plagiarism', p. 628.

88. Ibid., p. 625.

89. Ibid., pp. 628–9.

90. Ibid., p. 634.

91. Lang, 'Literary Plagiarism', p. 835.

92. Matthews, 'The Ethics of Plagiarism', p. 629.

93. Matthews, 'The Ethics of Plagiarism', p. 634; and Lang, 'Literary Plagiarism', p. 839.

94. Matthews, 'The Ethics of Plagiarism', p. 621.

95. Davenport-Adams, p. 902.

96. Martin Ross, letter to Longmans, 9 June 1913, MS. 17/917, Somerville and Ross Papers, Queen's University Belfast; and Miscellaneous newspaper cuttings, *c.*July 1913, MS. 17/917, Somerville and Ross Papers, Queen's University Belfast.

97. Edith Somerville, letter to J. B. Pinker, 18 October 1913, MS. 17/917, Somerville and Ross Papers, Queen's University Belfast.

98. G. Herbert Thring, letter to J. B. Pinker, 18 June 1913, MS. 17/917, Queen's University Belfast.

99. Thomas Longman, letter to Edith Somerville, 9 June 1913, MS. 17/914, Queen's University Belfast.

100. Ibid.

101. G. Herbert Thring, letter to J. B. Pinker, 18 June 1913, MS. 17/917, Queen's University Belfast.

102. Andrew J. Strahan, 25 June 1913, copy of Strahan's report in the hand of Edith Somerville, MS. 17/914, Queen's University Belfast.

103. Ibid.

104. Edith Somerville, letter to J. B. Pinker, 18 October 1913, MS. 17/917, Queen's University Belfast.

105. Thomas Edward Scrutton, *The Laws of Literary Property* (London: John Murray, 1883), p. 8.

106. Ibid.

107. William Wordsworth, letter to *Kendal Mercury*, 12 April 1838, in W. J. B. Owen and Jane Worthington Smyser (eds), *The Prose Works of William Wordsworth*, vol. 3 (Oxford: Clarendon Press, 1974), p. 312.

108. John Shortt, *The Law Relating to Works of Literature and Art* (London: Reeves & Turner, 1884), pp. 3, 9.

109. *Country Life*, 28 June 1913, newspaper cutting, MS. 17/914, Queen's University Belfast.

110. J. B. Pinker, letter to Martin Ross, 27 June 1913, MS. 17/914, Queen's University Belfast.

111. Andrew J. Strahan, 25 June 1913, copy of Strahan's report in the hand of Edith Somerville, MS. 17/914, Queen's University Belfast.

112. Scrutton, pp. 4–5.

113. 'Copyright and Libel', *TLS*, newspaper cutting, *c.*June/July 1913, MS. 17/914, Queen's University Belfast.

114. Edith Somerville, letter to Cameron Somerville, 23 March 1899, L.A.275.a–b, Edith Œnone Somerville Archive, Drishane House, County Cork, Ireland.

115. Edith Somerville, letter to Cameron Somerville, 20 October 1898, L.A.262.a, Edith Œnone Somerville Archive, Drishane House, County Cork, Ireland.

116. Edith Somerville, letter to Cameron Somerville, 26 January 1899, L.A.270.a–b, Edith Œnone Somerville Archive, Drishane House, County Cork, Ireland.

117. Edith Somerville, letter to Cameron Somerville, 2 August 1899, L.A.282.a–b, Edith Œnone Somerville Archive, Drishane House, County Cork, Ireland.

118. James B. Pinker, letter to Edith Somerville and Martin Ross, 8 March 1899, MSS. TCD 4276–7/60, Trinity College Dublin.

119. Ibid.

120. Edmund Yates, letter to Martin Ross, 25 July 1889, MS. TCD 4276–7/12, Trinity College Dublin.

121. Quoted in Lewis, *Somerville and Ross: the world of the Irish R.M.*, p. 134.

122. Quoted in Lewis, *Edith Somerville: a biography*, pp. 79–80.

123. Quoted in Lewis, *Somerville and Ross: the world of the Irish R.M.*, p. 134.

124. Edith Somerville, letter to Cameron Somerville, 9 October 1884, MS. L.A.58.a–b, Drishane Archive, Co. Cork, Ireland.

125. Quoted in Victor Bonham-Carter, *Authors by Profession*, vol. 1 (London: Society of Authors, 1978), p. 89.

126. Edith Somerville, letter to Cameron Somerville, 5 December 1888, MS. L.A.108.a–c, Edith Œnone Somerville Archive, Drishane House, County Cork, Ireland.

127. Somerville, *Irish Memories*, p. 129.

128. Ibid.

129. Ibid., p. 131.

4. Through Connemara and beyond

1. Quoted in Edith Somerville, 'Two of a Trade', in Geraldine Cummins, *Dr. E.Œ. Somerville: a biography* (London: A. Dakers, 1952), p. 182.

2. Anne Ruggles Gere, *Writing Groups: history, theory, and implications* (Carbondale: Southern Illinois University Press, 1978), p. 101.

3. Ibid.

4. Somerville, 'Two of a Trade', p. 186.

5. Sturgeon, p. 47.

6. Somerville, 'Two of a Trade', p. 186.

7. Ibid..

8. Edith Somerville, letter to Cameron Somerville, 6 January 1916, MS. L.A.938.a–c, Edith Œnone Somerville Archive, Drishane House, County Cork.

9. Ibid.

10. Edith Somerville, diary, 12 August 1902, MS. 17/874, Queen's University Belfast.

11. Somerville, *Irish Memories*, p. 133.

12. Edith Somerville, diary, 30–31 December 1888, MS. 17/874, Queen's University Belfast.

13. Somerville, 'Two of a Trade', p. 186.

14. Ibid.

15. Martin Ross, letter to Edith Somerville, 27 August 1889, mic. 140/40, Trinity College Dublin.

16. Emily Lawless, 'Iar-Connaught: a study', *The Cornhill Magazine*, vol. 45, no. 267, p. 319.

17. Edith Somerville, letter to Cameron Somerville, 11 December 1890, MS. L.A.137.a–b, Edith Œnone Somerville Archive, Drishane House, County Cork.

18. Lewis, *Somerville and Ross*, p. 154.

19. Catherine Nash, '"Embodying the Nation": the west of Ireland landscape and Irish identity', in Barbara O'Connor and Michael Cronin (eds), *Tourism in Ireland: a critical analysis* (Cork: Cork University Press, 1993), p. 90.

20. Glenn Hooper, 'Introduction', in Glenn Hooper (ed.), *The Tourist's Gaze: travellers to Ireland, 1800–2000* (Cork: Cork University Press, 2001), pp. xxii–xxiii.

21. Ibid.

22. James Buzard, *The Beaten Track: European tourism, literature, and the ways to culture, 1800–1918* (Oxford: Clarendon Press, 1993), p. 47.

23. Melissa Fegan, 'The Traveller's Experience of Famine Ireland', *Irish Studies Review* vol. 9, no. 3, 2001, p. 360.

24. Ibid.

25. Martin Ryle, *Journeys in Ireland: literary travellers, rural landscapes, cultural relations* (London: Routledge, 1998), p. 65.

26. Martin Ross, letter to Edith Somerville, 27 August 1889, mic. 140/40, Trinity College Dublin.

27. E.Œ. Somerville and V. M. Ross, *Through Connemara in a Governess Cart* (London: Virago, 1998), p. 30. All citations from *Through Connemara in a Governess Cart* have been taken from this edition and, henceforth, all references will be cited parenthetically in the text.

28. Martin Ross, letter to Edith Somerville, 27 August 1889, mic. 140/40, Trinity College Dublin.

29. Ibid.

30. Martin Ross, letter to Edith Somerville, 31 August 1889, mic. 140/42, Trinity College Dublin.

31. Edith Somerville, 31 January 1906, letter to Cameron Somerville, MS. L.A.528.a–c, Edith Œnone Somerville Archive, Drishane House, County Cork.

32. Malcolm Kelsall, *Literary Representations of the Irish Country House: civilisation and savagery under the Union* (Basingstoke: Palgrave Macmillan, 2003), pp. 139, 142.

33. Ibid., p. 142.

34. Blake Family, *Letters from the Irish Highlands* (London: John Murray, 1825), pp. xv–xvi.

35. Maria Edgeworth, *Tour in Connemara: and the Martins of Ballinahinch* (London: Constable, 1950), p. 72. Pierce Marvel is the central character in Maria Edgeworth's short story 'The Will', collected in volume one of her *Popular Tales* (1811). He is largely an enthusiastic, albeit injudicious, man full of schemes of improvement that generally fail until he unites himself with his more prudent cousin.

36. E.Œ. Somerville and Martin Ross, *In the Vine Country* (London: Vintage, 2001), p. 111.

37. Anon., *The Midland Great Western Railway of Ireland Tourists' Handbook: through Connemara and the west of Ireland* (Dublin: Sealy, Bryers & Walker, 1884), p. 56.

38. Somerville and Ross, *In the Vine Country*, pp. 116–17.

39. Martin Ross, letter to Edith Somerville, 27 August 1889, mic. 140/40, Trinity College Dublin.

40. Ibid.

41. Anon., *Midland Great Western Railway of Ireland Tourist Handbook*, p. 4.

42. Ibid., p. 3.

43. Ibid.

44. Anon., 'Modern Tourism', *Blackwood's Magazine*, vol. 64, no. 394, 1848, p. 185.

45. Ibid.

46. Ibid.

47. Buzard, *The Beaten Track*, p. 6.

48. Ibid., p. 150.

49. Edith Somerville, letter to Cameron Somerville, 4 August 1890, MS. L.A.584.a–b, Edith Œnone Somerville Archive, Drishane House, County Cork.

50. Somerville and Ross, *Irish Memories*, p. 216.

51. Sara Mills, *Discourses of Difference: an analysis of women's travel writing and colonialism* (London: Routledge, 1991), p. 86.

52. Quoted in Hilary Robinson, *Somerville and Ross* (Dublin: Gill and Macmillan, 1980), p. 74.

53. Violet Powell, *The Irish Cousins: the books and background of Somerville and Ross* (London: Heinemann, 1870), p. 35.

54. William Longman, letter to Martin Ross, 6 January 1904, MS. 4276–7/149, Trinity College Dublin.

55. James Duncan and Derek Gregory, 'Introduction', in James Duncan and Derek Gregory, (eds), *Writes of Passage: reading travel writing* (London: Routledge, 1999), p. 4; and Mary Louise Pratt, *Imperial Eyes: travel writing and transculturation* (London: Routledge, 1992), p. 4.

56. Lawless, p. 319.

57. Ibid.

58. Quoted in Lewis, *Somerville and Ross*, p. 165.

59. Pratt, p. 136.

60. E.Œ. Somerville and Martin Ross, 'In the State of Denmark', in *Stray-Aways* (London: Longmans, 1920), p. 161.

5. On opposite sides of the border

1. E.Œ. Somerville, untitled manuscript '[history of Somerville and Ross's spiritual correspondence]', n.d. [*c*.1940], MS. 17/904/13, Queen's University Belfast, p. 4.

2. Ibid., p. 5.

3. The Fox sisters later admitted that the spirit messages they had received in the form of rapping and knocking sounds had been effected by cracking their toe and finger joints together. Two useful accounts of the Fox sisters' lives and spiritualist practices can be read in R. Pearsall, *The Table Rappers* (London: Michael Joseph, 1972), and E. W. Fornell, *The Happy Medium: spiritualism and the life of Margaret Fox* (Austin: University of Texas Press, 1964).

4. One of the most complete and comprehensive accounts of Edith's personal spiritualist practices can be found in Maurice Collis, *Somerville and Ross: a biography* (London: Faber & Faber, 1968).

5. Diana Basham, *The Trial of Woman: feminism and the occult sciences in Victorian literature and society* (London: Macmillan, 1992), p. 150.

6. Quoted in Collis, p. 177.

7. Jem Barlow, 'A Memory of Martin Ross', *Country Life*, vol. 39, no. 995, 1916, p. 136.

8. Emmanual Levinas, *Existence & Existents* (Dordrecht: Kluwer Academic Publishers, 1978).

9. Colin Davis, 'Can the Dead Speak to Us? De Man, Levinas, Agamben', *Culture, Theory and Critique*, vol. 45, no. 1, p. 82.

10. Quoted in Roy Foster, *W. B. Yeats: a life*, vol. 2 (Oxford: Oxford University Press, 2003), p. 221.

11. Peter Goodrich, 'Laws of Friendship', *Law and Literature*, vol. 15, no. 1, 2003, p. 30.

12. Ibid., pp. 29–30.

13. Ibid., p. 30.

14. Ethel Smyth, Letter to Edith Somerville, 15 July 1919, MS. 17/878/2, Queen's University, Belfast.

15. Ibid.

16. Ibid.

17. Davis, p. 84.

18. Janet Oppenheim, *The Other World: spiritualism and psychical research in England, 1850–1914* (Cambridge: Cambridge University Press, 1985), p. 1.

19. Pamela Thurschwell goes on to talk about the 'uncanny nature of technological transmission as it was imagined at the *fin de siècle*'. Pamela Thurschwell, *Literature, Technology and Magical Thinking, 1880–1920* (Cambridge: Cambridge University Press, 2001), p. 3.

20. Ibid.

21. Peter Washington, *Madame Blavatsky's Baboon: a history of the mystics, mediums, and misfits who brought spiritualism to America* (New York: Schocken Books, 1993), p. 11.

22. Basham, and Alex Owen, *The Darkened Room: women, power and spiritualism in late nineteenth-century England* (London: Virago, 1989).

23. Owen, *The Darkened Room*, p. 4.

24. Ibid.

25. Basham, p. 124.

26. Owen reveals that Louisa was an unhappily married woman who suspected her husband of infidelity and who sought marital guidance and proof of her husband's unfaithfulness from her spirit communicators: 'for Louisa the writing expressed her most intimate concerns and reinforced her worse suspicions, and her spirit guides were eventually to support her in her endeavour to leave home ... These intimate and swiftly-penned dialogues with the unseen could prove devastatingly subversive in content, questioning the right of man's authority over woman and courting resistance to the established order.' Alex Owen, 'Women and Nineteenth-Century Spiritualism: strategies in the subversion of femininity', in Jim Obelkevich, Lyndal Roper and Raphael Samuel (eds), *Disciplines of Faith: studies in religion, politics and patriarchy* (London: Routledge, 1987), pp. 143–4.

27. Owen, 'Women and Nineteenth-Century Spiritualism', p. 144.

28. Jefferson Holdridge, *Those Mingled Seas: the poetry of W. B. Yeats, the beautiful and the sublime* (Dublin: UCD Press, 2000), p. 134.

29. Washington, p. 70.

30. R. Laurence Moore, *In Search of White Crows: spiritualism, parapsychology, and American culture* (Oxford: Oxford University Press, 1977), p. 111.

31. Henry James, *The Bostonians* (London: John Lehmann, 1952), p. 19. All subsequent references are taken from this edition and, henceforth, will be parenthetically cited in the main body of the text.

32. Theodor Adorno, 'Theses Against Occultism', in *Minima Moralia* (London: Verso, 1978), pp. 238–9.

33. Ibid., p. 239.

34. Quoted in Howard Kerr, *Mediums and Spirit Rappers and Roaring Radicals* (Urbana: University of Illinois Press, 1972), p. 40.

35. Washington, p. 12.

36. Moore, p. 106.

37. Ibid., p. 107.

38. Basham, p. 179.

39. Ibid.

40. Maureen O'Connor, *Female and the Species: the animal in Irish women's writing* (Bern: Peter Lang, 2010), p. 118; also see Roz Cowman, 'Lost Time: the smell and taste of Castle T.', in Éibhear Walshe, *Sex, Nation and Dissent in Irish Writing* (Cork: Cork University Press, 1997), p. 67.

41. Helen Sword, *Ghostwriting Modernism* (New York: Cornell University Press, 2002), p. 56.

42. Arthur Conan Doyle, *Pheneas Speaks: direct communications in the family circle reported by Arthur Conan Doyle* (London: The Psychic Press and Bookshop, n.d. [*c*.1927]), pp. 10–11.

43. Basham, p. 107.

44. Ibid., p. 3.

45. Somerville, '[history of Somerville and Ross's spiritual correspondence]', p. 1.

46. Oppenheim, p. 2.

47. Arthur Conan Doyle, *The New Revelation and the Vital Message* (London: Psychic Research Press, 1938), p. 13.

48. Ibid., p. 14.

49. Arthur Conan Doyle, *The History of Spiritualism*, vol. 1 (London: Cassell, 1926), p. 14.

50. Conan Doyle's poem 'Fate' is often used to confirm his spiritualist allegiance in relation to the death of his son. See Catherine Wynne, *The Colonial Doyle. British imperialism, Irish nationalism and the Gothic* (London: Greenwood Press, 2002), pp. 155–6.

51. Conan Doyle, *Pheneas Speaks*, p. 6.

52. Ibid., pp. 9–11.

53. Edith Somerville, diary, 13 August 1874, MS. 17/875, Queen's University Belfast.

54. E.Œ. Somerville, 'Extra-Mundane Communications', in E.Œ. Somerville and Martin Ross, *Stray-Aways* (London: Longmans, 1920), p. 273.

55. Edith Somerville, diary, 8 August 1874, MS. 17/875, Queen's University Belfast.

56. Somerville, 'Extra-Mundane Communications', p. 276.

57. Ibid. Although Somerville does not date these occurrences in her account, diaries suggest that these spirit-writing activities took place in the late 1870s.

58. Edith Somerville, diary, 5 and 22 February 1878, MS. 17/875, Queen's University Belfast.

59. Edith Somerville, diary, 3 April 1878, MS. 17/875, Queen's University Belfast.

60. Gifford Lewis, *Somerville and Ross: the world of the Irish R.M.* (New York: Viking, 1985), p. 183.

61. Edith Somerville, diary, 25 April 1878, MS. 17/875, Queen's University Belfast.

62. Edith Somerville, letter to Cameron Somerville, 6 September 1884, MS. L.A.56.a–b, Edith Œnone Somerville Archive, Drishane House, County Cork. See also Edith Somerville, diary, 30 August 1884, MS. 17/875, Queen's University Belfast.

63. Edith Somerville, diary, 2 January 1894, MS. 17/875, Queen's University Belfast.

64. Martin Ross, letter to Cameron Somerville, 27 May 1894, MS. L.C.5.a–c, Edith Œnone Somerville Archive, Drishane House, Co. Cork.

65. Somerville, '[history of Somerville and Ross's spiritual correspondence]', p. 5.

66. Ibid., p. 7.

67. Edith Somerville, diary, 16 October 1893, MS. 17/875, Queen's University Belfast. Lewis also comes to a similar conclusion: 'Edith's reaction to being used as an 'interpreter' by a spirit was one of interested appreciation – yet she often wrote scornfully of Uncle Kendal's "gubs" and "gubbing parties".' Lewis, *Somerville and Ross: the world of the Irish R.M.*, p. 182.

68. Collis, pp. 157–8. Collis gives the following description of Somerville's new friend: 'She was a woman in early middle age, unmarried, very slight of build, and not as poor as she made out. The Somervilles and Coghills had taken a fancy to her. When it was known that she was a medium, their interest in her increased. Her psychic powers were virtually that of a professional medium. Professor Coghill writes: "Her prominent blue eyes had an expression of permanent wonder, with a hint of coyness or slyness, one couldn't be sure which. How much she deceived herself and how much she deceived others, I shall never know."' Collis, p. 177.

69. Collis, p. 164.

70. Ibid., pp. 177–85.

71. Edith Somerville, diary, 16 June 1916, MS. 17/875, Queen's University Belfast.

72. Edith Somerville, letter to Alice Kinkead, 16 January 1917, MS. L.A.1386.a–b, Edith Œnone Somerville Archive, Drishane House, County Cork.

73. Collis, pp. 220–2. Also see Edith Somerville, diary, January/February 1924, MS. 17/875, Queen's University Belfast.

74. Lewis, *Somerville and Ross: the world of the Irish R.M.*, pp. 184–5.

75. Quoted in Edith Somerville, diary [back page insert], 1916, MS. 17/875, Queen's University Belfast.

76. Quoted in Somerville, 'Extra-Mundane Communications', p. 280.

77. Lewis, *Somerville and Ross: the world of the Irish R.M.*, p. 181.

78. Edith Somerville, letter to Ethel Smyth, 23 February 1921, MS. 17/878, Queen's University Belfast.

79. Edith Somerville, diary, 26 March 1921, MS. 17/875, Queen's University Belfast.

80. Edith Somerville, diary, 24 March and 22 April 1921, MS. 17/875, Queen's University Belfast.

81. Edith Somerville, letter to Ethel Smyth, 1 July 1922, MS. 17/878, Queen's University Belfast.

82. Edith Somerville, letter to Ethel Smyth, 9 August 1921, MS. 17/878, Queen's University Belfast.

83. 'All my letters had been neatly slit open, & on some envelopes the words "Censored by I.R.A." were written.' Edith Somerville, letter to Ethel Smyth, 28 February 1921, MS. 17/878, Queen's University Belfast.

84. Edith Somerville, letter to Ethel Smyth, *c*. September 1922, MS. 17/878, Queen's University Belfast. It should be noted that this was a particularly dangerous position to be in as the British naval forces were forbidden to intervene in the civil war that erupted after the July truce in 1921 between the Free State troops and the anti-treaty Irish republicans. The treaty was engineered by the Irish Dáil in Dublin and the British government in London.

85. Edith Somerville, letter to Ethel Smyth, 29 August 1922, MS. 17/878, Queen's University Belfast.

86. Edith Somerville, diary, 22 and 23 August 1922, MS. 17/875, Queen's University Belfast.

87. Edith Somerville, letter to Ethel Smyth, 13 August 1922, MS. 17/878, Queen's University Belfast.

88. Collis, pp. 214–15.

89. Edith Somerville, letters to Ethel Smyth, 16 and 21 February 1921, MS. 17/878, Queen's University Belfast.

90. Edith Somerville, letter to Ethel Smyth, 23 February 1921, MS. 17/878, Queen's University Belfast.

91. It is likely that Somerville met Cummins during a mass meeting of spiritualists at the Royal Albert Hall in November 1927. See Otto Rauchbauer, *The Edith Œnone Somerville Archive in Drishane: a catalogue and an evaluative essay* (Dublin: Irish Manuscript Commission, 1994).

92. Collis, p. 252.

93. Edith Somerville, diary, 29 November 1930, MS. 17/875, Queen's University Belfast.

94. Edith Somerville, diary, 5 December 1930, MS. 17/875, Queen's University Belfast.

95. Edith Somerville, letter to Cameron Somerville, 7 March 1933, MS. L.A.1210.a–c, Edith Œnone Somerville Archive, Drishane House, County Cork.

96. Edith Somerville, diary, 27 October 1934, MS. 17/875, Queen's University Belfast.

97. Collis, *Somerville and Ross*, p. 266; and E.Œ. Somerville and Martin Ross, *Notions in Garrison* (London: Methuen, 1941).

98. E.Œ. Somerville and Boyle Somerville, *Records of the Somerville Family of Castlehaven and Drishane: from 1174–1940* (Cork: Guy & Co., 1940).

99. Roy Foster, 'Protestant Magic: W. B. Yeats and the spell of Irish history', in Roy Foster, *Paddy and Mr. Punch* (Harmondsworth: Allen Lane, 1993), p. 220.

100. See Selina Guinness, '"Protestant Magic" reappraised: evangelicalism, dissent, and theosophy', *Irish University Review*, vol. 33, no. 1, 2003, pp. 14–27; and Julie Anne Stevens, 'Flashlights and Fiction: the development of the modern Irish short story', in *The Ghost Story from the Middle Ages to the Twentieth Century: a ghostly genre* (Dublin: Four Courts Press, 2010), p. 142.

101. Stevens, 'Flashlights and Fiction', p. 142.

102. Charles Kendal Bushe [séance conducted by Somerville and Cummins], notebook 16, 30 January 1932, MS. 17/904/1, Queen's University Belfast.

103. E.Œ. Somerville, *Some Experiences of an Irish R.M.* (London: Longmans, 1900), p. 7. All references to this book are taken from this edition and subsequent references will be cited parenthetically in the text.

104. Stevens, 'Flashlights and Fiction', p. 146.

105. Gerhardt Richter, 'Siegfried Kracauer and the Folds of Friendship', *The German Quarterly*, vol. 70, no. 3, 1997, p. 239.

106. Ibid., p. 240.

107. Martin Ross [séance conducted by Somerville and Cummins], notebook 17, 27 September 1937, MS. 17/904/2, Queen's University Belfast.

108. Stevens, 'Flashlights and Fiction', p. 144.

109. Somerville, '[history of Somerville and Ross's spiritual correspondence]', p. 14.

110. Ibid., p. 8.

111. Ibid., p. 28.

112. Stevens, 'Flashlights and Fiction', p. 141.

113. Ibid., p. 142.

114. Thurschwell, pp. 1–2, 10.

115. Daniel Pick, *Svengali's Web: the alien enchanter in modern culture* (New Haven: Yale University Press, 2000), p. 76.

116. MacFarlane, p. 46.

117. Sword, p. 8.

118. Moore, p. 106.

119. Somerville, '[history of Somerville and Ross's spiritual correspondence]', p. 3.

120. Ibid., p. 4.

121. Martin Ross [séance conducted by Somerville and Cummins], notebook 17, 21 October 1939, MS. 17/904/2, Queen's University Belfast.

122. Astor [séance conducted by Somerville and Cummins], notebook 16, 22 September 1931, MS. 17/904/1, Queen's University Belfast.

123. Martin Ross [séance conducted by Somerville and Cummins], notebook 16, September 1933, MS. 17/904/1, Queen's University Belfast.

124. Martin Ross [séance conducted by Somerville and Cummins], notebook 17, 27 September 1937, ms. 17/904/2, Queen's University Belfast.

125. Ross visited Tyrone House in March 1912 and gave the following description in a letter to Somerville of it and its former inhabitants: 'In the afternoon Tilly Redington and I drove over to Tyrone House. A bigger and much grander edition of Ross – a great square cut stone house of three stories, with an area – perfectly empty – and such ceilings, architraves, teak doors and chimney pieces as one sees in old houses in Dublin. It is on a long promontory by the sea – and there *rioted* three or four generations of St. Georges – living with country women, occasionally marrying them, all illegitimate four times over. Not so long ago *eight* of these awful half peasant families roosted together in that lovely house and fought, and barricaded, and drank till the police had to intervene – about 150 years ago a very grand Lady Harriet St Lawrence married a St. George and lived there, and was so corroded with pride that she would not allow her two daughters to associate with the Galway people. She lived to see them marry two of the men in the yard. Yesterday as we left, an old Miss St. George daughter of the last owner was at the door in a donkey trap – she lives near, in a bit of a castle and since her people died she will not go into Tyrone House or into the enormous yard or the beautiful old garden. She was a strange mixture of distinction and commonness, like her breeding, and it was very sad to see her at the door of that great house – if we dare to write up that subject!' Somerville later marked this passage in Ross' letter, 'Tyrone House: a possible subject for a book', and reproduces it in the introduction to the published edition of *The Big House of Inver*. Martin Ross, letter to Edith Somerville, 18 March 1912, in Gifford Lewis (ed.), *The Selected Letters of Somerville and Ross*, p. 294.

126. Hilary Robinson, *Somerville and Ross: a critical appreciation* (Dublin: Gill & Macmillan, 1980).

127. Martin Ross [séance conducted by Somerville and Cummins], notebook 17, 14 July 1940, MS. 17/904/2, Queen's University Belfast.

128. Martin Ross [séance conducted by Somerville and Cummins], notebook 17, 6 March 1940, MS. 17/904/2, Queen's University Belfast.

129. Gifford Lewis, 'Introduction', in E.Œ. Somerville and Martin Ross, *The Big House of Inver* (Dublin: A & A Farmar, 1999), p. xviii.

130. Martin Ross [séance conducted by Somerville and Cummins], notebook 17, 28 June 1939, MS. 17/904/2, Queen's University Belfast.

131. Martin Ross [séance conducted by Somerville and Cummins], notebook 16, 29 September 1933, MS. 17/904/1, Queen's University Belfast.

132. Edith Somerville, letter to Cameron Somerville, 18 January 1895, MS. L.A.177.a, Edith
      Œnone Somerville Archive, Drishane House, County Cork.

133. Martin Ross [séance conducted by Somerville and Cummins], notebook 17, 28 June 1939,
      MS. 17/904/2, Queen's University Belfast.

Afterword

1. Catriona Crowe, 'Testimony to a Flowering', *The Dublin Review*, vol. 10, Spring 2003, n.
    pag., http://thedublinreview.com/testimony-to-a-flowering, accessed 9 January 2015.

2. Qoted in ibid.

3. Patricia Ferreira, 'Claiming and Transforming an "Entirely Gentlemanly Artifact": Ireland's
    Attic Press', *Canadian Journal of Irish Studies*, vol. 19, no. 1, 1993, p. 97.

4. Julia McElhatton Williams, 'This Is (Not) a Canon: staking out the tradition in recent
    anthologies of Irish writing', *Journal of Women's History*, vol. 6, no. 4, 1995, pp. 228–9.

5. Quoted in Crowe, 'Testimony to a Flowering', n. pag.

6. Edna Longley, *The Living Stream: literature and revisionism in Ireland* (Newcastle:
    Bloodaxe, 1994), p. 35.

7. Preface [unsigned], in Angela Bourke, Siobhán Kilfeather, Maria Luddy, Margaret
    MacCurtain, Gerardine Meaney, Máirín Ní Dhonnchadha, Mary O'Dowd and Clair Wills
    (eds), *The Field Day Anthology of Irish Writing: Irish women's writing and traditions*, vols 4
    & 5 (Cork: Cork University Press, 2002), pp. xxxiii, xxxvi.

8. Julie Anne Stevens, *The Irish Scene in Somerville and Ross* (Dublin: Four Courts Press,
    2007), p. 9.

9. Augustine Martin, 'Prose Fiction, 1880–1945', in Seamus Deane, Andrew Carpenter and
    Jonathan Williams (eds), *The Field Day Anthology of Irish Writing*, vol. 2 (Derry: Field Day
    Publications, 1991), p. 1022.

10. Declan Kiberd, *Inventing Ireland: the literature of the modern nation* (London: Vintage,
     1996), pp. 69–82.

11. Declan Kiberd, *Irish Classics* (London: Granta, 2000), pp. 360–78.

12. Roy Foster, 'Nations, Yet Again: constructing or deconstructing an Irish canon?', *Times
     Literary Supplement*, no. 4643, 27 March 1992, p. 5.

13. Ibid.

14. Gerardine Meaney, 'Identity and Opposition: women's writing, 1890–1960', in Bourke et al.
     (eds), *Field Day Anthology*, vol. 5, p. 976.

15. Emma Donoghue, 'Lesbian Encounters, 1745–1997', in Bourke et al. (eds), *Field Day
     Anthology*, vol. 4, p. 1091.

16. Ibid.

17. Siobhán Kilfeather, 'The Whole Bustle', *London Review of Books*, 9 January 1992, p. 20.

18. Ibid.

19. Foster, 'Nations, Yet Again', p. 6.

20. Quoted in Yu-Chen Lin, 'Field Day Revisited (I): an interview with Seamus Deane',
     Concentric: Literary and Cultural Studies, vol. 33, no. 1, 2007, p. 212.

21. Eileen Battersby, 'Stalked by an Agenda', *Irish Times*, 5 October 2002, p. 10.

22. Ibid.

23. Rebecca Pelan, *Two Irelands: literary feminisms North and South* (New York: Syracuse
     University Press, 2005), p. xxi.

24. Gerardine Meaney, 'Identity and Opposition: women's writing, 1890–1960', in Bourke et al.
     (eds), *Field Day Anthology*, vol. 5, p. 976.

25. Ibid.

Bibliography

PRIMARY MATERIALS

Somerville, Edith, and Boyle Somerville, *Records of the Somerville Family of Castlehaven and Drishane: from 1174–1940* (Cork: Guy and Co., 1940)

—, and Martin Ross, *The Big House of Inver* (Dublin: A. & A. Farmar, 1999)

—, *In the Vine Country* (London: Vintage, 2001)

—, *Irish Memories* (London: Longmans, 1917)

—, *Some Experiences of an Irish R.M.* (London: Longmans, 1900)

—, *The Silver Fox* (London: Longmans, 1927)

—, *Stray-Aways* (London: Longmans, 1920)

—, *Through Connemara in a Governess Cart* (London: Virago, 1998)

MANUSCRIPT MATERIALS

Letters

Gregory, Augusta, letters to Martin Ross, 1906–1915, MS. 17/920, Somerville and Ross Papers, Queen's University Belfast

Gregory, William, letter to Mrs. Ross, 1889, MS. 17/920, Somerville and Ross Papers, Queen's University Belfast

Longman, William, letters to Martin Ross, MS. 4276-7/149, Trinity College Dublin

Longman, Thomas, letters to Edith Somerville, 1913, MS. 17/917, Somerville and Ross Papers, Queen's University Belfast

Pinker, James B., letters to Edith Somerville and Martin Ross, 1913, MS. 17/917, Somerville and Ross Papers, Queen's University Belfast

Ross, Martin, letters to Cameron Somerville, 1894–1910, MS L.C.5.a–c–L.C.10.a–c, Edith Œnone Somerville Archive, Drishane House, County Cork

—, letters to Edith Somerville, MIC 147, Berg Collection, NYPL, New York

—, letters to Edith Somerville, MIC 140/40, Somerville and Ross Papers, Trinity College Dublin

—, letters to Longmans, 1913, MS. 17/917, Somerville and Ross Papers, Queen's University Belfast

Smyth, Ethel, letters to Edith Somerville, 1918–1943, MS. 17/878, Somerville and Ross Papers, Queen's University Belfast

Somerville, Edith, letters to Alice Kinkead, 1895–1926, MS. L.A.1365.a–b– L.A.1538.a–b, Edith Œnone Somerville Archive, Drishane House, County Cork

—, letters to Cameron Somerville, 1879–1929, MS. L.A.1.a–c–L.A.1254.a–b, Edith Œnone Somerville Archive, Drishane House, County Cork

—, letters to Ethel Smyth, 1921–1930, MS. 17/878, Somerville and Ross Papers, Queen's University Belfast

—, letters to J. B. Pinker, MS TCD 3330–1/152, Somerville and Ross Papers, Trinity College Dublin

—, letters to Martin Ross, MIC 147, Berg Collection, NYPL, New York

Thring, G. Herbert, letters to J. B. Pinker, 1913, MS. 17/917, Somerville and Ross Papers, Queen's University Belfast

Wills, William, letters to Martin Ross, 1885–1890, MS. 17/876, Somerville and Ross Papers, Queen's University Belfast

Yates, Edmund, letters to Martin Ross, MS TCD 4276–7/12, Trinity College Dublin.

Diaries

Somerville, Edith, diaries, 1873–1948, MS. 17/875, Somerville and Ross Papers, Queen's University Belfast

Ross, Martin, diaries, 1875–1915, MS. 17/874, Somerville and Ross Papers, Queen's University Belfast

Misc.

Anon., misc., newspaper cuttings, 1913, MS. 17/917, Somerville and Ross Papers, Queen's University Belfast

Somerville, Edith, 'The Educational Aspect of Suffrage', 1912, MS. 17/898/d, Somerville and Ross Papers, Queen's University Belfast

—, untitled manuscript, history of Somerville and Ross' spiritual correspondence, *c*.1940, MS. 17/904/13, Somerville and Ross Papers, Queen's University Belfast

—, transcript of séances with Charles Kendal Bush, 1930–1941, MS. 17/904/1, Somerville and Ross Papers, Queen's University Belfast

—, transcript of séances with Martin Ross aided by Geraldine Cummins, 1930–1941, MS. 17/904/2, Somerville and Ross Papers, Queen's University Belfast

Somerville, Edith, and Martin Ross, autograph drafts of *Some Irish Yesterdays*, n.d., MS. 17/883, Somerville and Ross Papers, Queen's University Belfast

—, four commonplace autograph books recording characteristic Irish anecdotes, 1886–1945, MS. 17/881, Somerville and Ross Papers, Queen's University Belfast

SECONDARY SOURCES

Abrams, Howard B., 'Originality and Creativity in Copyright', *Law and Contemporary Problems*, vol. 55, 1992, pp. 53–94

Adorno, Theodore, 'Theses Against Occultism', in *Minima Moralia* (London: Verso, 1978), pp. 238–44

Alison, Archibald, 'The Copyright Question', *Blackwood's Magazine*, vol. 51, 1842, pp. 107–21

Anon., *Midland Great Western Railway of Ireland Tourist Handbook: through Connemara and the west of Ireland* (Dublin: Sealy, Bryers & Walker, c. 1880)

— , 'Modern Tourism', *Blackwood's Magazine*, vol. 64, no. 394, 1848, pp. 185–90

Arnold, Matthew, 'Copyright', *Fortnightly Review*, vol. 27, no. 159, 1880, pp. 97–113

Aswell, Duncan, 'Jame's Treatment of Artistic Collaboration', *Criticism*, vol. 8, no. 2, 1966, pp. 180–95

Badenhausen, Richard, *T. S. Eliot and the Art of Collaboration* (Cambridge University Press, 2005)

Barlow, Jem, 'A Memory of Martin Ross', *Country Life*, vol. 39, no. 995, 1916, p. 136

Barnard, Marjorie, 'The Gentle Art of Collaboration' in Hilarie Lindsay (ed.), *Ink No. 2*, 1977 (Sydney: Society of Women Writers), pp. 126–8

Barthes, Roland, *Image, Music, Text*, ed. and trans. Stephen Heath (London: Fontana, 1977)

Basham, Diana, *The Trial of Woman: feminism and the occult sciences in Victorian literature and society* (London: Macmillan, 1992)

Battersby, Eileen 'Stalked by an agenda', *Irish Times*, 5 October 2002, p. 10

Beer, John, 'The Unity of *Lyrical Ballads*', in Nicola Trott and Seamus Perry (eds), *1800: the new 'Lyrical Ballads'* (Basingstoke: Palgrave, 2001), pp. 6–22

Besant, Walter, 'On Literary Collaboration', *The New Review*, vol. 6, no. 33, 1892, pp. 200–9

— , *The Pen and the Book* (London: Thomas Burleigh, 1899)

Black, Jennifer Cognard, and MacLeod Walls (eds), *Kindred Hands: letters on writing by British and American women authors, 1865–1935* (Iowa City: University of Iowa Press, 2006)

Blackstone, William, *Commentaries on the Laws of England*, 4 vols, 1765–9 (London: Cavendish, 2001)

Blake, Family of (eds), *Letters from the Irish Highlands* (London: John Murray, 1825)

Bonham-Carter, Victor, *Authors by Profession*, vol. 1 (London: Society of Authors, 1978)

Boucharenc, Myriam, 'Plural Authorship in Automatic Writing', in Paul Gifford and Johnnie Gratton (eds), *Subject Matters: subject and self in French literature from Descartes to the present* (Amsterdam: Rodopi, 2000), pp. 100–14

Bourke, Angela, Siobhán Kilfeather, Maria Luddy, Margaret MacCurtain, Gerardine Meaney, Máirín Ní Dhonnchadha, Mary O'Dowd and Clair Wills (eds), *The Field Day Anthology of Irish Writing: Irish women's writing and traditions*, vols 4 & 5 (Cork: Cork University Press, 2002)

Brown, Terence, *The Life of W. B. Yeats: a critical biography* (Oxford: Blackwell, 1999)

Butler, Marilyn, *Maria Edgeworth: a literary biography* (Oxford: Clarendon Press, 1972)

Butler, Sandra, and Rosenblum, Barbara *Cancer in Two Voices* (San Francisco: Spinsters, 1991)

Buzard, James, *The Beaten Track: European tourism, literature, and the ways to culture 1800–1918* (Oxford: Clarendon Press, 1993)

Cahalan, James, *Double Visions: women and men in modern and contemporary Irish fiction* (New York: Syracuse University Press, 1999)

Caird, Mona, 'A Defence of the So-called Wild Women', *The Nineteenth Century*, vol. 31, 1892, pp. 811–29

Chartier, Roger, 'Figures of the Author', in Brad Sherman and Alain Strowel (eds), *Of Authors and Origins: essays on copyright law* (Oxford: Clarendon Press, 1994), pp. 7–22

Chon, Margaret, 'New Wine Bursting from Old Bottles: collaborative internet art, joint works, and entrepreneurship', *Oregon Law Review*, vol. 75, 1996, pp. 257–76

Cixous, Hélène, 'The Laugh of the Medusa', in Elaine Marks and Isabelle de Courtivron (eds), *New French Feminism* (Hemel Hempstead: Harvester, 1981), pp. 245–64

Colby, Robert, 'Authorship and the Book Trade', in J. Don Vann and Rosemary T. VanArsdel (eds), *Victorian Periodicals and Victorian Society* (Aldershot: Scholar Press, 1994)

Coleridge, Ernest Hartley (ed.), *The Complete Poetical Works of Samuel Taylor Coleridge Including Poems and Versions of Poems Now Published for the First Time*, vol. 1 (Oxford: Clarendon Press, 1912)

Coleridge, S. T., *Biographia Literaria; or Biographical Sketches of My Literary Life and Opinions*, ed. J. Shawcross, vol. 2 (Oxford: Oxford University Press, 1973)

Collis, Maurice, *Somerville and Ross: a biography* (London: Faber, 1968)

Conan Doyle, Arthur, *The History of Spiritualism*, vol. 1 (London: Cassell, 1926)

—, *The New Revelation and the Vital Message* (London: Psychic Research Press, 1938)

—, *Pheneas Speaks: direct communications in the family circle reported by Arthur Conan Doyle* (SW: The Psychic Press and Bookshop, c.1927)

Cronin, Michael, *Across the Lines: travel, language, translation* (Cork: Cork University Press, 2000)

Crowe, Catriona, 'Testimony to a Flowering', *The Dublin Review*, vol. 10, Spring 2003, n. pag., http://thedublinreview.com/testimony-to-a-flowering, accessed 9 January 2015

Cummins, Geraldine, *Dr. E. Œ. Somerville: a biography* (London: Andrew Dakers, 1952)

Davenport-Adams, W. H., 'Imitators and Plagiarists', *The Gentleman's Magazine*, 1892, pp. 502–627

Davis, Colin, 'Can the Dead Speak to Us? De Man, Levinas, Agamben', *Culture, Theory and Critique*, vol. 45, no. 1, pp. 77–89

Deazley, Ronan, *On the Origin of the Right to Copy: charting the movement of copyright law in eighteenth-century Britain, 1695–1775* (Portland: Hart, 1994)

Deleuze, Gilles, and Parnet, Claire *Dialogues II* (London: Continuum, 2002)

Dever, Maryanne, '"No Mine and Thine But Ours": finding M. Barnard Eldershaw', *Tulsa Studies in Women's Literature*, vol. 14, no. 1, 1995, pp. 65–74

Doan, Janice, and Hodges, Devon 'Writing from the Trenches and Collaborative Writing', *Tulsa Studies in Women's Literature*, vol. 14, no. 1, 1995, pp. 51–7

Duff, William, *An Essay on Original Genius* (London: E. & C. Dilly, 1767)

Duncan, James, and Gregory, Derek (eds), *Writes of Passage: reading travel writing* (London: Routledge, 1999)

Eagleton, Terry, *The Ideology of the Aesthetic* (Oxford: Basil Blackwell, 1990)

Edgeworth, The Family of (eds), *A Memoir of Maria Edgeworth*, vol. 1 (London: Joseph Masters, 1867)

Edgeworth, Maria, *Tour in Connemara: and the Martins of Ballinahinch* (London: Constable, 1950)

Ehnenn, Jill R., *Women's Literary Collaboration, Queerness, and Late-Victorian Culture* (Aldershot: Ashgate, 2008)

Eliot, T. S., 'Phillip Massinger', in *Elizabethan Essays* (New York: Haskell House, 1964), pp. 153–76

—, 'Tradition and the Individual Talent', in *Selected Essays* (London: Faber & Faber, 1975), pp. 37–44

Enfield, William, *Observations on Literary Property* (London: Joseph Johnson, 1774)

Farrell, Michael P., *Collaborative Circles: friendship dynamics and creative work* (Chicago: Chicago University Press, 2001)

Favret, Mary, *Romantic Correspondence: women, politics, and the fiction of letters* (Cambridge: Cambridge University Press, 1993)

Fegan, Melissa, 'The Traveller's Experience of Famine Ireland', *Irish Studies Review*, vol. 9, no. 3, 2001, pp. 361–71

Ferreira, Patricia, 'Claiming and Transforming an "Entirely Gentlemanly Artifact": Ireland's Attic Press', *Canadian Journal of Irish Studies*, vol. 19, no. 1, 1993, pp. 82–103

Fornell, E. W., *The Happy Medium: spiritualism and the life of Margaret Fox* (Austin: University of Texas Press, 1964)

Foster, Roy, 'Nations, Yet Again: constructing or deconstructing an Irish canon?', *Times Literary Supplement*, no. 4643, 27 March 1992, pp. 5–6

—, *Paddy and Mr. Punch* (Harmondsworth: Allen Lane, 1993)

—, *W. B. Yeats: a life*, vol. 2 (Oxford: Oxford University Press, 2003)

Foucault, Michel, *The History of Sexuality*, vol. 1 (London: Penguin, 2008)

—, 'What Is an Author?', in J. V. Harari (ed.), *Textual Strategies: perspectives in poststructuralist criticism* (Ithaca: Cornell University Press, 1979), pp. 73–81

Friedman, Marilyn, *What Are Friends For? Feminist perspectives on personal relationships and moral theory* (New York: Cornell University Press, 1993)

Gallagher, Catherine, *Nobody's Story: the vanishing acts of women writers in the marketplace, 1670–1820* (Princeton: Princeton University Press, 1994)

Genosko, Gary (ed.), *Deleuze and Guattari: critical assessments of leading philosophers* (New York: Routledge, 2001)

Gere, Anne Ruggles, *Writing Groups: history, theory, and implications* (Carbondale: Southern Illinois University Press, 1978)

Gillies, Mary Ann, *The Professional Literary Agent in Britain, 1880–1920* (Toronto: University of Toronto Press, 2007)

Gisborne, Thomas, *An Inquiry into the Duties of the Female Sex* (London: T. Caldwell & W. Davies, 1797)

Goodrich, Peter, 'Laws of Friendship', *Law and Literature*, vol. 15, no. 1, 2003, pp. 23–52

Griggs, Earl Lesley (ed.), *The Collected Letters of Samuel Taylor Coleridge, 1785–1800*, vol. 1 (Oxford: Clarendon Press, 1956)

Guinness, Selina, '"Protestant Magic" reappraised: evangelicalism, dissent, and theosophy', *Irish University Review*, vol. 33, no. 1, 2003, pp. 14–27

Hargrave, Francis, *Argument in Defence of Literary Property* (London: W. Otridge, 1774)

Hegel, Georg, *Philosophy of Right*, trans. S. W. Dyde (New York: Cosimo, 2008)

Heinemann, William, 'The Middleman as Viewed by a Publisher', *Athenaeum*, 3446, p. 663

Hill, Alan G. (ed.), *The Letters of William and Dorothy Wordsworth*, vol. 5 (Oxford: Oxford University Press, 1969–88)

Hickey, Alison, 'Coleridge, Southey, "and Co.": collaboration and authority', *Studies in Romanticism*, vol. 37, 1998, pp. 305–49

—, 'Double Bonds: Charles Lamb's Romantic collaborations', *English Language History*, vol. 63, 1996, pp. 735–71

Holdridge, Jefferson, *Those Mingled Seas: the poetry of W. B. Yeats, the beautiful and the sublime* (Dublin: UCD Press, 2000)

Holston, James, *Insurgent Citizenship: disjunctions of democracy and modernity in Brazil* (Princeton: Princeton University Press, 2008)

Hooper, Glenn (ed.), *The Tourist's Gaze: travellers to Ireland 1800–2000* (Cork: Cork University Press, 2001)

Howitt, Anna Mary, 'The Sisters in Art', *The Illustrated Exhibitor and Magazine of Art*, vol. 2, 1852

James, Henry, *The Bostonians* (London: John Lehmann, 1952)

—, 'Collaboration', *The English Illustrated Magazine*, vol. 9, 1892, pp. 911–21

Jaszi, Peter, 'On the Author Effect: contemporary copyright and collective creativity', in Martha Woodmansee and Peter Jaszi (eds), *The Construction of Authorship: textual appropriation in law and literature* (London: Duke University Press, 1994), pp. 29–56

—, 'Towards a Theory of Copyright: the metamorphoses of "authorship"', *Duke Law Journal*, vol. 455, 1991, pp. 455–502

Kahn, Zorina, *The Democratization of Invention: patents and copyrights in American economic development, 1790–1920* (Cambridge: Cambridge University Press, 2005)

Kant, Immanuel, *Anthropology from a Pragmatic Point of View*, ed. Robert B. Loudon (Cambridge: Cambridge University Press, 2006)

—, *Critique of the Power of Judgement*, ed. Paul Guyer (Cambridge: Cambridge University Press, 2000)

Kaplan, Carey, and Rose, Ellen Cronan 'Strange Bedfellows: feminist collaboration', *Signs*, vol. 18, no. 3, 1993, pp. 547–61

Kelsall, Malcolm, *Literary Representations of the Irish Country House: civilisation and savagery under the Union* (Basingstoke: Palgrave Macmillan, 2003)

Kennedy, Duncan, 'The Structure of Blackstone's *Commentaries*', *Buffalo Law Review*, vol. 28, 1978, pp. 205–382

Kerr, Howard, *Mediums and Spirit Rappers and Roaring Radicals* (Urbana: University of Illinois Press, 1972)

Kiberd, Declan, *Inventing Ireland: the literature of the modern nation* (London: Vintage, 1996)

Kilfeather, Siobhán, 'The Whole Bustle', *London Review of Books*, 9 January 1992, p. 20

Koestenbaum, Wayne, *Lyrical Ballads* in *Double Talk: the erotics of male literary collaboration* (New York: Routledge, 1989)

Laird, Holly, *Women Coauthors* (Chicago: University of Illinois Press, 2000)

Lang, Andrew, 'Literary Plagiarism', *The Contemporary Review*, 1887, pp. 831–40

Lawless, Emily, 'Iar-Connaught: a sketch', *The Cornhill Magazine*, vol. 56, no. 267, 1882, pp. 319–33

Leonardi, Susan J., and Pope, Rebecca A., 'Screaming Divas: collaboration as feminist practice', *Tulsa Studies in Women's Literature*, vol. 13, no. 2, 1994, pp. 259–70

Levinas, Emmanuel, *Existence & Existents* (Dordrecht: Kluwer Academic Publishers, 1978)

Lewis, Gifford, *Edith Somerville: a biography* (Dublin: Four Courts Press, 2005)

—, *Somerville and Ross: the world of the Irish R.M.* (New York: Viking, 1985)

—, (ed.), *The Selected Letters of Somerville and Ross* (London: Faber & Faber, 1989)

Lin, Yu-Chen, 'Field Day Revisited (I): an interview with Seamus Deane', *Concentric: literary and cultural studies*, vol. 33, no. 1, 2007, pp. 196–220

Linton, E. Lynn, 'The Girl of the Period', in *The Girl of the Period and other Social Essays*, vol. 1 (London: Richard Bentley & Son, 1883), pp. 1–9

—, 'The Wild Women as Social Insurgents', *The Nineteenth Century*, vol. 30, October 1891, pp. 596–605

Locke, John, 'The Second Treatise of Government: an essay concerning the true original, extent, and end of civil government', in Peter Laslett (ed.), *Two Treatises on Government* (Cambridge: Cambridge University Press, 1988)

London, Bette, *Writing Double: women's literary partnerships* (Ithaca: Cornell University Press, 1999)

Martin, Augustine, 'Prose Fiction, 1880–1945', in Seamus Deane, Andrew Carpenter and Jonathan Williams (eds), *The Field Day Anthology of Irish Writing*, vol. 2 (Derry: Field Day Publications, 1991), pp. 1005–32

Masten, Jeffrey, *Textual Intercourse: collaboration, authorship, and sexualities in renaissance drama* (Cambridge: Cambridge University Press, 1997)

Matthews, Brander, 'The Art and Mystery of Collaboration', *Longman's Magazine*, vol. 15, 1890, pp. 157–70

—, 'The Ethics of Plagiarism', *Longman's Magazine*, vol. 8, October 1886, pp. 621–34

May, Christopher, 'Cosmopolitan Legalism Meets "Thin Community": problems in the global governance of intellectual property', *Governance and Opposition*, vol. 39, no. 3, 2004, pp. 393–422

Mazzeo, Tilar J., *Plagiarism and Literary Property in the Romantic Period* (Philadelphia: University of Pennsylvania Press, 2007)

MacFarlane, Robert, *Original Copy: plagiarism and originality in nineteenth-century literature* (Oxford: Oxford University Press, 2007)

McGann, Jerome J., *The Romantic Ideology: a critical investigation* (London: University of Chicago Press, 1983)

Mills, Sara, *Discourses of Difference: an analysis of women's travel writing and colonialism* (London: Routledge, 1991)

Moore, R. Laurence, *In Search of White Crows: spiritualism, parapsychology, and American culture* (Oxford: Oxford University Press, 1977)

Moore, T. and Sturge, D. C. (eds), *Works and Days: from the journal of Michael Field* (London: John Murray, 1933)

Moorman, Mary, *William Wordsworth: a biography*, vol. 1 (Oxford: Clarendon Press, 1957)

Nash, Catherine, '"Embodying the Nation": the west of Ireland landscape and Irish identity', in Barbara O'Connor and Michael Cronin (eds), *Tourism in Ireland: a critical analysis* (Cork: Cork University Press, 1993), pp. 86–112

Ong, Walter, *Orality and Literacy: the technologizing of the word* (New York: Routledge, 2002)

Oppenheim, Janet, *The Other World: spiritualism and psychical research in England, 1850–1914* (Cambridge: Cambridge University Press, 1985)

Owen, Alex, *The Darkened Room: women, power and spiritualism in late nineteenth-century England* (London: Virago, 1989)

—, 'Women and Nineteenth-Century Spiritualism: strategies in the subversion of femininity', in Jim Obelkevich, Lyndal Roper and Raphael Samuel (eds), *Disciplines of Faith: studies in religion, politics and patriarchy* (London: Routledge, 1987), pp. 130–53

Owen, W. J. B., and Worthington Smyser, Jane (eds), *The Prose Works of William Wordsworth*, vol. 3 (Oxford: Clarendon Press, 1974)

Parks, Stephen (ed.), *Four Tracts on Freedom of the Press, 1790–1821* (New York: Garland, 1974)

Patterson, Lyman Ray, *Copyright in Historical Perspective* (Nashville: Vanderbilt University Press, 1968)

Pearsall, R., *The Table Rappers* (London: Michael Joseph, 1972)

Peterson, Linda H., *Becoming a Woman of Letters: myths of authorship and facts of the Victorian market place* (Princeton: Princeton University Press, 2009)

Pick, Daniel, *Svengali's Web: the alien enchanter in modern culture* (New Haven: Yale University Press, 2000)

Pinker, James B., interview, *The Bookman*, vol. 14, no. 79, April 1898, pp. 9–10

Pelan, Rebecca, *Two Irelands: literary feminisms North and South* (New York: Syracuse University Press, 2005)

Powell, Violet, *The Irish Cousins: the books and background of Somerville and Ross* (London: Heinemann, 1970)

Pratt, Mary, *Imperial Eyes: travel writing and transculturation* (London: Routledge, 1992)

Prickett, Stephen, *Coleridge and Wordsworth: the poetry of growth* (Cambridge: Cambridge University Press, 1970)

—, *Wordsworth and Coleridge: 'The Lyrical Ballads'* (London: Edward Arnold, 1975)

Prins, Yopie, *Victorian Sappho* (Princeton: Princeton University Press, 1999)

Rauchbauer, Otto, *The Edith Œnone Somerville Archive in Drishane: a catalogue and an evaluative essay* (Dublin: Irish Manuscript Commission, 1995)

Raymond, Janice, *A Passion for Friends: towards a philosophy of female affection* (Boston: Beacon Press, 1986)

Richter, Gerhard, 'Siegfried Kracauer and the Folds of Friendship', *The German Quarterly*, vol. 70, no. 3, 1997, pp. 233–46

Robinson, Hilary, *Somerville and Ross* (Dublin: St Martin's Press, 1980)

Rose, Mark, *Authors and Owners: the invention of copyright* (Cambridge, MA: Harvard University Press, 1993)

—, 'The Author as Proprietor: *Donaldson v. Becket* and the genealogy of modern authorship', *Representations*, no. 23, 1988, pp. 51–85

Roseneil, Sasha, 'Foregrounding Friendship: feminist pasts, feminist futures', in Kathy Davis, Mary Evans and Judith Lorber (eds), *The SAGE Handbook of Gender and Women's Studies* (London: SAGE, 2006), pp. 322–42

Ryle, Martin, *Journeys in Ireland: literary travellers, rural landscapes, cultural relations* (London: Routledge, 1998)

Saint-Amour, Paul K., *The Copywrights: intellectual property and the literary imagination* (New York: Cornell University Press, 2003)

Saunders, David, *Authorship and Copyright* (London: Routledge, 1992)

Saunders, Max, 'Secret Agencies: Conrad, collaboration and conspiracy', in Silvia Bigliazzi and Sharon Wood (eds), *Collaboration in the Arts from the Middle Ages to the Present* (Aldershot: Ashgate, 2006), pp. 94–125

Schellenburg, Betty A., *The Professionalization of Women Writers in Eighteenth-Century Britain* (Cambridge: Cambridge University Press, 2005)

Scrutton, Thomas Edward, *The Laws of Literary Property: an examination of the principles which should regulate literary and artistic property in England and other countries* (London: John Murray, 1883)

Seville, Catherine, *The Internationalisation of Copyright Law: books, buccaneers and the black flag in the nineteenth century* (Cambridge: Cambridge University Press, 2006)

—, *Literary Copyright Reform in Early Victorian England: the framing of the 1842 Copyright Act* (Cambridge: Cambridge University Press, 1999)

Shaw, Margaret, 'Constructing the "Literate Woman": nineteenth-nentury reviews and emerging literacies', in Michael Timko, Fred Kaplan and Edward Guiliano (eds), *Dickens Studies Annual: essays on Victorian fiction*, vol. 21 (New York: AMS Press, 1992), pp. 123–44

Sherman, Brad, and Bently, Lionel *The Making of Modern Intellectual Property Law: the British experience, 1760–1911* (Cambridge: Cambridge University Press, 1999)

Shortt, John, *The Law Relating to Works of Literature and Art* (London: Reeves & Turner, 1884)

Shiach, Morag (ed.), *Virginia Woolf:* A Room of One's Own *and* Three Guineas (Oxford: Oxford University Press, 2000)

Shoenfield, Mark, *The Professional Wordsworth: law, labor, and the poet's contract* (Athens, GA: University of Georgia Press, 1996)

Showalter, Elaine, *A Literature of their Own: from Charlotte Brontë to Doris Lessing* (London: Virago, 1999)

Southey, Robert, *The Poetical Works of Robert Southey* (New York: D. Appleton, 1839)

Stevens, Julie Anne, 'Flashlights and Fiction: the development of the modern Irish short story', in *The Ghost Story from the Middle Ages to the Twentieth Century: a ghostly genre* (Dublin: Four Courts Press, 2010), pp. 137–54

—, 'The Irish Landscape in Somerville and Ross's Fiction and Illustrations, 1890–1915', PhD diss., Trinity College Dublin, 2000

—, *The Irish Scene in Somerville and Ross* (Dublin: Four Courts Press, 2007)

—, 'The Staging of Protestant Ireland in Somerville and Ross's *The Real Charlotte*', in Aaron Kelly and Alan Gillis (eds), *Critical Ireland: new essays in literature and culture* (Dublin: Four Courts Press, 2001), pp. 188–94

Stillinger, Jack, *Multiple Authorship and the Myth of Solitary Genius* (Oxford: Oxford University Press, 1991)

Stivale, Charles, 'Pragmatic Machinic: discussion with Félix Guattari', 1985, www. dc.peachnet.edu/~mnunes/guatarri.html, accessed 25 August 2012, n. pag.

Sturgeon, Mary, *Michael Field* (London: Harrap, 1922)

Surrey, Janet, 'Relationship and Empowerment', in Judith Jordan, Alexandra Kaplan, Jean Miller, Irene Stiver and Janet Surrey (eds), *Women's Growth in Connection: writings from the Stone Center* (New York: Guidford Press, 1991), pp. 97–132

Sword, Helen, *Ghostwriting Modernism* (New York: Cornell University Press, 2002)

Thurschwell, Pamela, *Literature, Technology and Magical Thinking, 1880–1920* (Cambridge: Cambridge University Press, 2001)

Tingley, Stephanie A., '"A Letter is a Joy of Earth": Emily Dickinson's letters and Victorian epistolary conventions', *The Emily Dickinson Journal*, vol. 5, no. 2, 1996, pp. 181–99

Tuchman, Gaye, and Fortin, Nina E. *Edging Women Out: Victorian novelists, publishers, and social change* (New Haven: Yale University Press, 1989)

Warburton, William, *A Letter from an Author, to a Member of Parliament, Concerning Literary Property* (London: John & Paul Knapton, 1747)

Warter, John Wood (ed.), *Selections from the Letters of Robert Southey*, vol. 3 (London: Longmans, 1856)

Washington, Peter, *Madame Blavatsky's Baboon: a history of the mystics, mediums, and misfits who brought spiritualism to America* (New York: Schocken Books, 1993)

Wiley, Michael, 'Romantic Amplification: the way of plagiarism', *English Language History*, vol. 75, no. 1, 2008, pp. 219–40

Williams, Julia McElhatton 'This Is (Not) a Canon: staking out the tradition in recent anthologies of Irish writing', *Journal of Women's History*, vol. 6, no. 4, 1995, pp. 220–32

Wollstonecraft, Mary, *A Vindication of the Rights of Men with A Vindication of the Rights of Woman* ed. Sylvana Tomaselli (Cambridge: Cambridge University Press, 1995)

Woodmansee, Martha, 'The Genius and the Copyright: economic and legal conditions of the emergence of the "author"', *Eighteenth-Century Studies*, vol. 17, no. 4, 1984, pp. 425–48

Wordsworth, William, and Coleridge, S. T. *Lyrical Ballads*, ed. W. J. B. Owen (Oxford: Oxford University Press, 1995)

Wright, Edward, 'The Art of Plagiarism', *The Contemporary Review*, 1904, pp. 514–18

Wynne, Catherine, *The Colonial Doyle: British imperialism, Irish nationalism and the gothic* (London: Greenwood Press, 2002)

Yeats, W. B., 'A General Introduction for My Work', in *Essays and Introductions* (London: Macmillan, 1961)

York, Lorraine, 'Crowding the Garrett: women's collaborative writing and the problematics of space', in Marjorie Stone and Judith Thompson (eds), *Literary Couplings: writing couples, collaborators, and the construction of authorship* (Madison: University of Wisconsin Press, 2006), pp. 185–95

—, *Rethinking Women's Collaborative Writing: power, difference, property* (Toronto: University of Toronto Press, 2002)

Young, Edward, *Conjectures on Original Composition: in a letter to the author of Sir Charles Grandison* (London: R. & J. Dodsley, 1759)

Zaczek, Barbara, *Censored Sentiments* (London: Associated London Presses, 1997)

Index